VOID

Library of
Davidson College

YOUNG LIVES AT STAKE

The Education of Adolescents

Young Lives at Stake

The Education of Adolescents

by

CHARITY JAMES

with a Foreword by

CHARLES E. SILBERMAN

Agathon Press, Inc.
NEW YORK
1972

First published 1968 by
William Collins Sons & Co. Ltd.
London and Glasgow

This edition published 1972 by
Agathon Press, Inc., New York

© 1968 by Charity James

© 1972 by Charity James

All rights reserved. No portion of this
book may be reproduced, stored in a retrieval
system or transmitted, in any form or by any
means, electronic, mechanical, photocopying,
recording or otherwise, except for purposes
of brief quotation, without permission of
the publisher. For information, address

Agathon Press, Inc.
150 Fifth Avenue, New York, N.Y. 10011

Library of Congress Catalog Card Number: 77-166550

ISBN 0-87586-035-4

Printed in the United States of America

Contents

FOREWORD by Charles E. Silberman	vii
AUTHOR'S PREFACE TO THE U.S. EDITION	xiii
PREFACE TO THE ENGLISH EDITION	7

PART ONE
INTRODUCTORY
  1. Education for a Well-spent Youth ... 12

PART TWO
A NEW STYLE OF SECONDARY SCHOOL
  2. Everybody Can Grow ... 42
  3. Collaborative Learning ... 52
  4. Rationale of Curriculum ... 78
  5. Enquiry, Making, and Dialogue ... 98

PART THREE
IDEA IN ACTION: THE COLLABORATIVE SCHOOL
  6. The Organization of the Curriculum ... 125
  7. Diversity without Divisiveness ... 171
  8. Evaluation, Appraisal, and Counselling ... 212
  9. Changing Roles in a Changing Situation ... 230

GLOSSARY	252
INDEX	255

For Claire James

Foreword

Agathon Press has performed a valuable service by making Charity James' *Young Lives at Stake* available to the broad American audience. Few people in England or the United States have thought as hard or as cogently about secondary education as has Charity James; perhaps no one has thought as productively about the education of early adolescents—about the youngsters who, in most American school systems, attend the junior high.

In some ways, Mrs. James suggests in her Preface to this edition, *Young Lives at Stake* is not an easy book for most American readers to approach. The reason, I think, is that it is a very English book. Charity James' concern for the quality of life, in school and out; her concern for the nature of human relationships, between teachers and students, between students and students, and between teachers and teachers—all this is as characteristically English as are the flowers that grace almost any English schoolhouse. ("The gentleness of the English civilization," George Orwell wrote, "is perhaps its most marked characteristic.") And the paradox that lies at the heart of her inquiry—why can't school be as humane and joyous for adolescents as it is for young children—takes as a given the revolution that has transformed English primary education since World War II.

In good measure, however, it is precisely because *Young Lives at Stake is* so English that it is so useful—and so important—for American readers. In the last several years, after all, we have come to recognize that there is much to be learned about teaching and learning from the best English practice, especially at the primary level. As a result, Americans are trooping through English infant and junior schools in staggering numbers, and teachers and administrators in every part of the United States are trying to adapt what they have seen or heard of English practice to their own classrooms and schools. And what Charity James proposes for secondary education is a logical extension of the best primary school practice.

Having done my share to popularize informal education, I can only welcome the extraordinary interest that has developed. In an institution as resistant, and seemingly as impervious, to change as the American public school, moreover, a certain amount of faddism can play a useful role. Up to a point, that is to say, faddism may be the solvent of institutional rigidity and lag: administrators and school board members who might otherwise oppose or even sabotage the desired changes may be persuaded, instead, to jump on the new bandwagon.

But only up to a point! In the growing popularity of informal education, or "the open classroom," as it is coming to be called, there is a clear and present danger that faddism may go too far—that educators and parents alike may adopt the forms without understanding the substance. Classrooms divided into "interest areas" instead of rows of clusters of desks and chairs, individualized learning instead of whole-group instruction, multi-age grouping instead of homogeneous age grouping, architecturally designed open spaces instead of the familiar "egg-crate" design—all of these can be useful pedagogical techniques. But none are ends in themselves.

Charity James' genius is that she never forgets the ends. That means, among other things, that she never forgets to place the students and their needs first, and the institution's needs second. It means that she recognizes, with Dewey, that education is inescapably a moral enterprise, and that she recognizes, with Socrates, that education "is not about something casual, but about the proper way to live." Hence the title of the book, which reveals her priorities. "For discovering, accepting, and confirming the self," she wrote in the Preface to the English edition, "adolescence is a critical period. And the stakes are higher than they have ever been: on the one hand, not 'failed O-level' or 'failed B.A.,' but 'failed humanity,' and on the other, new possibilities of richly enjoyable living by people who are more fully, generously, and diversely persons than we with our long training in parsimony can even imagine. *We must not miss this moment. Young lives are at stake.*" (Emphasis added.)

Thus, the project out of which *Young Lives at Stake* emerged ended up quite differently from the way it began. The project started as an attempt to develop better means of meeting the needs of young school leavers—what we call "dropouts." It ended as an attempt to transform the education of *all* adolescents, college-bound as well as school leavers, rich as well as poor. Professor James acknowledges that "Radical reappraisal, not just a patching, is needed to ameliorate the disadvantages in school of those who suffer from obvious social and cultural handicap." But it would also be wrong "to ignore the damage that we do to children who are thought of as academically successful." What is needed is "an education that is appropriate for adolescence." To do this requires radical change, for "At present there is no model of secondary schooling that is remotely in line with our growing understanding of what human living might become." As the project developed, therefore, its members defined their goal in simple but sweeping terms: "To make school a good place to live in" for everyone.

Nothing could be more Deweyan than this insistence on viewing schools not (or not simply) as preparation for life, but as life itself. And nothing could be more English than the insistence that life in school be pleasant and humane as well as stimulating. "Are we allowing millions of people in schools, children and adults, to spend their time disagreeably," Professor James asks, "when it is quite unnecessary that they should do so?" Throughout the book, she insists on examining pedagogy not only in its own terms but in terms of its human implications. Thus, having contrasted a picture of a good typical infant school with a good typical secondary school, she writes, "These are not differences simply of method. They are different ways in which lives are being spent. They represent fundamental differences of values between the two institutions."

Professor James' concern with the quality of school life extends to teachers no less than students. "Teachers' lives are at stake, too," she writes. "They should be experiencing the same kinds of support, respect, and optimism about themselves that we ask them to accord to young people." What she urges, therefore, is not a child-centered school but rather a person-centered school.

Young Lives at Stake is a book about curriculum as well as school climate and organization. Those who want a "how-to" manual will be disappointed; those who want to be helped to think creatively about curriculum will be richly rewarded.

The most frequent question teachers ask about curriculum, at least in English schools, Mrs. James suggests, is "When to teach what?" But this, she argues, is "a misleading question." It is misleading because it assumes, falsely, that there is a single optimum route which all children should traverse through a given area of knowledge. The assumption ignores the fact, as Mrs. James writes, that "We can no longer induct young people into agreed certainties; we have to coopt them into uncertainty." And the question reflects a tendency to think of students as the objects of the teaching process. "Once we learn to think of students as the subjects of their own sentences, we free them. For it becomes clear that each must have the freedom to follow routes that are appropriate to him: what for him may be a shortcut, a closure readily achieved, may well for others seem roundabout . . . students move in their own directions and they arrive by different routes." Thus the question "When to teach what?" must be changed to "When to teach what to whom?"— And this in turn suggests a further rephrasing, into the question Professor James puts forward: "When should this child learn what?"

American teachers, whether of young children or adolescents, will find her discussion of individualization particularly rewarding—particularly her critique of what commonly passes for individualization, which is no more than to vary the rate at which students traverse the same course. For learning to be truly individualized, there must be a recognition "that students have needs which are not related to teachers' norms." To recognize this fact, however, is not to surrender the essential adult role. On the contrary, Professor James warns repeatedly of "the danger that a change from a relatively authoritarian model, if it is not supported by a theoretical understanding of the need for change, may lead simply to laissez-faire practices."

She warns of another danger as well: that individualization may be construed as isolation. "To go overboard for individualized learning in the sense of incompanionate learning would be a grave danger," she argues. Although "we need the chance for students to follow their bent, it does not follow that they must be asked to move as isolates." On the contrary, she calls for programming on the basis of individual needs or interests for part of the school day, and on the basis of youngsters working with their peers in groups of varying size for another part of the day. "There is no need for 'either-or' thinking here," she insists. "Both group work and individual work are important and the need is to have a far more flexible and opportunist view of the school day than either class lessons or individualized programming can allow." And her discussion of various kinds of grouping, together with her construct of the "fourfold curriculum," provides the theoretical basis for reform at the upper elementary as well as secondary school level.

In a book as far-ranging as this, needless to say, any reader is likely to find much with which he disagrees as well as agrees. To this reader, for example, Professor James exaggerates the degree and extent of the so-called "knowledge explosion," and thus exaggerates the obsolescence of the traditional academic disciplines. This, in turn, leaves me vaguely dissatisfied with her treatment of how teachers might relate the structure of the disciplines (or their subject matter) to students' individual and group interests and concerns. I wish, too, that she would have provided more concrete illustrations of how her curricular approach could be, or has been, carried out in practice. But it is pointless, and a little foolish, to complain that an author did not write a different book when the one she *has* written is as profoundly stimulating as this one. We are all in Charity James' debt.

CHARLES E. SILBERMAN

New York
September, 1971

Preface to the U.S. Edition

A YOUNG FRIEND of mine had a disturbing experience in his early twenties. He remembered nothing of his childhood, but wherever he went, if he crossed a street, for instance, he felt there was a small child following behind him, weeping. I have something of the same feelings about *Young Lives at Stake*. Having now taught for a year in the United States, and with the prospect of a year's study and development work in American schools, I am thinking today in terms of American needs. This is a book I wrote a while ago, and in another country. Yet when American teachers, students and administrators suggest to me that it could be useful over here I think they may be right.

It is certainly different in intention from much contemporary American literature advocating radical educational reform. Books and articles are usually of one of three kinds: they provide perspicacious analyses of what is wrong with American schools, they offer appreciative narrative of visits to innovative schools, or they give personal witness of what a dedicated teacher can achieve. They say, "Don't do this. It is evil, and for these reasons," or "I saw this. It was splendid," or "I did this. In spite of these mistakes which I made it was marvelously rewarding."

Considered diatribe, delighted description and authentic autobiography are all absorbing to read, and are much needed. But I think there is also a place in the world's movement towards reform and survival for a few books like *Young Lives*. In writing it I was trying to provide sustained theoretical argument in favour of radical reform of every aspect of schooling, and to show how education based on humane theory can work out in practice. The relation of practice and theory is very close, and the arguments against shocking or meager practices are given mainly in order to clear the ground for a positive proposal.

Looking at it today I see that this book gives a considerable challenge to the general reader without giving fair warning that it's doing so. The style at first makes it seem pretty straightforward and easygoing, and then suddenly you find yourself in the middle of some quite detailed practical, technical, or philosophical material. This is partly because I was attempting to relate theory and practice, but partly also because of the order of presentation. It deals *seriatim* with many different facets of school, with adult expectations of them, with curriculum, with classroom procedures, appraisal and so on; and all the way through, the same switch from negative to positive argument is repeated: "This won't do, this is damaging for these reasons, I hope we have heard the last of the other. Look at the deeper significance of our actions and I think you will agree that our priorities should be as follows. Now here are some ways in which they might be embodied in practice (or are being so). Now for the next aspect." Analytically, this is a good design, but the constant switchback is quite hard on the reader.

There seem to be two remedies. One is for readers not to be at all puritanical about the way they read it, to skip parts they aren't interested in, or to use it in a nonlinear way rather like a handbook. The other is for me to fill a gap by giving a short summary of some of the central ideas. Some are only implicit in the argument because I intended to follow *Young Lives* with another book in which underlying beliefs were to be more fully developed. Other ideas listed are pretty fully worked out, but I would rather not assign chapters or pages to them because they are fundamental to the book as a whole. As the reader will notice throughout the book, I like to give lists and I do so because they make it possible for readers to build their own patterns of relationships between ideas, so here is a **summarized list:**

* The most important thing about a school is its fabric of human relationships. If these aren't loving, truthful and hopeful, and if human diversity isn't respected and enjoyed, then you can change the curriculum and the shape of the classroom as often as you like, but the cows won't come home.
* Today, most schools are what I would call bossocracies or are rigid bureaucracies. The value they represent is power, not growth. They mirror a social condition outside the school which is destructive to human dignity and ultimately endangers the species. Schools should be mirrors of our hoped-for future, living communities in which socially we are producers not alienated from the products of our social labours.
* The secret of a living community is twofold. First, it must be at risk. People in schools need to be free to make mistakes without shame. One of the worst things about our schooling is that everyone plays safe. Secondly, it requires "organic solidarity" based on the collaboration of small groups. The basic concept of the collaborative school is one of small groups of teachers and teachers, students and students, students and teachers.
* If a school is to be a fit place for people to be in, it must be porous, with much movement in and out of the community. The school as a total institution is out; the school as a community of younger with older can still be serviceable, if the social fabric and patterns of expectation are brought into line with the true needs of adolescents and other humans, and if it draws on the wider community without being subservient to it.
* We are now at a stage in human development where we can afford to take note of the true character of our extraordinary species, and in truth cannot afford not to. Look at any competent infant and you will find him or her exploratory, creative, aware. Look at any of the young people that our culture has damaged, and you will find them apathetic, passive, or insensitive to others and them-

selves. People in schools need to engage in the "living behaviors" of enquiry, making and dialogue—risky behaviors that require the supportive fabric of a living community.
* Any fixed curriculum (and especially one based on knowledge as known rather than knowledge as knowing) is out of date, and always will be, and this is good although a difficult challenge, since it means that teachers and students, with all the help they can muster, have the task of exploring and creating a curriculum appropriate to themselves.
* By a beautiful coincidence, adolescents engaging in a heuristic, creative, expressive and sensitive education need teachers to work together in small groups, since if you seriously ask any worthwhile questions you are going to get into the wide-ranging studies that I called Interdisciplinary Enquiry (IDE) and Making (IDM). Teachers have to group together to pool their strengths if they are to help students in IDE to formulate and develop ideas and to use a wide range of forms of expression, ranging from math to the dance, as they are needed. Artists should see themselves as central and essential to this experience. This collaboration, and other forms of grouping that become natural as a school develops, give teachers, no less than their students, the opportunity for continuing growth.
* The distinction between cognitive and affective education is untenable.
* Most traditional schools treat students as creatures to be processed, often in terms of teachers' objectives. Many innovative schools treat them as consumers who are thus still dependent on a bureaucracy.
* If you value diversity in growth then appraisal will be in terms of relative strengths. This is important not only because students need intrinsic success and personal acknowledgment, but also because it is vitally important that they discover the circumstances and rhythms of life that best suit them.

* There is value in thinking of learners and learning in terms of a four-cell system that I called the fourfold curriculum. In this students can engage in open enquiry (IDE), can work within the deliberate demarcation lines in narrower fields of study, can get help according to special needs and can move into studies of special interest to them.

Perhaps I might add here that today I would alter the balance of the book. At the time I introduced IDE, in 1965, emphasis on the structure of disciplines was at its height, and I knew from experience that it was essential to offer a sound epistemological argument for interdisciplinary studies. I had only formulated the notion of the fourfold curriculum in the course of preparing for this book and wasn't yet fully aware of its implications. Today it seems to me that recognition that students have needs which are not related to teachers' norms is very important. It seems so obvious that it shouldn't need mentioning, but in fact most schools say, "You ought to be able to do this, but you can't, so you need remedial help" (or "so we can write you off"), whereas we should be saying, "Everyone develops in different orders and at different rates, and everyone throughout life needs remedial help in some study or other. You recognize this particular need—possibly we have helped you to see it—so it is up to us to enable you to cope with it."

* Teachers' lives are at stake too. They should be experiencing the same kinds of support, respect and optimism about themselves that we ask them to accord to young people.

* By implication this book demythologizes educational reform. It sometimes seems from the literature as if only Renaissance men and women, people with immense verve and intellect, can achieve the changes that are needed. The English teachers who have been working out these ideas are good heads or good teachers but few of them would see themselves as spectacular people. Their strength lies in the fact that their priorities are humane and firmly grounded, that they are willing to abandon naivete in order

to achieve reform, and that they are aware of the changes that can be wrought by collaboration.

This is not a book about hating schools, nor is it another harrowing of the teacher. I think we have to see the educational revolution as an enormous step forward in the history of our species, and therefore inevitably difficult and threatening to many people. I can't hate teachers for performing the tasks, even what I called the assassinations, that are demanded of them by our economy and culture. The narrow, rigid ones, like our alienated pupils, are one tip of the iceberg of our very chilly society.

As for the schools, of course I think they are coming to an end in their present form: a short, sharp compulsory education will come to seem very odd indeed as lifelong access to learning and resource centers and to wider sources of enjoyment become the norm. I don't happen to feel particularly moral about it. In fact, I don't like moralizing about changes in our social institutions which seem to me to be inevitable much more than I like using moralistic arguments to support reactionary institutions. The need seems to me to be for action to improve the condition of youth, wherever you find your relative strengths are most useful, whether it is struggling to humanize existing schools by changing their fabric of relationships, and all that follows from that, or moving out to set up innovative programs of other kinds, This is a matter of temperament and circumstance, not of a dogmatic either-or. *Young Lives* is written in terms of the first situation, but much of it has relevance for the second.

I have been wondering if the deliberate Englishness of the book is going to make difficulties for American readers. I hope the Glossary (page 252) will solve some immediate problems. Beyond that, I think it's important to make some distinctions. I put forward some ideas as being true of all human beings, as for instance the insistence on "living behaviors." Then again, some material seems to me to be common to modern Western societies. I would include in this the importance of groups in effecting change, and also many of the evils of our education, such as divisiveness and the distortion of schools by the economy. Some of the school procedures that I attack, such as the incoherent dribble of class lessons on subject-disciplines narrowly conceived, and especially the failure to recognize the changed role of teachers —these seem to be common to both countries because much of our education has common roots.

On the other hand some of the problems are different. Schools in both countries are highly competitive, but the pressures come at different stages and in rather different forms. Also, some of the details in the specific proposals are inappropriate, although the underlying problem is similar. Throughout, I was deliberately building on English strengths and hoping to mitigate English faults. American strengths and weaknesses are different, so even if the underlying values are shared the educational changes are likely to differ. *Young Lives* should be seen as a highly political book, dealing with the art of what was possible in England in the late 1960s. For instance, I proposed retaining age-grouping for much of the time because to the English secondary teacher it's familiar, and not another confusing factor. It might not be appropriate here, though surely much better than grading. Even for England, the book was intended throughout to suggest starting positions, not finality.

To many readers it will seem that what I propose is an extension of the British primary school. The fact is that in our Pilot Courses for experienced teachers, in which we worked out possibilities for reform, we weren't thinking about primary schools at all. We were trying to look with eyes experienced yet innocent at the adolescents we knew, at ourselves and our colleagues, at parents, at the changing social and cultural patterns. What we came up with turned out to be a logical extension of the best primary education. But we were creating, not copying, and it has become increasingly clear to me that if our thinking was lively and adventurous it was because among ourselves we were working in the spirit of exploratory and creative education. I am sure this is the way for Americans also, and in particular that a greater trust of teachers is essential.

So I hope people here will find this book useful, and also *Collaborative Learning** by a friend and former colleague, Edwin Mason; I hope some will want to get IDEAS, the publication edited by a third originator of our work, Leslie Smith (see p. 11). But to copy these proposals, which after all are not novel, just freshly seen and perhaps freshly interrelated, is not to be exploratory, creative or sensitive to American youth. Struggling through problems in collaborative groups is what open education is all about. The outward results might for a time seem similar, but the inner experience is totally different, can't be copied, can hardly be conveyed. It's fun and pain, it is risk and realization, it is the real stuff of learning.

CHARITY JAMES

Boston, Mass.
Summer 1971

---

*Agathon Press, Inc., New York, 1972.

Preface

THIS BOOK IS a record of some of the things I have learned during the last three years about immediate possibilities for educational innovation in England. Since January, 1965, when the Department of Education and Science invited Goldsmiths' College to undertake a full-time Pilot Course for experienced teachers to consider the needs of young school leavers, the unit which has now become the Curriculum Laboratory has been in continuing dialogue with groups of head teachers and senior staff from secondary schools. Over seven courses, each lasting eleven weeks, we have explored a range of problems much wider than can be represented here. We have concluded that the education of *all* adolescents should have a high priority in educational change, no less than the education of statutory leavers, education in socially deprived areas, or even education of younger children.

If this country cannot get its secondary education right we shall continue to diminish the possibilities of primary schooling; and radical reappraisal, not just a patching, is needed to ameliorate the disadvantages in school of those who suffer from obvious social and cultural handicap. But beyond that there is an urgent need to seek an education that is appropriate for adolescence, since this is in modern societies a vitally important period of growth, when new ranges of personal development can be explored and new qualities of personal relationships established. At present there is no model of secondary schooling that is remotely in line with our growing understanding of what human living might become or is relevant to our context of continuing change. To make school a good place to live in has been the task we have set ourselves, together, over these last years. Although this book is deliberately confined to a statement of the English situation I believe that our work has significance for other countries.

My proposals are practical, immediate and in some respects subject to rapid obsolescence. Whatever the long-term future of schools (if indeed they have a long-term future as compulsory environments for young people to grow up in), and whatever radical changes are made in buildings and technological aids for learning and for banking and retrieving data, the problems I discuss stem from features in our lives that are with us already, the changing relationships between the generations, for instance, the expanding sense of human power to control the environment, the loss of shared cultural certainties. The changes in mood and direction that I propose do not wait on further social and cultural change in the future. They are possible and necessary now.

Our continuing dialogue with teachers and the adventurous experimentation that is coming out of it in schools, both as a direct result of shared decisions and through the welcome our common ideas have received elsewhere, combine to give me a confident belief that in this country we are in a superb position for educational innovation. There is a desire for change among many teachers, which needs only that some should have (for the first time in our educational history) a little time to settle down to examine possibilities. And the tradition of English teachers' freedom in matters internal to the school, even if it has not been greatly exploited in the past, enables them to create relatively unhampered a new way of life in school once they find that they, their pupils, and the community in which they live enjoy doing so together.

That the need for change is urgent we can hardly doubt. A teacher bounded by the present lives in the past. Rather as a creative artist cannot permit himself to be the mouthpiece of commonly understood social consensus, but has to discover a new vision through patiently working with his material, so the creative teacher contributes fully to the making of tomorrow's culture not by enslaving himself to the current demands of today's society but by being open to the needs and potential of the young.

Today's teachers are perhaps uniquely fortunate, if they have the faith to see it. Just because the dangers of a society that is not person-centred are so great today, now that the species can achieve genocide or can organize totally manipulated *used* communities, the message for teachers is clear. They must seek to make education fully human, drawing out the strengths and talents of all young people so that they can acquire the intellectual, practical, and social skills they need, but above all helping them to find within themselves the resources that alone can help them to live at ease with a changing world.

For discovering, accepting, and confirming the self, adolescence is a critical period. And the stakes are higher than they have ever been: on the one hand, not "failed O-level" or "failed B.A.," but "failed humanity," and on the other, new possibilities of richly enjoyable living by people who are more fully, generously, and diversely persons than we with our long training in parsimony can even imagine. We must not miss this moment. Young lives are at stake.

My thanks are due to all the members of our Pilot Courses, for all have contributed to our collaboration. In quoting from our Pilot Course Reports I have been able to name some of the anonymous contributors, but there were many others; and only a diary could record the moments when after weeks of uncomfortably casting about we suddenly came to see a new possibility, or when an idea that had seemed too radical to be mooted was calmly accepted by one or other of these experienced teachers and thereby made available to the group.

I cannot name all the course members, but I must name my colleagues in the Curriculum Laboratory, although I could not hope adequately to express what I have gained from being with them. We have had a series of distinguished American

Visiting Professors. Their combined effect, both by their professionalism and by their surprise at what we have thought obvious, has been to teach us to become less insular in our expectations of what schools might be, without ever suggesting that we should adopt transatlantic models. Individually, the contribution of each has been unique. On the first Course, Dr. G. D. Phillips, Chairman of the Foundations of Education Department at Boston University, shattered the mould of our habitual thinking and thereby made it possible for us to create new solutions to problems freshly seen. I know of noone else with the vigour and vision to have done this for us. Then Dr. Florence Roane, a distinguished black educator, helped us to understand how a movement based on group process might develop. Later Dr. Jack Abramowitz brought long experience of work with the socially handicapped, and Dr. Mary Caroline Richards, an artist of a wide diversity of gifts and searching humanity, helped us to arrive at new understanding of our inner resources. Now we are joined by Dr. J. B. Macdonald, Professor of Social Foundations and Curriculum in the University of Milwaukee-Wisconsin, whose determination for freedom, profoundly felt and thought, reminds us all of the dangers of a conforming society. These have been our welcome and generous visitors. Among our English colleagues we have looked throughout to the support and understanding of Dr. D. R. Chesterman, Warden of Goldsmiths' College.

With the permanent members of our tiny unit my working relationships are so close that it is hard to acknowledge one attribute without feeling that I diminish the total person whom I know. On every page I find echoes of what they are. Edwin Mason has brought to our common thinking a deep understanding of what human living might be and of the degradation and irrelevance of many of our present ways, together with a poet's power to reveal our daily experiences to us. Leslie Smith, who as a headmaster created one of the most perceptive, humane, and light-hearted schools in England, makes miracles seem commonplace by knowing how to set about them. Sam Mauger, our newest recruit, already refreshes us with his directness and clarity of vision. Finally, Mrs. Mary Darby, Secretary to the unit, supports and guides us all through all our difficulties, including mine with the final stages of producing this book. We are what in this book I call a "focus-group," and I am deeply grateful for all that this means.

This book stems from continuing dialogue with these friends and colleagues. Nevertheless I would not ask anyone else to take responsibility for the views expressed in it. For this reason, and because I do not believe this to be a period in which we should seek to make lapidary and authoritative statements, I have chosen to write in a direct and personal style.

October, 1967

CHARITY JAMES
Director, University of London
Goldsmiths' College Curriculum Laboratory

NOTE: Many of the ideas in this book found their first expression in the reports prepared by the various Pilot Courses for Experienced Teachers at the Curriculum Laboratory of the University of London Goldsmiths' College. Their titles are as follows:

No. 1: *The Role of the School in a Changing Society.* C. M. James and G. D. Phillips, eds., 1965.
No. 2: *The Raising of the School Leaving Age.* A. E. Mason, ed., 1965.
No. 3: *The Education of the Socially Handicapped.* A. E. Mason, ed., 1966.
No. 4: *14-18: The Education of the Young School Leaver.* K. Rudge, ed., 1966.
No. 5: *New Roles for the Learner.* A. E. Mason, ed., 1967.
Nos. 6 & 7: *Curriculum and Resources in the Secondary School.* D. Hoffman, M. C. Richards, and A. E. Mason, eds., 1968.

The University of London Goldsmiths' College also publishes on behalf of the Curriculum Laboratory a periodical called IDEAS, edited by Leslie A. Smith, that gives accounts of work in implementing the Fourfold Curriculum as it develops. For further information on these publications, address the Editor of Publications, The University of London Curriculum Laboratory, 6 Dixon Road, London S.E.14, England.

Chapter 1

Education for a Well-spent Youth

GROWN-UP: You don't like school? I wonder why not.
5-YEAR-OLD: Well, it's such a waste of time, for one thing.
GROWN-UP: You don't like school? I wonder why not.
5-YEAR-OLD: Well, I can't read and I can't write and they won't let you talk.

IF I OPEN a book about the education of adolescents with comments by two dissatisfied five-year-olds, it is certainly not with the intention of mocking good infant schools, which I believe point the way through to the rest of us. On the contrary, I have chosen them, rather than any other excerpts from the massive concordance of quotations on the pros and cons of school, for two reasons. First, here are two children who between them suggest how their education might be programmed. One hints at the marvellous dimensions of possibility in his offhand phrase, "for one thing." Here is someone who had world enough if only he were allowed the time to explore it, and thereby come to realise his own possibilities, instead of being trapped in the clinical corridors of the time-sense of industrialized adults. Here is the demand for *intrinsic motivation*, for *education through involvement*, for *living in the present* with full enjoyment. The second child, less visionary, more convivial by disposition, or in that moment of time or during that phase in his development, found school too refined and private a place. He wanted to be able to talk to his fellows. Here is the demand for establishing human relations through good *communication*, a hint perhaps (though not developed) of the possibilities of *collaborative learning*. And he wanted to communicate in his own way, which at that time was by talking. Here is the demand for *development through relative strengths*. Finally the very difference between their requirements points to the *diversity* of needs, talents, and interests of the young.

Most of us, hearing their comments from friends as I did, would feel very regretful that these two children were obviously at unusually poor infant schools. Yet if five or ten years later they made comparable criticism of school, would their parents, teachers, and prospective employers accord them comparable sympathy? This is the second reason for quoting them. They suggest a fundamental question: is there any reason other than tradition why we permit to the young child an intrinsically motivated exploratory and constructive education, yet deny it to the adolescent?

CHILD-CENTRED ATTITUDES—a quiet revolution

During the present century there has been a quiet revolution in our treatment of young children, a gradual removal of physical restraint and a withdrawal from judgmental attitudes. Demand feeding, gentle weaning, a more permissive attitude towards toilet training, sandpits to get dirty in, water for sensual delight, these early experiences are followed at best by an interest-centred, creative primary education, which is officially sanctioned[1] if not always practised.

All this is evidence of a major cultural change. The rationale may not always be widely understood and the deeper motivation is open to different interpretations. We may choose to attribute the change, for instance to a late flowering of 19th century romanticism; or to a vulgarization (usually in the good sense of that word, but sometimes indeed an oversimplification as in regard to repression) of psychoanalytic theories; or we may look to economic causes, to a gradual

e .g. *Children and their Primary Schools* (The Plowden Report, H.M.S.O., 1966) weakening of the insistence on postponed gratifications as thrift loses its moral grip or as parents begin to sense that an affluent society can afford golden days for children. Perhaps it is simply that having fewer we value them more and observe them more closely. Whatever the explanation may be, the facts are clear: prevailing attitudes to childhood are increasingly child-centred and increasingly child-trusting. Modern primary education has greatly benefited by this change. It has also greatly contributed to it. We have an admirable model for primary education, one that is respected all over the world, and it is based on perceiving and trusting children.

THE CONTRAST WITH ADOLESCENCE

The harsh world of the adolescent, in school at any rate, still awaits its spring. Indeed, the discordant dissatisfactions of much of our secondary education may become more intense. The contrast between education in childhood and in adolescence may well increase when the habit of drilling children for selection at 11-plus wears off and junior schools come more fully to recognize their freedom to give children an opportunity for active participation in a permissive atmosphere. At a time when the sharp distinction between primary and secondary education is growing rather fuzzy at the edges with different Local Education Authorities experimenting with middle schools (9 to 13) and with transfer at 12-plus rather than 11-plus, it is worth remembering the historical background of the breaking up of the all-age elementary school. In 1926, when it was recommended by the Hadow Report, despite a good deal of rationalizing overfroth about surging adolescence, the fact was that 11-plus was a convenient age for a break in schooling because it divided the last six years of statutory schooling neatly into two halves. It is worth remembering also that Sweden has all-age schools today.

Certainly there is no justification in terms of human development for the sharp discontinuity in social experience to which we subject young people in the years embracing or preceding puberty. We have some consensus of opinion as to how childhood might be well spent, in school and out of it, and the opinion is coherent. Yet it seems that although individually many teachers and most parents are increasingly humane and relaxed in their relationships with adolescents, and observant of their needs, the demands that society makes on young people through its secondary schools are neither.

THE SCHOOL DAY—*a caricature?*

If for a moment we forget our preconceptions about secondary schooling and imagine ourselves able to start afresh, can we really be content with the way in which our young people's days are spent? Would we allow them, if we had the choice, to spend this time in squads (groups is too rich a word) being addressed or grilled by adults, one adult after another, and in a totally incoherent order? Would we not wish them, at an age apt for what Allport has called "propriate striving"[1] (the development of a momentum towards personally recognized goals) to have the chance to undertake some major task during a school day, or week, or year? Would we not like them to learn to work cooperatively rather than in a moral climate so competitive that sharing is denigrated as "cheating" and actually punished? Would we really wish them to find much of their satisfaction in having some others to be better than? Animals, we are told, rescue their wounded. Who rescues the children at the bottom of the heap, the bottom children in the bottom stream? Sometimes a kindly, occasionally a superbly imaginative remedial teacher; certainly, never their peers in higher streams.

Today parents increasingly see themselves as advisers to their adolescent and indeed younger children and aim to work with them cooperatively. Parents are warned that the young must learn to face frustrations if they are to become

---

[1] cf. G. W. Allport, *Becoming* (New Haven, Yale University Press, 1960), pp. 47-51

self-directed, but also symbiosis, the reality situation of collaborative living, presents ample frustration without the need for parents to put themselves on pedestals of unimpeachable virtue and unquestionable authority. How then can we explain the typical stance of the teacher (usually himself or herself a parent, so this is a problem of the institution, not the person)? There he stands like a Victorian paterfamilias instructing his flock, and without even the pleasure of warming his coat-tails, believing that he must always know the answers, that on his authority the discipline of thirty-odd young people directly depends. How have teachers allowed themselves to be manoeuvred, or trapped, or fossilized, into a position which accords so ill with our contemporary understanding of the relationship between the generations, not to mention our grasp of group dynamics, according to which he invites hatred as a dominant father or contempt as a scapegoat. It is a triumph of many teachers that in such a social context they can maintain their humanity.

Again, how do we explain a youth-time arbitrarily divided into spasms of thirty, forty, or forty-five minutes, punctuated by the clanging of bells, and often followed by a massive flocking in and out of corridors? How do we reconcile this planned incoherence with our knowledge of the different rhythms of learning different individuals have, of their different ways of thinking and learning, of their different degrees of P-factor (perseveration, mercifully permitted to be amoral, unlike those hardened virtues, persistence and perseverance)? How can we hope that any young people will in school time engage in any worthwhile creative thinking if they are never allowed to brood, to stay at something a little longer, to move on in apparent restlessness to minor chores while the ground is fallow for "negative capability"?

Again, is it really a requirement of equality of educational opportunity in a mass society that young people should have to prove themselves equal to sitting down periodically in a room with a clock in order to inform their elders of familiar facts? In allowing them to spend precious time mugging up facts for us, is it we who are the mugs? For even if such examinations were skilfully and scientifically planned—and the level of competence shown in most internal tests and many external examinations is a national disgrace—do they really give us much information beyond examining the ability to pass examinations? Do they tell us more than what teachers could tell us? Worse still, do they not invite teachers no less than pupils to look at the young as sums of their performances? What does it profit an employer to know that X achieved A in physics, B in woodwork, C in French in a public examination? What he needs is a recognizable profile, indicating the person's personal style, the qualities of accuracy, or fluency of ideas, or quality of ideas, or skill at handling complex material (or accurate memory, perhaps, but this is not usually so important today with the availability of data banks of all kinds). But if that is what we need, would not young people's youth be better spent if our purposes were effective diagnosis, leading to the identification of strengths? And if this were our purpose would we not decide that quite different methods of appraisal would be saner?

If we really thought of young people as people, would we go on playing Bingo with their lives, demanding that they should be able to produce all the necessary pieces to match the standardized pre-ordained picture of what a satisfactory young person would be? At breakfast they seem to be quite different from one another, and again at tea, and we are well satisfied. Why ask them all to do the same things (or as nearly so as possible) in the time between? Are there so few things to know and to do that we must insist on these and no others?

If we were once again to look at adolescents with innocent eyes, unblinkered by tradition, would we not want them to spend this time in part at least in discovering themselves, and enabling them to communicate their findings to others, using the many windows on to themselves that our culture can provide—not only speaking up in the occasional "class-discussion," but working in cooperative groups, seeking and exploring materials which at that moment seem supremely interesting, drawing on phantasy to enrich self-understanding and the perception of others, using the behavioural sciences to study the behaviour of human beings?

And would we not be seeking to help them now (and ourselves also) to understand better what it is like to live in a technological society? Would we not be trying to help them to become the kinds of people who will be able to solve the appalling problems of the human misery that is part—to some young people perhaps the most noticeable part—of the culture that we transmit? Could anyone claim that our secondary education as it is today is one which will help them to meet collaboratively and with courage the problems that will crowd in on them?

Is my description of the school day a caricature, or is the school day in many schools a caricature of living? Secondary education is so strange a process, one without parallel among other creatures, and the change from our model of primary schooling represents so sharp a slashing of the growing human being's experience, that we have to ask on what grounds, psychological or sociological, we can explain it, and whether we can defend it at all. Are we allowing millions of people in schools, children and adults, to spend their time disagreeably when it is quite unnecessary that they should do so?

Of course there are students who enjoy their secondary schooling much of the time. It is even possible to think that a majority of them do so for the greater part of the time; but this seems improbable, in view of the fact that such little research evidence as we have suggests that in one area of Britain at least, whereas home meets reasonably satisfactorily the expressive, as against the instrumental, needs of midadolescents of 15 and 16, school lamentably fails. Professor Musgrove's study[1] of young people in a Northern conurbation shows that school failed to meet their hopes and expectations for emotional security, freedom, friendship, sense of competence, support from adults, identity with a group and sense of

[1] F. W. Musgrove, "The Social Needs and Satisfactions of Some Young People," *Brit. Jour. of Ed. Psych.*, xxxvi (February and June, 1966)

purpose. With school rapidly replacing the extended family as the institution to which young people of the small nuclear family must turn for additional stable adult figures, even when the relationships with parents are all that could be desired, this failure is disastrous.

Home, according to this study, was far more satisfactory, and the author's summary of reasons given is significant: "At home you can be natural; individuality is recognized."[1] The implied plea to the school to let this too be a place where you can be yourself recalls those five-year-olds, reminds us that (although we have not research evidence to prove it) there are primary schools where individuality is recognized. These are schools where it is not for the child to find out what the teacher wants and give it to him, but for the teacher to observe what the child is becoming and help him to find what he needs. We do not want a society where only in the "privatization" of home life can we be ourselves. If we are not ourselves at school, and later at adult work, then we cannot be ourselves at home either; we bring too many anxieties, channel our emotional needs too narrowly, demand too much of home, diminish our expectations of what we might become by looking in the one favourable mirror we know.

Granted that for much of the time school is a strain—for neither pupils nor teachers can be themselves—is the sacrifice of precious life-time necessary? I have no wish to denigrate teachers. On the contrary, even as I write I have in mind the generosity and concern of very many teachers, who see their students through periods of great difficulty with their homes. It is not the individual behaviour of teachers or parents that I am concerned with—there are some good and some bad in both groups, and most teachers are parents also. The problem is whether the school as a socializing institution is adapting itself, as perhaps the home is, to the changing needs of today. The difference is that whereas millions of homes, by drawing in on themselves, can through millions of unplanned adjust-

---

[1] ibid. p.66

ments make havens of themselves against a bleak and stormy world, school is necessarily a public institution, which has public pressures on it. On the other hand it has one vast advantage in change over the family: it is in the hands of a profession which can if it wishes revolutionize its ways of work.

Schools are dysfunctional at the moment partly because they are acting in response to public pressures which are largely ignorant and in some ways unconsciously destructive. By taking to heart and mind the findings of educational and other social research, and by using modern opportunities for easy communication, the teaching profession could create a model and practice of secondary schooling that was more agreeable to all its members and met the functional requirements of society more effectively than anything we have had during our short history of mass schooling. The power and the opportunity are there, properly and within the professional scope of teachers, to work toward a new model, more coherent, pleasant and more efficient, which will carry the goodwill of the rest of society with it.

Having made this statement of faith in the possibility of change, I must also recognize that there are obstacles. The first obstacle is the suspicion, conscious and unconscious, felt by all social classes (though often on different grounds) that schools and teachers inevitably attract unless they open their doors to the community and become a loved and established part of it. There is inevitably some rivalry between school and home, and a good deal of fear among parents lest their children are not at the best possible school, and it takes a lot of overcoming. It is significant that all the schools which are working successfully on the lines that I shall be describing have for a long time been accepted by parents as good schools which can be trusted.

The same is true of relations with employers. Students who attend good schools (and I do not at all mean selective schools necessarily) have a double advantage: they receive a better education and employers are more apt to accept them and their teachers' evaluation of them. To change from good to better is a great deal easier than changing the whole image of a school.

The second obstacle to change cannot be proved, but the possibility that it is there must be faced. How can we explain the difference between the education of the child and that of the adolescent? Is one reason that we, and by this I mean all adults, see less to envy in childhood whereas, on the other hand, it would be surprising if there were no punitive element in our attitudes to adolescents? In a rapidly changing society a very natural envy of old for young is strengthened by reminders of rapid obsolescence both of machines and persons, and the middle-aged are denied the pedestal which was their reward in more static times. We find it hard to keep up; it is easier for the young and they are better looking and more energetic than we are into the bargain. Parents marry sooner, their children mature earlier, and the rivalry is rapid and unmistakable. What easier way of cutting them down to size than to send them to schools where they must be sedentary and silent at an age when they are full of talk and physical vigour, acquiescent when they most need to discover what personality they may have to assert, impersonal when the tides of altruism and rebellion are now flowing most strongly?

If there is jealousy, there is likely also to be fear, for the young represent many of the urgent forces to which many adults have scrupulously denied consciousness for half a lifetime. Freud commented that we ought to educate children to face the danger and hostility they would meet in adult life.[1] Perhaps we are, as a society, doing just that: giving them an experience-based education of a grim kind.

Whatever credence we choose to give to these possibilities, we can at least see that it would be a very natural human ploy to get the best of both worlds: at home to be a good parent with a happy convivial relationship in which you could safely spoil the young, confident in the assurance that you had

---

[1] S. Freud, *The Future of an Illusion* (1927), tr. W. D. Robson-Scott (1928, rev. ed. 1962, Hogarth Press and Institute of Psychoanalysis), p. 49

handed over the authoritarian elements in your parental role to experts.[1] Then turn against the experts and side with your children and the world is yours. The teacher with his back to the blackboard also has his back to the wall.

It may be, then, that secondary school is among other things the institution through which adults express their deep unconscious rejection of the young and of the aspects of themselves which they are afraid of. What is certain is that it is for many parents the battle-ground on which their rivalry is played out. This is the negative aspect of a change whereby the education system has very properly become the main selective agency by which future status and earning capacity is determined. It is worth remembering how rapidly in the first quarter of the century many parents recognized the potential importance of the 1907 Regulations permitting free (as opposed to scholarship) places in selective schools. The Board of Education of the time had no expectation of the competition there would be for these places,[2] but parents were quick to see their importance. In a society dedicated to acquisitive egalitarianism this is inevitable. What is lamentable is that there is so little flexibility of outlook, so that it is not the youngster's present needs that are observed but only his supposed future profit. No wonder there is evidence of acute role conflict and negative self-concepts among older secondary school students undergoing this process.[3]

---

[1] Many teachers know that this is not phantasy. One headmaster told me of a visit from a parent. "Two of your boys were behaving disgracefully the other day," she said. "What are you going to do about it?" Baffled, he answered "But they're both your sons, aren't they?" "Yes," she said. "Now, what are you going to do?"

[2] cf. Olive Banks, *Parity and Prestige in English Secondary Education: a study in Child Psychology* (Routledge and Kegan Paul, 1955), Ch. 5 esp.: "The popular demand for secondary education ... increased enormously during and after the First World War at a rate beyond the capacity of the local education officers to supply. The resulting competition for free places destroyed all hopes of a secondary education for the 'average' elementary school child except as a fee-payer." (p. 69)

[3] cf. F. W. Musgrove, *Brit. Jour. of Ed. Psych.*, XXXVI (1966), 143-149, and "Role Conflict in Adolescence," op. cit., XXXIV (1964); also Douglas A. Pidgeon, ed., *Achievement in Mathematics* (National Foundation for Educational Research in England and Wales, 1967), Ch. 4

It is most certainly arguable that one of the effects of bonding school to parental ambition is that we are likely as a nation not to be drawing out the less conformist, more creative kinds of talent that the world so greatly needs. My point here is that it may well be that in some respects young people have less chance of spending their youth in richly rewarding ways in a meritocratic society than in periods which had no thought of equality of opportunity. As parents invest more of their emotional capital in their small families[1] the pressure on teachers to deliver the goods, acquisitively speaking, increases. Moreover, two factors add to the pressure. First, there is the drive of the "status dissenters" who see school as a second chance to overcome the frustrations of their own lives: D. F. Swift suggested, for instance, a few years ago that the best chance of passing the 11-plus was to be the child of a pessimistic lower-middle class clerk,[2] and Jackson and Marsden put forward the view that much of the pressure was from the "sunken middle class" wishing to regain status through the grammar school.[3] Such parents are likely to be prepared to believe that an educational system is good for their children although disagreeable—perhaps in some cases because it is disagreeable, since life to them is like that. These can be influential parents bringing constant pressure on a school.

A second more general factor is parental ignorance. Secondary education has not been re-thought as a whole for generations. The teaching profession has not offered a creative alternative to parents. In fact there is every reason to hope that when changes are formulated that will make education more satisfactory for young people, they will gain support from parents. For we are in a special sense a developing nation, and there is widespread anxiety about education. "Today," write Hanson and Brembeck in surveying education in developing

---

[1] cf. F. Zweig, *The Worker in an Affluent Society* (Heinemann, 1961)
[2] In D. F. Swift, "Who Passes the 11+ ?" *New Society*, III (5th March, 1964)
[3] B. Jackson and F. Marsden, *Education and the Working Class* (Routledge and Kegan Paul, 1962)

nations, "in the modernizing world, there is widespread feeling that too much education is irrelevant, out of touch and out of tune with modern life, dysfunctional in terms of the services it is currently being called upon to render...."[1]

The anxiety is justified. Education must be dysfunctional when it is so little related to the differing needs, concerns, and life tasks of the young, but it is also becoming increasingly clear that the system is failing even by the most hard-headed and short-sighted terms of reference. Many parents seem complaisant about their children's dissatisfactions at school only because they know of no alternative. When they become aware that reforms which embody practical good sense as well as a sound theoretical structure can also make schooling far more suited to their children's individual needs they give full support.

Similarly if we were to offer employers a creative alternative to the present evidence we give them of a pupils' accomplishments, based on new styles of school records, we should be meeting their requirements far more successfully than we can at present either for those who are taking examinations or for those who do not.

It may be necessary to continue for a time with certification at 16, although this is curiously old-fashioned behaviour which most advanced countries manage very well without; but following the lead of Certificate of Secondary Education (Mode 3) which is internally set but externally moderated, we can collaborate with General Certificate of Education Boards, so as to produce an examination which can be concerned with major areas of investigation on inter-disciplinary lines.[2] Again, the pressure of competition for places in higher

---

[1] John W. Hanson and Cole S. Brembeck, edd., *Education and the Development of Nations* (Holt, Rinehart and Winston, 1966), p. 250

[2] I have suggested, for instance, that much of the material individually examined could be brought into a coherent whole by seeing it in a context, such as "Living in a Technological Society," and my colleague, L. A. Smith, is evolving techniques for this purpose, in collaboration with an interested G.C.E. Board. If part of this work is Mode 3, it will be an admirable extension of work pioneered by the Southern Regional C.S.E. Board, and others, in developing work in "environmental studies."

education distorts our entire secondary schooling. In this context, we must see the wastage rates at University as very high. A wastage of some 14 per cent. would be negligible in a country with an open University system; here, it must be considered high and therefore a cause of great concern. Schools are challenged to create a kind of schooling that involves young people more in their work, leaves more growing power in them, more positive self-concepts. Similar changes are both possible and necessary in those Universities which have not for generations examined their own preconceptions.

Writing on behalf of the members of the first Pilot Course for Experienced Teachers at Goldsmiths' College I said:

> The school is seen by society as a place where children are selected and prepared for the labour market. They are shaped in their formative years not according to their developmental needs but so that they may fit into pre-ordained niches, a system in any case doomed to failure since the shape and number of niches are constantly changing. They are classified and labelled according to their anticipated market value, and this essay in astrological prediction continues despite our knowledge that it attempts the impossible. The pressure of parents, employers, and Universities constrict the school with a strait-jacket of examinations. Yet we have evidence from these same agencies that the products of the schools disappoint. Small wonder, when the system has extruded those who by sex or class prefer to opt out of this obstacle race, and when the criteria for selection give credit to convergent thinking and a willingness to conform to conventional patterns of attainment.
>
> Our primary concern in this report has been with the well-being of children and teachers in school, but we cannot ignore the fact that the wastage of the nation's talent chronicled by numerous English researches and implied by the new American studies in creativity may destroy this country's ability to survive alongside the expanding economies of others. It may even now be too late.[1]

The field is open for change. Teachers are not accountable for the fact that secondary schooling is dysfunctional. The teaching profession would be at fault, however, as a profession, if it neglected the opportunity that there is today to promote

[1] First Report, p. 22. The Reports of the various Pilot courses, referred to thus in the footnotes, are listed on page 252.

change. It is a remarkable fact that this first Pilot Course in 1965 was the first opportunity experienced secondary teachers had had to hold a prolonged conference on educational policy. It is encouraging that through the seven pilot courses we have held up to 1967 experienced teachers have made, or welcomed into their own thinking, proposals that amount to a complete reappraisal of the human relationships, the organization, and the curriculum of the school, of its attitudes to teachers and pupils, and of its place in the community.

Two years later I was able to comment:

> People sometimes have said to us that there have been many other "progressive" or liberating movements in education before the one that derives from the Pilot Courses at Goldsmiths. If these have flourished for a while only to die away, why should this one root? I believe that it has a better chance because it is the outcome of collaboration of teachers across a whole range of schools with others in a College of Education, and also because I have seen how as each course tackles the whole problem afresh and also moves in to examine some aspect in far greater detail, the whole style of schooling proposed stands up to this continuous analysis and appraisal by very experienced professionals, and is strengthened and enriched by it.[1]

It is in this context of collaborative thinking and as a result of seeing these new ideas in action in many schools that this book has its being. All the changes described here *are* being made, gradually but with determination. Readers may not welcome all of them. Nor should they: the work goes on through dialogue, and that involves disagreement. But all must welcome the energy, confidence, and concern for human well-being that is going into bringing the secondary school into line with the needs of the young, of their teachers, and of all of us.

[1] Fifth Report

REALISM ABOUT THE ECONOMIC FUNCTION OF EDUCATION

In thinking about educational planning little is gained by seeing the schooling outside its social context. That the schools have an increasingly important part to play as a selective agency is sociological fact. It is hardly surprising that teachers, feeling under an obligation to provide the education that will enhance the employment prospects of their students, have accepted the role of trainers for the meritocratic stakes. A drawing aside of University gowns, a dismissal of utilitarian aims for education, may be theoretically ennobling, but it does not help teachers to meet this powerful environmental press constructively. The alternative we offer has to be realistic as well as imaginative. To insist that education has no ends beyond itself, beyond the production of educated persons, becomes merely an argument in favour of the status quo, unless it is based in a prophetic vision of what educated behaviour might be in the context of a developing culture. My hope is to show that, properly understood, the economic and social demands of society and our embryonic desire that adolescents, like their younger brothers and sisters, should have an education appropriate to human growth are not irreconcilable: on the contrary what society, even in its most workaday aspects, needs today is that young people should have the kind of education which is to them at the time rewarding, intrinsically interesting, and relevant to their concerns. The reason is that we are no longer in a primitive industrial state, which needed large numbers of "living tools."[1] We are rapidly moving towards a fully technological society, which can hand over the processing of physical material and of data to technological tools. We can afford free men, and we need them.

Young people are right even in terms of future economic functions to look for emotional security, freedom, friendship,

---
[1] Aristotle's description of slaves

sense of competence, support from adults, identity with a group, and a sense of purpose. Our education will not be functioning well until they find these in the school as well as in the home, and in a schooling which is more oriented to the future than millions of homes can be.

THE NEEDS OF THE ADULT WORLD

A. THE NEED TO DEVELOP TALENT

The changing needs of a technological society ought to be more manifest to the British than to other advanced countries, where they may be masked by the possession of rich natural resources. For years it has been a cliché that in this country our resources must be those of human talent—fish, coal, and now natural gas not being sufficient.

Our schools should develop talent to the fullest. But this cannot be done by a system which is narrowly addicted to the avoidance of waste. At one time it was possible to see education as fitting children into ready-made niches in an adult world which stood at the end of the school drive like a vast columbarium, patiently awaiting its urns. It is possible no longer because, as the Crowther Report underlined,[1] young people will have to fill many roles in their working lives. We cannot foresee what these will be, and so if they are to survive we have to be "wasteful," providing them with a broad general education. This point the Crowther Council recognized and it is further stressed by the existence of the new Industrial Training Boards which will provide for the initial training of all young entrants into industry and commerce. But Crowther did not establish the more important point that it is not only a general mechanical ability that changing employment demands, but a general optimism and flexibility, which will enable the young to meet change with confidence and competence now and as they grow older. They need experience in meeting problems,

[1] *15 to 18* (H.M.S.O., 1959), para. 163

and in solving them by going to good sources of evidence. If their first experience of solving major problems is met in adult life, the effect may well be traumatic, and will confirm the tendency to cling to what is familiar. It is worth "wasting time," would be worth "covering the ground" of the established syllabus (if one thinks in such terms) more slowly, if in the process young people could learn to live on the flexible "if-then" basis which changing social forces demand.

It is worth remembering that at any moment in Sweden 1 per cent. of the working population is undergoing retraining, but change is true not only of those required to change jobs. It is true of the requirements of much of the work itself. Modern technology will increasingly demand not the living tools of industrial enslavement but self-directed and adaptable persons. It is arguable that earlier phases of industrialization within a capitalist framework demanded the kinds of processing which our schools provided. It is true no longer.

What we need today is a kind of schooling which will identify a variety of talents, including creative talents, and this is not cheaply done. Successful firms reduce their running costs to a minimum, but they are generous in capitalization and research. We have to think big in education also. Thinking big, in terms of a florescence of talent, means two things. First, we need to be willing to suspend judgment as to where the talent lies until the last possible moment. Secondly, we have to create an environment sufficiently diversified for different kinds of talents to emerge and at different times. The first of these requirements our present educational system manifestly fails to meet. Our habit of streaming—we alone of advanced countries stream even in the infant school—represents a hubristic claim by adults to be able to identify talent at an early age. This was a tenable position (though in fact unsound) forty years ago, when it was possible to believe in the fixed I.Q., and it is fair to recall that the 11-plus test was in its time an effort towards justice to ensure that children with a high I.Q. would not be penalized by poor schooling in their chances for an entrance to a selective school. But, in the last fifteen years or so streaming has become merely ignorant, as the effect of environment on intellectual performance has been established beyond doubt. One could almost say today that streaming is as arbitrary a process as Russian roulette, if it were not that it has one feature that is anything but arbitrary, for it strengthens the position of those who already have the advantage of coming from a home environment that is supportive to education.

Nor can we claim that our secondary schools are nurseries for varying styles of talent. On the contrary, they grossly favour a certain kind of intelligent behaviour, the kind of child who can perform imposed tasks efficiently, who finds routine work tolerable or even enjoyable—and not merely as a rest from more arduous and more satisfying self-directed enterprises, but as a way of life. Our education favours also the quick child, who can move rapidly from one teacher's way of thought to the next, bringing with him no disturbing flicker of interest in the subject he has just left. It favours the conformist, not the kind of creative talent which is based on what R. B. Cattell has called "the high dispositional dominant individual", who "leads those below and kicks those above him . . . [and] expects a high level of individual independence for everyone in groups." Such people "establish a more democratic and free society perhaps because of this need for autonomy for everyone. . . . "

Does this matter? Do we need to encourage such personalities? It seems that for the sake of our economy we do, for Cattell goes on " . . . creative scientists and artists tend to score high on dominance . . . (It) is definitely affected by environment, being fed by social success (and therefore higher in higher social status persons)."

Yet he suggests the discomfort of such children in school today:

> The more dominant child . . . learns more slowly than the submissive . . . Whereas with post-graduate University students and scientific researchers, the reverse is true. The more dominant turns out to be

more creative ... the docility and imitativeness which makes a good examination-passer are not what makes a good independent, critical thinker. Some may regard this finding as obliquely exposing something wrong with our school system. This is not necessarily true: perhaps class teaching is only possible with some degree of docility.[1]

Another conclusion is possible, very different from that of Dr. Cattell's final sentence. It is that if there is a choice to be made between independent, critical, and creative thinking and class teaching, then it is class teaching that must go.

This comment on the nature of creative talent, which I choose from a mass of evidence produced by fifteen years of studies of creative processes, is significant for English education in another aspect. It suggests that a system which may do little harm to the "higher social status person," whose social standing acts as a counterpoise, will be particularly damaging to those whose social circumstances do not encourage dominance. One might add, thinking of the many instances every teacher must be familiar with of awkward pupils who have gone on to make a success outside school, that it is particularly damaging also to those who have not the smoothness of social skill to present their need for independence in a socially acceptable manner. Another small pointer, that deserves further research study, suggests that possibly one of the reasons why there is less successful creative talent developing in our schools among girls than among boys, is that girls may lack the social basis for establishing this particular personality factor. Wallach and Kogan in their study of the "creativity-intelligence dimension"[2] found that among 10-year old boys and girls it was the "high creative, low intelligence" girls (intelligence being represented by breadth of grasp and analytical powers) who were least at ease. Their work suggests to me the hypothesis that the girls may have needed the support of high intelligence as well as high creativeness to give them the

---

[1] Raymond B. Cattell, *The Scientific Analysis of Personality* (Pelican Books, 1965), pp. 90-92
[2] Michael A. Wallach and Nathan Kogan, *Modes of Thinking in Young Children* (New York, Holt, Rinehart and Winston, 1965)

assurance required for success within an educational system which does not of itself give social support and emotional well-being to the creative child, since it asks for correct answers, on the dot when they are asked for, and does not seek out those who ask good questions.

If we want a society where ascribed status (by wealth or heredity) is little challenged, despite an egalitarian appearance, where the persons who come up through the educational system to acquired status are likely to include a large proportion temperamentally suited to be the obedient handmaids of tradition, where those who are potentially creative but socially unprivileged are likely to opt out of education, where there is the greatest likelihood of power residing either with the socially secure or with functionaries who do not require much autonomy themselves and cannot see why others should need it, where the functionary is the boss rather than the assistant to the creative thinker—if that is what we want, if that is what we think is likely to keep our economy going, we may congratulate ourselves on our educational system.

Those of us who do congratulate ourselves on our educational system tend to do so on the basis of the eminent marketability of our most successful products. What we fail to notice is that one reason (among many, of course,) for the brain drain is that many of these exceptionally able people find themselves too much hemmed about by the restrictive attitudes of others. May this be (among other things, of course,) that whereas the "high creative, high intelligence" person has come through the system to the top successfully, the next layer includes too many of the less questioning, more small-minded, of the "high intelligence, low creatives"?

Whatever the final status of the creativity studies they are important reading for the many people, including many teachers, who often find themselves accused of power-hunting when they want everyone to have the freedom they need themselves, who find themselves raising questions when others are satisfied with answers received and understood, who find it difficult to accord to routine data the respect considered due to them but are often effective at working out new systems or making the old system work if it is absolutely necessary, who often find themselves saying "I would like to sleep on that" rather than having an answer ready. Often such people feel there is something a bit wrong with them. The fact is that they are likely to be highly or fairly creative people who do not know their own strength. "Possibility is a fairer house than prose," said Emily Dickinson. They have been talking possibility all their lives, while the others have been talking prose.

To say this is not to say that our education system should go overboard in a search for creative talent, but rather that we should redress the present balance which unduly favours more docile personalities. We should seek for and respect the relative strengths of *all* children, bearing in mind also that there is evidence of creative reponses in all children, and that in a time of social and cultural change when the old answers no longer serve one very well, the more these responses are developed in childhood and adolescence the more at ease will the adult be in the flux of circumstance.

A study of the requirements of the adult world, and particularly of the economy, suggests two further lines of development for the secondary school. The first is a need to break down the distinction made between theoretical and applied studies and to reduce the greater status within the school hierarchy that is accorded to "pure" than to applied knowledge. Those who like to think in terms of an élite may learn from the Swedes, who have suggested that today the élite are those with theoretical-practical gifts. There is a place certainly for the pure theorist. But what we signally fail to do is to recognize sufficiently the value of exploratory and creative work that links theory to practice. The Nuffield proposals for improved science teaching have shown that far too much teaching of natural science has been instruction in dogma rather than an invitation to explore the natural world. Too much of our engineering also has been taught didactically, just as much of the craft work done in schools is the copying of other people's designs.

Altogether there has not been enough chance to identify problems, to invent solutions, to move readily from facing a practical problem to seeking an hypothesis in theory to account for it, and back to the practical again. But beyond this, there has been far too little cooperation between the natural science and the engineering and craft departments. A good deal of the separation must be put down to some supposition that one is superior to the others. Nationally, one of our causes for anxiety is that there are not enough people coming forward to take up places in higher education in either science or technology. The reasons for this await more research than they have had so far. One possibility that is worth considering is suggested by the finding of Dr. Liam Hudson,[1] that a greater number of the more "divergent" students are opting for the humanities, the social and behavioural sciences than for natural science or technological studies. May this be because in one's teens the material in which many students can be most readily inventive is technical, and that out of ample experience of creative work in the workshops, particularly for the thirteen-year-old boys and upwards, would flow a far greater interest in both pure and applied science in mid-adolescence, which would show itself particularly in sixth form studies?[2]

The other requirement of a changing economy is of more far-reaching importance.

It is a profoundly mistaken view to suppose that a divisive society is economically viable. We need to think big in our respect for potential talent not in order to achieve a better

---

[1] Liam Hudson, *Contrary Imaginations: a psychological study of the English schoolboy* (Methuen & Co., 1966)

[2] Members of the Schools Council's Project Technology are already confident that from the work being done in their project schools a new type of talent is emerging that is overlooked by traditional approaches. See *Technology and The Schools*, Schools Council Working Paper no. 18, H.M.S.O. 1968, p. 2. (What careers choices are made by pupils displaying these abilities remains, of course, to be seen.)

élite but in order to create a continuum of understanding between all members of a modern society, and this not simply from a sense of social justice but as a form of progress necessary to a developing society. We have far too often in our minds a roughly equilateral triangle as our model of employment, with the small managerial group supported by large numbers of unskilled labourers, and in between a smaller number of semi-skilled and even fewer skilled workers. Our model should be (it if is to be linear) of a Cleopatras's needle, with a diminishing unskilled underclass and increasing numbers of people involved in intermediate positions (including tertiary services) which require skills of communication and some enterprise.

Furthermore there is a great need for all of us to have some comprehension of the scientific forces that are changing our lives, as well as for people working in industries to have some understanding of the theoretical structure underlying their practical work. M. Reuchlin, editor of the Council of Europe's study of pupil guidance in Europe, has suggested the need for a unified culture in a scientific age:

> Culture, above all in its scientific forms, ... becomes every day more of a collective creation, and if its greatest heights could only be achieved by a limited élite, cut off from the rest of the population by a wide moat, this élite would become sterile and atrophied. In most underdeveloped countries there exists a minority of highly cultured individuals, but their presence does not suffice to promote the cultural development of these countries... It is therefore a defensible idea that any assessment of a country's cultural heritage should take into account the number of people who gain access to each cultural level.
>
> School systems that set out to raise by a few degrees the cultural level of the greatest number can therefore bring to this heritage a more important contribution than systems inspired by the idea of "enlightened aristocracy."[1]

To sum up, in a scientific age an élite culture is a dead culture; to be effective today, a society requires an inclusive culture in which scientific attitudes are widespread.

Finally (to stick to a linear hierachical model which is

[1] M. Reuchlin, *Pupil Guidance: Facts and Problens* (Council for Cultural Cooperation of the Council of Europe, Strasbourg, 1964), pp. 72-3

conveniently familiar, even though we should be moving beyond it to a more organic concept of society), communication needs to be horizontal as well as vertical. As moving a society along its path becomes a more and more complex task requiring more and greater expertise, and as more and more new sciences are developing, there is a great danger of the people most profoundly engaged in the techniques and logistics of change and development becoming silenced by their inability to communicate with each other. Lord Jackson of Barnley, speaking as a technologist, gives one example of this need:

> ... It must often appear, and indeed it is not infrequently a fact, that the anticipation of and the preparation for the consequences of technological change lag considerably on the urge to achieve it. ... in my belief the technologists themselves have an important part to play, by focusing early attention on the likely sociological effects of what they are seeking to achieve, and by ensuring that the knowledge and experience of sociologists and others are brought to bear in joint consideration of the problems involved. We must aim for a much closer identification of the social scientists with emergent technological possibilities, so that there may grow alongside innovation and change the ability to anticipate and to plan ahead the resolution of the human problems associated with it.[1]

George Stephenson, one of our archetypal inventors, was a one-man band. He could not only design a train engine but determine the best route for it to take. He is not the model for today. Today the need for interdisciplinary and interprofessional dialogue between experts is acute in every field. The difficulties in finding ways of communicating even between sciences that are closely akin are familiar and formidable. Those between professions which vary in status and self-regard are at least as severe. The problem is not an easy one, and its solution does not lie at school level. But at school at least the foundations could be laid. Students could begin to concentrate more of their time on an analysis of the conceptual framework, learning to see how they could cooperate

---

[1] From an abridged version of the Presidential Address to the British Association, 1967, in *New Scientist* (31st August, 1967), p. 429

on major problems with others of different cognitive styles and different bents, and less of their time on introverted separatist studies and on memorizing data peculiar to these; could see it as a matter of normal behaviour that they should seek ways of making their findings communicable. Students cannot do this *in vacuo*, but only where their teachers also are growing towards such interdisciplinary collaboration with one another.

B. AN INCLUSIVE OR A DIVIDED CULTURE

If I have concentrated on the changing requirements of adult society in relation to our working lives (i.e. our paid working lives) it is because any educational proposals which were not economically realistic would have no chance of acceptance in a heavily populated island that can offer little in the way of primary produce. M. Reuchlin's comments on the need for a common culture show that the distinction between the economic and the general viability of a culture is one that is justified only for analytical purposes. In terms of making educational reform a practical possibility the irrelevance and inappropriateness of much of our traditional educational practice to modern working conditions is the most persuasive argument that can be mustered; in terms of our hopes for human beings and our fears for them there are other reasons for reform which are more significant.

For if we are moving towards an economy which requires a greater partnership between the professions and disciplines and between all levels of skills, we can make this the threshold to the common, inclusive culture that Britain has never had. What is more, we can no longer dare to allow the rift between "the two nations" to continue, for today the power that an élite has to manipulate the rest is too great. Education may properly be a selective agency but it must cease to be a source of social division. To require this is to call for a major reversal of our educational procedure.

The movement towards comprehensive education is a move

towards a social justice which is necessary for national survival. But it must be said that putting all the pupils behind one wall is not enough. It is quite possible for a comprehensive school to be as nastily divisive as any selective system. The comprehensive system makes possible the ground base of a common culture. It does no more. It is the whole patterning of personal relationships, the organization of the school and the curriculum itself, which determine whether comprehensiveness is less or is even more divisive that the tripartite, where that was accompanied by strong support for the secondary modern schools.

A streamed school, a streamed staff—these are no longer economically permissible if we are trying to search for talent effectively. But beyond this the even more fundamental change has to be made, a change which most teachers, concerned with the well-being of pupils here and now, will welcome; if we are to be a society that is unified without the unification being imposed by a powerful élite, we must require our schools to provide experience of shared consideration of matters of social concern. The First Pilot Course made this a central point of the "Education Bill of Rights for Adolescents."[1]

> Today's fragmented time-table presents the pupil with an experience of reality as incoherent as a political map. We should re-create the school day, bearing in mind the following considerations:
> (a) To understand the significance and application of key concepts of our culture is far more important than acquiring factual information.
> (b) Much of the information accorded to adolescents in school is quite irrelevant to their needs and interests.
> (c) They welcome the opportunity to examine problems that deserve attention. These must not be simply topics: at this age they need to study topics in the context of a major theme.
> (d) A problem-solving approach is vital. By using the social and natural sciences, mathematics and language, the arts in co-operative enquiries, adolescents will learn to appreciate them.
> (e) Every adolescent has a right to share in these integrated studies.

---

[1] W. J. Preece, M.B.E., First Report, p. 2

They are not a sop for the 4th or 5th year "failures", but should occupy some half of the day from the first year onwards.

Selection and streaming according to meagre kinds of assessment gives social experience that is anti-social. It denies adolescents the opportunity to find themselves in relation to a wide diversity of persons. It also wastes talent, since many accept and fulfil the pessimistic predictions of adults.[1]

Our education has been far too closely geared to the immediate prospects of individual employment and far too blind to other aspects of community life, aspects which alone will make for a viable economy but which have their own greater value. Otherwise it could not have so long ignored the need of the young to become well-informed members of the national culture. And this could only happen in a country where, despite an admirable parade of well-established democratic institutions, power has been the prerogative of an undisturbed élite. Justice has been seen to be done without the cost of actually doing it.

C. A PARTICIPANT DEMOCRACY

Most countries make it a major requirement of their schools that they shall concern themselves with the civic education of students. This concept does not appear in any public pronouncement on English education. Certainly the Newsom Report and the subsequent Schools Council documents on the Raising of the School Leaving Age[2] have stressed the importance of an education in the humanities for the non-élite pupil but the reasons adduced for it do not include any reference to our need to become a well-informed electorate. They are important and excellent reasons, but it does not look as if the idea of our being members of a participant democracy is central to them. Yet there is American evidence to show that even the nine-year-old is in some sense "homo politicus." I need hardly say that I am not here arguing for compulsory

[1] First Report p. 2 (contributed by C. M. James)
[2] Schools Council Working Papers Nos. 2 and 11

civics to match compulsory religious instruction, for this would be entirely against the tenor of my proposals for curriculum. But I do suggest that if we are to take seriously the ideal of a common culture, so long as the vote and pressure groups remain important ways in which people can express their wishes it is reasonable for society to ask that young people should have had some experience of a participant democracy as part of their socialization.

But the pay-off is this: "Democracy . . . remains a sham in the degree that authoritarianism in administrative and pedagogical routines prevails over sharing, free discussion, and mutual decision-making."[1]

You cannot learn to be a member of a democracy by being a subject of an oligarchy or a dictatorship. A true civic education for our young people demands a radical reform in the personal relationships of the school, in the distribution of power, and in the concept of leadership. The model of the school polity today is an autocratic model.

Here again, from the acknowledged needs of adult society it emerges that our model of secondary schooling not only may be allowed to change, as so many teachers wish it to do, but must be required to change if it is not to become a dead cell in our social system.

THE NEEDS OF ADULT SOCIETY *inseparable from those of the young*

I have followed a line of argument which emphasizes the recognized needs of the adult world and especially our economic needs, not because I believe this to be the proper starting-point for a book on education but because by doing so it may be possible to avoid the charges of being unrealistic, which make it easy to write off good educational proposals. If we are truly realistic we shall surely see that today technology not only makes possible a new diversity and individuality among

---

[1] Theodore Brameld, *The Remaking of a Culture: Life and Education in Puerto Rico* (Harper and Row, 1959), p. 405

its users, and new standards of collaboration and mutual care—it also demands them. Perhaps for the first time elders need not exploit and process the young into Procrustean conformities, and the familiar dreams of educators are not utopian in the melancholy English sense of being too good to hope for but in the sense that proclaims the possibility now of making a good place for human beings to live in. The only way we can do this is to become good people to live with. And this in turn means that we must learn to be good at being ourselves.

In this context of change and possibility, teachers are no longer the transmitters of an elders' culture. They are first and foremost agents of young people's growth into themselves; they belong to the profession most closely concerned of all with our human future, dedicated to mankindness.

Society as a whole cannot easily recall that each of its child-members has only one life to live. Teachers should not easily forget it.

As a member of an inventive society which sees increasingly clearly that theory without practice is empty and practice without theory is blind, I do not propose in the following chapters to elaborate these statements of belief, but prefer to show ways in which they can be articulated in the every-day *living* of people in schools. In due course, schools as institutions set apart from the rest of the community may well wither away, as adults gain a greater freedom to continue in processes of learning and re-learning for playful as well as work-based reasons. In the meantime, the first steps in a new direction will be to enrich and humanize living *in* schools. Out of this will come a new openness between a school and the wider community of which it is part, and to talk of living in *schools* will no longer seem to suggest a special kind of living.

Chapter 2

Everybody Can Grow[1]

A PERSON-CENTRED SCHOOL

Some of the characteristics of a well-spent youth are accessible to some pupils in some schools. But until they become the central features of the vision that a school has for all its members (pupils and teachers) most pupils and most teachers will live in the pressure and discomfort that are inevitable in any way of life that is dysfunctional. The way ahead is not towards a "child-centred" education that involves a sacrifice of devoted adults on the altar of youth, with the teacher clad in a robe of moral purity of Quintilian's design (for it was he who said "the teacher must be morally perfect"). People never live above their spiritual income to the extent this would demand without a strain which is damaging to themselves and the young. We have to aim at a school where a more natural symbiosis is possible for older and younger people, where the teacher expects to grow also. We need, in fact, a *person-centred school*, just as our pattern for adult life will be increasingly symbiotic, and increasingly open to the needs of persons.

The changes that are required are both formidable and easy: formidable because teachers and pupils have lived in an unnatural mould for so long, but easy because the relationships and the curriculum are more natural—or if that is begging too vast a question—are more in line with cultural trends of which we are at least dimly aware.

NEW ROLES FOR THE LEARNERS

The curriculum that is required is one which is intrinsically interesting, not necessarily from moment to moment, of course, for we are considering the education of people who are coming to or have arrived at an age when their involvement in large-scale projects can carry them through the periods of drudgery that are part of any enterprise. The experience that is needed is one of collaborative learning in which the very diverse gifts of human beings, different both in style and degree, can be recognized by the young themselves, and they are not taught patterns of contempt or despair, or that Whiggish benevolence to the inferior which destroys the morality of the giver as well as the morale of those at the receiving end. This will mean great variety and flexibility of working by small working-parties. If the scale of the problems is to be appropriate to young people who are participant members of a very complex society the problems to be examined will have to be complex also, and will need all the resources of talent and expertise that students and teachers can muster: increasingly they will call on the new sciences and the new arts, in which the vigorous forces of our society are engaged, to clarify the issues. For the reason for the change is the context in which we live. We can no longer induct young people into agreed certainties; we have to coopt them into uncertainty.

TEACHERS ARE PEOPLE TOO

If students are engaged in a heuristic and creative education, which is largely undertaken in small working parties (or as we have come to call them, "clusters" of pupils), working with some autonomy, it is clear that the role of the teacher changes

---

[1] This was the title chosen by Edwin Mason, who directs courses and conferences in Goldsmiths' Curriculum Laboratory, for a day conference held in February, 1967, when teachers who are working towards the reforms described in this book explained or demonstrated their work to teachers from all over Britain.

from being that of an instructor,[1] giving a class lesson. He becomes rather a facilitator, an impresario, and a consultant. He spends much less of his time preparing organized lessons and marking children's attempts at precisely similar tasks which he has to set them (although there is a place for both these processes), much more on thinking about the kinds of question that are likely to arise in the course of a substantial period of study of some major problem, much more on seeing what contributions he and his colleagues can make to its solution. His specialism is acknowledged. He is not asked to dabble rather helplessly with a variety of topics of which he knows nothing or little. But he is an expert working in a context of collaboration not of solitude. He has to work collaboratively with his colleagues just because the kinds of question that will arise among lively groups of adolescents are beyond his competence to help them to answer or to develop. But he also has to work collaboratively with his students (and this is where our proposals are strongly at variance with many suggestions for team-teaching). He has to work collaboratively with his pupils because his knowledge, hard won as it is, is becoming obsolete far too rapidly for him to hope to keep up with all aspects of any evolving subject-discipline. It is an age-old cliché that in school we have to learn how to learn. Teachers can now demonstrate this skill, freed from the need to look like pantomaths.

The Second Pilot Course made this point succinctly:

> In most secondary schools throughout the world the work is seen as limited to what the teacher can encompass. Once we start to think of creative learning it becomes the first task for teachers to foster this process. Therefore the child-teacher relationship must be one of a partnership of equals in discovery. Although the teacher is likely to have a greater degree of knowledge or skill in a particular field and has a professional role which demands concern for the child's growth towards his potential, behind this lies the intrinsic equality of teacher and child as persons. This must be recognized if originality, experiment-

---

[1] Throughout this book I use "instruction" in the sense of didacticism not in the general sense of, for instance, J. S. Bruner in *Toward a Theory of Instruction* (Harvard University Press, 1966)

ation, initiative, invention and non-conformity are not to be stifled. The teacher must not only permit the advice and information he gives to be questioned: he must actively encourage it.[1]

The freedom to be fallible is a delicious freedom, but like every other freedom worth having it is a threat. It ceases to be a threat to individual self-esteem and to assurance of professional competence only if it is part of the way of life of the school. Members of the First Pilot Course referred from their own wide experience to the danger that a change from a relatively authoritarian model, if it is not supported by a theoretical understanding of the need for change, may lead simply to laissez-faire practices: "A more liberal relationship between pupil and teacher is indeed developing, as is a more democratic interchange of ideas between head teachers and staff; but the reasons for this are not always fully understood, and where there is an inadequate rationale for behaviour actions tend to be capricious. Hence in some schools the old security is lacking and a new security has not yet emerged."[2]

It is only when staff and pupils see education as a process of invention and discovery that security is assured.[3] Then teachers report their work more satisfying, their confidence greater, than it has ever been before, as one would expect, for their activities are no longer unauthentic.

USING OUR RELATIVE STRENGTHS

English secondary education has three important strengths, and it is vitally important to our proposals for reform that these should not be discarded, but welcomed and re-deployed. One of the most fruitful concepts in a period of change is that of *working through relative strengths*, which was formulated by Leslie Smith in relation to pupils' development, but which has a

---

[1] G. N. Clark, Second Report p. 21, "Fostering Creative Behaviour"
[2] First Report, p. 20
[3] This does not mean that an entire staff has to be converted to this viewpoint before any part of the work of the school can change. The way through may more often be by small-scale experiment among those who are ready to change.

general strategic validity (see below, page 227). The three relative strengths that I have in mind are:

* The tradition of the Pastoral Role of the teacher.
* The tradition of strong specialist teaching.
* The tradition of the freedom of a school to plan its own curriculum.

These are the assets which are already making reform possible in a number of schools. In another country with different traditions, even if it were stronger in some or many respects, the route to change might have to be different, might perhaps even be slower than seems likely in England, where already there are signs of a ferment for change among teachers.

Other countries have other strengths, a powerful tradition of research, for instance, a national recognition of the importance of education to a developing community (however relatively advanced), closer communication between the local community and the school, or perhaps some system which may permit the necessary democratic control of education as a public institution without requiring professional educators, whether teachers or administrators, to wrestle endlessly with the ignorance or prejudice of the local representatives of the electorate. In these areas we are weak, but it is more profitable to look to our strengths than to agonize about our weaknesses.

A. THE PASTORAL ROLE OF THE TEACHER

There is a long tradition of the teacher's pastoral role, and with it that school is more than a machine for learning in. It is seen as a place for living in, in which the values of the school society are no less important than its academic results. If schools do not at present meet the expressive needs of their pupils adequately this is to be expected in a period when the increasingly dominant role of the school as a selective agency has set its other values awry. An Anglo-American study by Dickson and Wiersma (*New Society*, Aug. 1966) shows English student teachers rating relatively high for their concern for children. Very many teachers are dedicated to the pastoral aspect of their work, and know or believe that they are doing essential service to their pupils; many are rewarded by a continuing affection and regard of those who have known them.

Even teachers who are bitter or contemptuous seem to be so partly because their offers of guidance or improvement have been spurned. Very often the rejection is due to an unbridged gap between middle-class and working-class assumptions of which neither side is fully aware. It is right that the difficulties of the working-class child caught up in the middle-class culture that is a feature of most schools have been powerfully chronicled, for one of the worst failings of schools has been their refusal to accept what so many of their children can offer. But there has been too little understanding of the continuing bafflement and exasperation of the teacher in the same situation. One teacher came to a Pilot Course for this reason "The inspector was coming and I asked the girls to bring flowers so that the classroom would look attractive. One girl brought one rose, and that was all. I want to know why." This is the response of a kindly and spirited teacher. It is very different from other talk that many of us have heard: "These children are the dregs, Mrs. James. There's nothing you can do." "I wouldn't have that lot to *my* home." Or, to a colleague from a headmaster in the North whose grammar school was "going comprehensive": "You'll find you cannot trust these boys; they never tell the truth." These comments also, inhuman and ignorant as they may be, are the reactions of pastors—albeit failed pastors—not of people purely concerned with academic success. Each side makes an offer; each side rejects; each side suffers. The difference is that it is the teachers who can *create* an environment in the school where all offers are acceptable. Many of them, after all, are familiar from childhood with the values of their pupils, even though these have been overlaid with the values of their acquired status; and all can read the ample sociological literature that is available.

For the fact is that neither middle-class nor working-class values are appropriate to an inclusive and creative culture. One of the most important aspects of the new pastoral role of teachers is to evolve with their students the basis for a more appropriate way of looking at human behaviour, one based on sharing and on mutual confidence.

The pastoral role—redeployment

It often happens in a period of growth that early developments although much admired are less satisfactory than later achievements. I believe this to be so with the concept of the pastoral role. It is fossilized. In recent history its origin is two-fold, one face for each of the two nations. On the one side, schools involved in the creation of the larger élite required by the last century's expansion established a tradition of deep concern for character-building which would give moral justification to the pupil's subsequent claim to authority and privilege, and guide him to use them with discretion if not wisdom. On the other, the provision of elementary schooling was "in origin, a discipline" as R. H. Tawney expressed it[1] "half redemptive, half repressive, for the lower orders": the battle of Waterloo, won on the playing fields of Eton, was not to be lost to a mob on the grimmer fields of Peterloo. The concept of the pastoral role has of course moved on since then; new tasks have been added, such as the need of the remedial teacher to protect the weakest in the competitive life of a school and to forearm him against the bitterness of the future. And many teachers, it has to be said again, provide very effectively the stability of adult relationship that young people require in mid-adolescence.

Nevertheless the role remains by and large that of the guardian of a static moral code, in which there are known moral answers and a teacher can be expected to know them. The result is that we see ourselves too often not as perceivers of the child as he is here and now but as judges, seeing how far

[1] R. H. Tawney, *Equality* (Allen and Unwin, 4th edition, 1952), p. 138

he has gone on a road of moral improvement whose end we know. To quote an article in which I argued this case on values in rather greater detail:

> ... I would like to quote one of the wisest of the many wise things said to me by experienced teachers on our "courses" ... As he left, one teacher, now a headmaster, said "All my life I have wanted boys and girls to be what I wanted them to be. Now I want them to be what they *are*." This willingness to demoralize oneself, as it were, stopping oneself short in acts or attitudes which invade the personal space of the students, is a characteristic of the new mood of teachers today.[1]

"Judge not that ye be not judged" is a good pull-up for teachers working with adolescents, giving us pause.

B. THE TEACHER AS SPECIALIST

Although I shall be concerned a great deal in the chapter on curriculum with the role of the teacher as a subject-specialist this strength must be mentioned here, if only to avert misunderstanding. It is sometimes supposed because of our interest in interdisciplinary studies, that the teachers I represent want to "do away with subjects." This is totally incorrect. On the contrary, I do not believe that we would be able to develop Interdisciplinary Enquiry (Chapter 6) if we had not a strong tradition of specialism. What I do propose is that in any curriculum which seeks to engage young people in worthwhile studies of man and society on a heuristic, not an instructional basis, part of the function of the specialist is to contribute, as he alone is able, to the examination of these problems. This is in line with the collaborative study on inter-disciplinary and inter-professional lines which is increasingly important in adult life (see above, pp. 35-36) and which should not be denied in the schools.

The stronger the specialist and the more acute his sense of the style of discipline the more valued will he be in these collaborations. Nevertheless, teachers vary by temperament as well as by training or environment along a continuum

[1] C. M. James, "A Shared Search for Values," *Learning for Living* (Sept. 1967)

ranging from a broad interest in the way that their special interests illuminate other studies and are illuminated by them, through to a narrower focus more concerned with a subject in isolation, which is sometimes called more scholarly. Breadth need not be shallow, nor is depth necessarily narrow. These tendencies are differences of cognitive style and aptitude which should be respected, —must be respected in a person-centred school.[1] In the Four-fold Curriculum that I propose (pp. 125ff.) the one is more apt for Interdisciplinary Enquiry and Interdisciplinary Making, the other for Autonomous Studies, although it is to be hoped that the most dedicated specialist in the narrower sense will act at times as consultant to a group of students and teachers in IDE and IDM.

C. THE SCHOOL'S AUTONOMY

We must not be naive about the celebrated freedom of the English teacher with regard to curriculum. Few teachers are more subjected to the demands of external examining boards, which until now have assumed that not only the setting but the marking of papers in public examinations must be taken out of the hands of the candidates' teachers. For the élite, or its penumbra, quality control has been strictly exercised in this way, and although G.C.E. boards have often left fairly vague the territory to be covered it is melancholy to report that Mode 1 C.S.E., syllabuses, which are externally examined and marked, are often almost obsessionally detailed. As to the education of those not taking examinations, too often freedom seems to have been little more than freedom from help. Too often also the almost haphazard nature of our schooling has meant that excellent ideas have been developed in a school

---

[1]The difference may turn out to correlate with convergence and divergence (cf. L. Hudson, who says that the converger "is prone to compartmentalize one topic from another," op. cit. Penguin edition, 1968, p. 103); but there is certainly a place for the competent convergent thinker in an interdisciplinary focus-group of teachers, and the signs that teachers who are initially antagonistic to collaboration often become friendly to it after they have seen satisfactory outcomes or been involved as consultants are in that case all the more welcome.

owing to the imagination and drive of an individual teacher, but he moves on, and a year later you would not suppose that he had passed that way.

Moreover, the great mythological dragon of our profession, a national curriculum, may not be so constrictive as we assume. A recent study of mathematics teaching by International Evaluation of Achievement (IEA) showed Swedish teachers feeling remarkably unhampered by their national curriculum.[1] No call for St. George from them.

It is quite possible, in fact, that all in all our "freedom" has been favourable neither to pupil nor teacher. Nevertheless I believe it is vital for the future. Anarchy can be opposed to useful order, but it can also be the contrary of an imposed and inorganic system of command. In this latter sense, a situation which allows a school to embark on creative ventures with social norms reached by the agreement of its members and with a curriculum that is appropriate to their interests, talents, and concerns, may be anarchic but it is also the best seedbed for experiment. In this situation, it is noticeable that inspectors and advisers increasingly see themselves as consultants giving supportive leadership to teachers. If they were in the habit of creating curriculum guides for use by the schools, and if teachers were in the habit of looking up to them, hungry to be programmed, the vigour of collective ferment would have to be achieved in some different way. As it is, it remains a vital task for L.E.A's, Colleges of Education, and teachers' centres to service teachers with what they find they need, to refresh them with ideas, materials, and skills. But basically we have found that teachers do not have to look far for resources for change, and become confident in themselves and each other. This is the resource which the habit of a divided time-table and a tradition of benevolent paternalism have combined to mask, leaving the teacher in the chilly isolation of the formal classroom.

---

[1]Torsten Husén. ed., *International Study of Achievement on Mathematics*, International Project for the Evaluation of Educational Achievement (IEA) Phase 1 (Almquist and Wisksell and John Wiley and Sons), vol. II, pp. 175-6

Chapter 3

Collaborative Learning

SETTING THE SCENE

If you close your eyes and picture a good infant school, you will probably visualize children immersed in a whole diversity of pursuits, some dressing up, some collected together to have a story read to them, some in the shop, some literally immersed or partly so in complicated experiments with water. They are working but it looks like play. If you close your eyes and picture a good typical secondary school your second picture may well be of young people engaged in craft, or singing, or acting or dancing, but your first will surely be of passing through long corridors, and glancing in at rows of children sometimes being questioned, sometimes writing, sometimes being addressed, but all in any one room doing the same thing, and always sitting nose to nape, behind their desks, eyes down to book or front to teacher. They are working. It does not look at all like play.

These are not differences simply of method. They are different ways in which lives are being spent. They represent fundamental differences of values between the two institutions. It is not superficial to start by looking at such externals. Our best primary education is based on a belief that we should observe children with care and expertise, allowing them to reveal their interests and their potential through individual or group work, as far as possible programming their own learning by drawing what they need, with the teacher's direct help at times, from a very rich and stimulating environment. The model is one of elicitation, a feminine model perhaps.

In contrast, the model of the secondary school remains didactic: there the teachers are penetrating the children's ignorance with knowledge which they believe to be requisite for responsible adult life. Motivation to learn is obtained partly from the intrinsic interest of the material, and very often from the lively presentation by the teacher. But more fundamentally students are motivated by their knowledge that if they are to do well they must meet fixed adult requirements at fixed points in time. The values which are revealed by the secondary school scene are values proper to a static culture. If we are looking for autonomous members of a free society we shall not get them this way.

What kind of picture should one have of learning in a secondary school? Four models suggest themselves:

1. The Separate Class Lesson
2. Team-teaching
3. Individualized Learning
4. Flexible Grouping

1. THE CLASS LESSON

The class lesson represents two assumptions, the first about relationships, the second about knowledge. The first is that secondary school is a place for imposing the adult will on the young (good adults with good will, but imposed). The second is that knowledge is to be carved up cold, heated in a tasty gravy of good teaching, and served to the young. (This I shall deal with under curriculum.)

The imposition of the adult will on the young is enforced day by day by the class lesson, in which some thirty or more children with different needs, interests, potential, and cognitive styles are required to perform identical tasks. The class lesson may have its place as one of a wide repertoire of teaching techniques. It can never be a learning technique. Despite a generation of psychological studies of "individual differences," these are ignored. The use of this didactic technique and the fact that it ignores essential differences between human beings together do violence to adolescents' learning, to their "propriate striving."[1] This is not the process of education; it is educational processing.

A routine of class lessons makes perception of persons almost impossible. For one thing it narrows the possible kinds of response that an individual can make. He is invited to respond in eager attentiveness to teacher and task. Three other responses are more probable, as anyone who has followed groups of children through the average school day could testify, from his own experience and his own feeling of despair and boredom. The first is an excessive dependence on teacher. The second is rebellion. The third is acting a part. All these are responses to a situation where the fundamental value represented by the institution is *power*.

Dependence on the teacher is likely to be the behaviour of the adolescent who is over-dependent anyway on adults and can be expected to have real difficulties in reaching autonomy. This experience will not help him. The second may be the response of the genuinely dominant and creative personality. But what it is inviting him to do is to create a rival power structure. The choice of dependency or rebellion is one all too familiar in our adult world, and in industrial relations. It invites some to become functionaries of an established static system, drives others to set up rival systems which mirror the autocracy against which they are uniting. Put people in a squad and they are likely to become awkward.

The third response is to solve the problem by truancy, an emotional and often intellectual truancy which is only roughly masked by the pupil's physical presence in the classroom. This truancy has its uses, certainly, for it provides the opportunity the young need to brood, to meditate on their real concerns of sexual development, personal relationships, or occasionally of some invention or hobby far away from

[1] G. W. Allport, *Becoming*, pp. 45-51

the lesson. But this is hardly an economical use of anyone's energy, least of all the teacher's. Class teaching encourages a dangerous split in personality between the real psychic life and the surface mask, for it does not permit the pupil to commit his whole personality to an endeavour of his own choice. It denies to him our most precious commodity, truth in personal relationships, encourages unauthenticity, the development of a false person which in the end the individual cannot distinguish from reality, except that he feels dissatisfied and void. This too is familiar enough behaviour in adult life, one would have thought, for schools to be seeking to avert it. The way of life of the traditional secondary school is grounded in it.

A routine of class lessons diminishes the professional skill of the teacher as an expert in child development, not only because it narrows the responses of pupils in this way, even for the best and most "democratic" teacher, but for another even more obvious reason. It simply is not possible to perceive in the round pupils whom one meets perhaps twice a week: one's view is limited to seeing how far they meet or fail to meet one's expectations. No peripatetic teacher, however humane and perceptive, can see a child as much more than a productive unit, for the class lesson does not provide enough opportunities to show hidden or latent facets of the personality. Nor does the class lesson permit the student to reveal himself to his fellows, except in so far as he emerges as good, naughty, or indifferent. Finally, in a class lesson the student cannot find out about himself. The required tasks, being basically extrinsic to his personality, do not invite him to discover new interests, to discover how he works best, what kind of behaviour seems to be thought useful by his peers, in what situations his leadership is appropriate, and in which he is best to follow others. On the contrary it demands that he become increasingly dependent on outside incentives, praise, blame, marks, peer-popularity or dislike, and increasingly dependent for his self-esteem on his success in matching up or refusing to match up to adult requirements.

Having extruded from the classroom most of the individuality of some pupils and important and relevant aspects of all of them, many schools, since they care very much for their pupils' well-being, seek to provide opportunities for personal meeting and friendship in the social life of the school, which by tradition in a good English school is vivid and fertile. The pastoral role of the teacher is thus channelled off on to his duties as form teacher or house tutor, or to his meetings with pupils in clubs or expeditions or school journeys abroad. "We get to know children on expeditions, when we get away from school, so we try to arrange a number of these." "It is important for teachers to work with school clubs so that they can see the children in a different context" —where they "can be natural," in fact. The school is filled with young people all day long who are aching to discover and reveal themselves, for this is fundamental to human growth. Yet this essential process is seen as extra-curricular or extra-mural. This is a reductio ad absurdum of an education. Alas, it is also a reductio per absurdum, a reduction of the confidence, coping powers, and self-image of the young through making them spend their time in an "absurd," a dysfunctional institution.

What is unsatisfactory for students' growth inevitably damages the growth of the teachers. The class lesson puts teachers in a power situation, yet many are brought into teaching by a deep concern for the young. It cannot be right that those who teach the student-teacher find themselves preparing their students for practice as if they were preparing commandos for action. Again, the class lesson is a demanding technique; if the teacher is to keep up with all the relevant information about his discipline the demands are impossible. Moreover, so generalized a technique largely ignores the special strengths and weaknesses of teachers. For some, presentation to a group is enjoyable, but many experienced teachers have told me that they feel they can be well pleased if even one lesson in a week or so is really fulfilling.

And the regular class lesson is a very isolated way of spending adult life. "A man among boys, a boy among men," we are told, yet there are plenty of other men or women about in the school. It is strange indeed that we have chosen to cut ourselves off from them and did not long ago for the sake of our own growth and enjoyment of adult company move into collaboration with our colleagues. The isolated teacher suffers from self-imposed cultural deprivation.

2. TEAM-TEACHING

Some of the disadvantages of this cultural deprivation are counteracted by team-teaching, and it is is not surprising that moves towards teamwork have rapidly become fashionable all over the world. Team-teaching in the usual sense is a formal presentation to a large group by one member of a team of teachers of material which is then discussed and worked through by tutors with smaller groups of pupils. This is the first primitive stage of evolution towards the kind of mutual support that teachers need in a period of rapid obsolescence of knowledge. It is an economical form of planning, ensuring that instruction can be handed over to the individual who most nearly of all the members of a staff can "encompass" the material required by students. Since the task falls on different individuals in turn, each has a chance of preparing a well-balanced presentation, supported by the film, strip, concept loops, display material, and so on that he may need.

This is what teachers, at any rate in England today, are likely to mean by team-teaching, but the term may refer to a quite different situation much closer to the vigorous work of small "clusters" of children, with the teachers in a variety of roles, as observers, consultants, "grouping experts," that I shall be describing as "flexible grouping." The very fact that the phrase is variously interpreted demonstrates that team-teaching is a method, not an attempt at a true reappraisal of the way of life of a school. To engage in team-teaching of the kind which I have described as the most usual form is to do little more than rationalize the chaos of isolated class-teaching, in order to achieve didactic effectiveness.

I have little experience of team-teaching of this kind in school, but my experience of it in other educational fields, including the pre-service education of teachers, suggests that in schools also it is likely to be profoundly unsatisfactory. Some of the disadvantages can be briefly listed:

The presenter or lecturer presents the material according to his particular mental set, and from then on tutor and tutor-group have no choice but to accept it as the way in which the material ought to be presented, or to rebel. The tutor is reduced to the level of a middleman whose own processes of thinking are not fully exploited for the same reason. There may be dialogue at a pre-planning session between lecturer and tutors but there is no dialogue between lecturer and students. The lecturer becomes an authority figure whose authority is even less often in question than if he were with a lively class. Thus the disadvantages of the class lesson are magnified.

This is the kind of teaching which may easily stem from cooperation between teachers who in isolation might well be found working their pupils' passage through one text-book. But even when one makes a genuine effort to open up other possible ways of looking at material, the ingenious questions one suggests for discussion are often not those that students in fact find it profitable to ask, and one is not there to be flexible in meeting their needs and profiting by their difficulties and insights. What is more, any presentation that is to hold the interest of a large audience must always be geared to around the median level of listeners.

We need to look elsewhere than to team-teaching in the sense of cooperative instruction to find a way of life which will make good use of the lively questioning of interested minds. It is true that the tutor has the very great advantage of being able to get to know his tutor-group far more thoroughly than is possible in the isolated teacher's round of class-lessons. The group has the possibility of free exchange of ideas with him, provided that he is independent or impolite enough to allow his own group to colonize their own chosen spots in the territory prepared for them in the presentation. But his difficulty is that he is likely to be rather out of his depth. In class lessons "he could be on top of his subject-matter but not on terms with his students, since he met them too seldom to perceive their potential with any subtlety. Now he knows his pupils better, but cannot enjoy the confidence of assured expertise, *nor convey it to them.*"[1]

Team-teaching of this kind institutionalizes the choice of the lesser evil, if it is seen as a main plank in a school's teaching programme. On the other hand for the occasional presentation it is a useful technique which makes a good "starter" for pupils' autonomous work, or as a "watershed" lesson, which summarizes achievement of the course already run and suggests possible directions for the future. But it is a technique, and it should not be elevated beyond that status. It is not a way of life.

3. INDIVIDUALIZED LEARNING

In England we are used to thinking in terms of class lessons shared by children within an age group. Some schools stream —and I will suggest later some reasons why this is an outmoded procedure (pp. 181-5, below). Some schools are more subtle in the way they divide children, trying to fit them with pupils within their year-group who are at about the same level of work by "setting" them in different classes according to their achievement in different subjects. These (and the American system of grading) I shall discuss in greater detail in Chapter 7. But there is a proposal which takes further than either streaming or setting the idea of tailoring lessons to the needs of the individual learner, and which is flexible enough to have some of the advantages of setting without some of its disadvantages. This is the proposal, adapted by Douglas Pidgeon[2] from some

---

[1] A. E. Mason in Fifth Report, p. 37
[2] Douglas A. Pidgeon, "Learning in Secondary Schools," *New Society*, v (10th June, 1965)

American developments, for individualized learning programmes, carefully related to each student's level of achievement in the separate disciplines. Unlike team-teaching, which at base is simply a tidier version of separate class lessons, this is a serious attempt to build on individual strengths, to recognize different routes of learning of different individuals, and to break up the whole field of the fixed curriculum and assembly line class teaching which have gone to make for the processing of human beings in school.

Individualized studies will be an increasingly important aspect of forward-looking secondary schools over the next decade or more. Skilled teaching will more and more consist in diagnosing a student's present needs and suggesting the course of learning most appropriate to him, whether through specially prepared assignments or through the sophisticated use of programmed learning techniques and technological aids. But to go overboard for individualized learning in the sense of incompanionate learning would be a grave error in England at this time. Our pupils have too little experience of mutual perception and acceptance, too long a history of being manipulated by competition, for this to be the right step. And our failure as a community to communicate with each other is too melancholy a feature of our social, industrial, and commercial life for the schools to dare to ignore its warning.

We need the chance for students to follow their bent. It does not follow that they must be asked to move as isolates. The answer I propose is two-fold, and it will emerge in my discussion of grouping. The first step is to recognize that within flexible grouping there will be times when a student will need to work on his own. But in the shared work of a Main Group of some 150 one of the important skills of the teacher is to match pupils for short periods according to their needs of the moment. This will involve sometimes putting a very advanced pupil with one less advanced, to their mutual benefit,[1] some-

---

[1] For the value of heterogeneous "pairing" see below, p. 183

times recognizing that their particular lines of enquiry will be helpful to each other, often simply relying (as the young often need and wish) on friendship grouping. To pull out of this complex one solitary variable, achievement, and emphasize this alone is to over-emphasize it. Moreover, the experience of group process among contemporaries alongside whom one is growing up is a vitally important benefit of flexible grouping which should not be sacrificed.

The second step is to recognize that programming on the basis of individual needs or interests across age groups can be one part of the school day, and working alongside one's peers another.[1] I envisage that where a third or a half of the school day is spent on flexible grouping in interdisciplinary work an increasing part of the remainder will be spent on "orbital" work in interest-based, mixed-age groups which are related to individual achievements, or on consultation with specialists.

There is no need for "either-or" thinking here. Both group work and individual work are important, and the need is to have a far more flexible and opportunist view of the school day than either class lessons or individualized programming can allow. The development of special skills can well be reinforced by "orbital" work, but it is in flexible groupings of people accustomed to work together that full personal development, cognitive and psycho-social, is most likely to be achieved.

4. FLEXIBLE GROUPING

I have criticized class-teaching and similarly team-teaching as being techniques for imposing adult ways of knowing and thinking, not ways of inducing self-directed learning.

I have criticized class-teaching as under-estimating individ-

---

[1]The proposals for a Fourfold Curriculum are given on pp. 125ff. Of this, two cells—Interdisciplinary and Autonomous (i.e. intra-disciplinary) studies are undertaken in small "clusters" on a basis of (roughly) chronological age, while two, Remedial (i.e. need-based studies for *all* students) and Orbital (or Special-interest) Studies are individually programmed.

ual differences between pupils, and as effectively depersonalizing classes.

I have criticized the usual forms of team-teaching as requiring large numbers of human beings to think according to the supposedly authoritative categories of the lecturer making the presentation, thus reducing the opportunity for challenge, and limiting the contribution of the group to a discussion of what has been given, as opposed to the valuable task of planning enquiry.

I have criticized (although with greater approval) the individualized routing of learning for emphasizing one variable, individual differences in learning, thereby undervaluing the importance of collaboration in both its expressive and instrumental aspects and thus ignoring the young person's need to establish his identity within a known social group and ignoring also the tremendous vigour of active cooperative groups.

My value assumptions, the requirements that I make of flexible grouping, are thereby made clear enough. I am seeking an education in which young people are actively engaged, and not eternally manipulated to learn by extrinsic rewards, in which they are decision-makers not merely decision-followers, and in which their perception of each other and of themselves as persons with individual differences that are to be respected and understood is a major concern of the collaborative process. For the rest of this chapter I want to try to analyze the kinds of relationships and the ways of working which should be congruent with these values.

For the purpose of clarification I shall distinguish three models of students' relationships and ways of working, and with them the consonant role models of teachers.

MODEL A. PUPILS AS EXECUTANTS; TEACHERS AS IMPRESARIOS

The first essential step in breaking away from the class lesson is to alter the geography of the class-room. Before you can begin you have to remove the row of desks, for these are suitable only for didactic teaching. Much of the work is done, as in a primary school, at tables in groups; and the basic working-party ceases to be the class of 30 or more and becomes the inner flexible group of 1, 2, 3, up to 7, which in the Goldsmiths' Curriculum Laboratory we have come to call a "cluster."[1] If at any time it seems appropriate for a whole class to work together in an undifferentiated group, they do so in a circle, or, failing that, a hollow square, for if the intention is that their work shall be a shared experience it is important that they should be able to see each others' reactions and engage in useful conflict of ideas, rather than all either competing for the teacher's attention or opting out. All in all, the pupils look less and less to the teacher, more and more at the work in hand, and the classroom becomes a workshop in which young people work together. There may well be a good deal of moving about from one classroom to another, but from the microcosmic point of view what matters is the engagement of groups of students in the work in hand.

This is the classroom typical of much activity education, with children working together on plans which have been devised for them because teachers think the subject matter important and relevant to their pupils, and because through these activities they will be able to arrive at new concepts or acquire new skills. Everybody is busy, everybody is doing something, and if the teacher is skilful each child is having some experience of success. Engagement in such activity can have great therapeutic value for the child who has studied only in the solitary confinement of his desk and who never learned to ask questions of his material, only to answer those posed for him by other people. Alas for the reputation of our primary schools: many of the secondary schools now introducing group work find that the eleven-year-olds from some primary schools have already forgotten how to ask questions.

---

[1] L. A. Smith, *IDEAS*, No. 1 (University of London Goldsmiths' College, March 1967) See also pp. 192-3, below.

The weakness of this model

This model is creditable, yet it does not begin to meet the needs of young people living in modern society as active participants in the nation's decisions and as people who in their life-times make important personal choices. Grouping does not create a culture appropriate for full personal development unless two other criteria are met. First, members of the groups have to be genuinely participants in decision-making about the direction and intentions of their work. Secondly, the purposes of the work need to be more than purely instrumental. It is these needs that are represented in Models B and C.

For the moment it is worth noticing that model A is the level of thinking approved by the Schools Council's Working Paper on Humanities for the Young School Leaver.[1] In so far as the concept of grouping is introduced there, it is of small numbers of children undertaking elements of a complex study which is pre-planned by the teacher. Even the elementary tasks involved are assignments handed out to them, not ploys chosen by the young themselves as relevant and interesting. The whole concept is authoritarian, an instructional course masked as an "Area of Enquiry." We have a long way to go, it seems, even in the more liberal of our official thinking about the education even of our senior adolescents, before we can begin to invite them into partnership with their teachers in collaborative studies. True participation, in school as in adult life, which is supposed to be the basis of democratic practice, involves much more than being one more number on the roll: it involves a share in decision-making, and education should make it increasingly possible over the ten years of compulsory schooling to trust children to become partners in their own education. We move of necessity to Model B.

[1] *Society and the Young School Leaver*, Schools Council Working Paper No. 11 (H.M.S.O., 1966). It is only fair to add that the subsequent plans for the provision of resources for this project under the guidance of Dr. L. Stenhouse are much more truly "enquiry-based", or at least "discovery-based".

MODEL B. PUPILS AS DECISION-MAKERS; TEACHERS AS ENABLERS

Here the teacher, as the person charged by society with the first phase of the cooption of the young into adult society, sees himself less as an organiser, more as a consultant to students in their self-directed enterprises and increasingly as a fellow-learner. This is, of course, a very radical change of role from that of the instructor or even that of the impresario. The description is not that of some "child-centred" education, in which the teacher may find himself so averse from officially guiding the progress of the work in hand that he is in fact left either with a laissez-faire situation or with the need secretly to manipulate the work towards an end pre-ordained by him; that is a form of Model A.

The relationship which is to be established in Model B is a symbiotic one, in which teachers openly play their part, as older and better informed, but as equals. They do not as it were ask "What would everyone like to do?" and then notice only those who come up with the desired, convenient suggestions. At first they suggest areas worth investigating, which they believe will be interesting and useful but they are ready to change course if they are proved mistaken. Later, and especially with students who for several years have been used to working in this way, it is possible to leave more and more the choice of the area of investigation to them. The essential feature of Model B is a truthful acknowledgement of function, as it is seen by teachers and students. The relationship may very well vary between schools, and within schools, according to the disposition and viewpoint of teachers and of the dominant tendencies of different groups of students. But it is open to discussion, and teachers in this sense recognize an accountability to their co-learners, the students, and not only to the adult world.[1]

In Model B, at its most elementary, if a group of students

---

[1] For an excellent analysis of the working relationships of pupil and teacher, see Nuffield Junior Science Project, E. R. Wastnedge, ed., *Teacher's Guide 1* and *Teacher's Guide 2*, esp. the latter, pp. 239-245

is engaged on Interdisciplinary Enquiry within an area of investigation (say, some aspect of life in a technological society, or of human growth and development in childhood and adolescence) students formulate the questions they want to answer, identify the problems which they want to solve, create hypotheses for their solutions, test them, and revise the hypotheses. They are, that is, deeply involved in the planning of their work. Increasingly, as they become more assured they need also to plan not only the overt but the inner objectives of a period of work, to see what skills they need to acquire and for what reason, and to evaluate how far the work has achieved the desired objective and what their next requirement is, as a Main Group, as a "cluster," as individuals. (see pp. 182, 189, below)

The only share in decision-making which most English secondary pupils enjoy today is when as individuals at 14 (and far too early for most) they make a choice of a course which will narrow their education for the purposes of an examination at 16, or choose one of a semi-vocational character. The criterion of choice has been largely extrinsic, the choice often haphazard because the school's counselling services have been inadequate. The habit of everyday choosing on a basis of good information is far more important than these occasional major decisions as an initiation into a life in which such factors as increased mobility, a greater understanding throughout society of the partnership involved in "democratic marriage," and greater financial freedom to choose one's way of life, will make more personal choices more pervasive, quite apart from the public choices in which we all need to engage.

It is the exercise of these small daily choices that Model B makes possible, no less than cooperation in major decisions. Hence there is an immediate feedback in the daily work, an important reinforcement of learning, as students come increasingly to discriminate between those decisions that have been well-conceived and satisfying and those that have proved unrewarding.

There is another aspect of choice which the schools have to look to, particularly in view of the adolescent's growing concern with his identity. Since human beings can envisage their own potential development, which is different from their immediate interests, they need to become mature participants in their own education. It is often said of working-class children that they are unable to postpone gratification, but one reason is surely that no bridge has been created between two realms of choice, the immediate and the more remote.

Participation in decision-making can be achieved far more easily than it often is even in schools which take seriously the need to encourage it. "We are treated like children. We don't make any decisions about the school or about our education or about ourselves." This was the comment not of rebellious early leavers but of sixth-formers in their last year at an established grammar school. It is commonplace among younger pupils, for some schools even deliberately postpone choices so that these become a sixth-former's privilege, and this is another expression of an authoritarian outlook.

We come back to the same point: the structure of the English school is not devised for change.

Change that continues, change that is due to more than the efforts of an impresario can come only from personal interchange, from the "collective ferment," as Durkheim called it, of small groups working together in dynamic interplay of individual with individual and group with group. Carl Rogers has made this point on the basis of a number of studies of self-directed groups:

> If the individual or group is faced by a problem;
> If a catalyst-leader provides a permissive atmosphere;
> If responsibility is genuinely placed with the individual or group;
> If there is basic respect for the capacity of the individual or group;
> Then, responsible and adequate analysis of the problem is made; responsible self-direction occurs; the creativity, productivity, quality of product exhibited are superior to results of other comparable methods; individual and group morale and confidence develop.[1]

[1] Carl R. Rogers, *Client Centred Therapy* (Boston, Houghton Mifflin, 1951), pp. 63-4

When teachers create this permissive atmosphere, inviting the young to be responsible persons, the young behave responsibly, and the whole character of the school society changes.[1] This process is so fundamental that it cannot be left to the sixth form, channelled off into clubs or negated by a view of cooption of the young that involves no more than handing over certain autocratic powers to prefects (even if the prefects are elected). The creative, exploratory group, engaged in dialogue between older and younger, between "clusters" with different trends of interests, creates a ferment in which schools report that all kinds of vigorous learning that had seemed too difficult suddenly become natural and easy. It is not surprising that this should be so, since students and teachers at last have the opportunity to exercise together the fundamental human behaviours of enquiry, making, and dialogue, and to experience the supportive assurance of working in a group where truth prevails.

In this situation the teacher sees himself more and more as part of an enabling service. Here it is necessary to forestall misunderstanding by saying that the teacher's contribution is positive throughout. Grouping is not teaching: it is a way of making better learning possible. Teachers need to pre-plan a broad area of investigation and the phases of study within it even if it is chosen in collaboration with students. This is necessary if they are to discover the many fruitful lines of enquiry that may emerge, and prepare the necessary resources. They will also have an eye to the kinds of learning that may emerge, the techniques of disciplines, the methods of enquiry and problem-solving, and the establishment of conceptual understanding through a variety of experiences. They will have been thinking about their specialist contribution. They will above all have been focusing on individual students'

---

[1] It is the unanimous impression of teachers whom I have consulted that in this collaborative social context discipline problems of a traditional kind largely disappear. This would be in line with the study of social climates of Lippitt and White; cf. White, R.K. and Lippitt R. "Leader Behaviour and Member Reaction in Three Social Climates" in Cartwright, D. and Zander, A. *Group Dynamics* (Row, Paterson, 1953).

COLLABORATIVE LEARNING

individual needs. For this reason I call these collaborative groups of teachers not "teams" but "*focus*-groups," as a reminder that it is through them that the school focuses its attention on its students.

MODEL C. STUDENTS AS PERSONS: TEACHERS AS PERSONS

In Model B I have tried to suggest the changed relationship that develops between pupils, between teachers, and between pupils and teachers, even when a group is seen simply as a task-related group looking outwards towards executive action. Model C is not an alternative to this but a completion of the concept of grouping.

When a group is simply a task-related team and does not concern itself also with the well-being of its members, they are in fact submitting to being used for the group's instrumental purposes and do not gain their full personal stature. Only the "useful" part of them is recognized; the rest, being ignored, does not receive full stimulus to growth. This is another limiting factor in much team-teaching. It is recognition of the need to experience group process that led me as a secondary reason to call the collaborative groups of teachers "focus-*groups*." It is in the total acknowledgement of the members of groups, the mutual perceptions of its members, that emotional security develops. We return to the need to be oneself, and one's self is much more than a member of a working team.

If we take seriously Freud's dictum that mental health is evidenced in an ability to work and an ability to love,[1] and if we believe that cooperative study in groups is the way in which pupils should spend a good deal of their day, a serious purposiveness towards loving as well as working must be part of the groups' norms. We have in the school in fact, as one would expect of what is after all part of life, not a preparation

[1] i.e. productive loving and working. From a conversation of Freud quoted by Erik H. Erikson, Childhood and Society. W. W. Norton and Co., Inc., 2nd ed., 1953, P.264

for it, the opportunity to bring together two aspects of living that are too often divorced from one another. Thereby incidentally we shall play our part in making it possible for the young as they grow older to reconstruct adult living according to something of the same values, as no paternalist system of schooling can do. For if working without loving, in the sense of an openness to and concern for the other, is only partly profitable, so too is loving without working. We have here a pattern of the problems of adult life that arise if the work place is a place only for impersonal working and home only the place for the consumption of loving as of other benefits, a natural tendency as home has ceased to be an economic productive unit. Bruno Bettelheim's comment on work with disturbed children is relevant to all human living: "I had to learn once again that love is not enough; that the good life can be achieved for individual and society only if, in addition to 'love,' it is also based on the constructive, healing, personality building (not just "ego" building) propensities of work."[1] Similarly David Riesman has spoken of the weaknesses of groups that are excessively concerned with internal morale,[2] as opposed to productive work. Once again we have to avoid an "either-or," although in the English school, with its traditional separation of intellectual from social development, the counterpoise needed now is to emphasize the need of young people, and older too, to discover themselves and each other.

Work in isolation may produce a competent community in instrumental terms but not a caring one, and hence on the long haul it is likely to achieve less excellence in work also. There is plenty of evidence that active group work does not of itself relieve fears or result in mutual support. John Holt's study of work in a progressive primary school in the United States indicates how hard children find it to abandon the fear of being found failing. If only the energy that they spent in defending their personality had gone to coping with the mathematics, what strides could have been made. Holt in

[1] Bruno Bettelheim, *The Informed Heart* (Free Press of Glencoe, 1960), p. 31
[2] David Riesman, *The Lonely Crowd* (Yale Univ. Press, 1950)

fact reports the tremendous advances made by a boy in the equivalent to an Educationally Sub-Normal or Special school when he was released from his paralysing fear by the faith of a visiting expert.

> He was tall, pale, with black hair. I have rarely seen on a human face such anxiety and tension as showed on his. He kept darting looks around the room like a bird, as if enemies might come from any quarter left unguarded for more than a second.
>
> Then as I watched, the dark-haired boy saw! Something went "click" inside his head and for the first time, his hand visibly shaking with excitement he reached without that terror for the right rod. It worked. The tongue going round in the mouth and the hand clawing at the leg under the table doubled their pace ... "It fits. It fits,' he said and held up the rods for all of us to see.

John Holt describes the respect Dr. Gattegno showed, "a conviction that under the right circumstances [these children] could and would do first class thinking", a respect very different from the attitudes children can meet in teachers, to which some will respond with fear, others with hatred and despair:[1]

> "Eyes like worms that crawl with no mercy.
> Eyes that condemn as ignorance
> Our ideas, and in front of the world
> Interrogate, and cast to dogs
> How can one receive education from those
>   who do but push forward criticism?
> Let us rebel, us the opposed, and cast out
>   these wage-pulling civil-criticizers
>   and form our own schools
> The which teach the beauty of all rough and tidy."

(Boy 14. An illiterate-looking, almost unreadably misspelt entry which ended: Please excuse spelling, no-one will educate me.")[2]

The gifted teacher can at times do a great deal to relieve children of fear of failure, enabling the child to redirect his aggression from self-hatred to action by re-stating a problem in a way which makes it meaningful; by drawing a child's attention from what he finds himself unable to do and guiding it towards what he can do; and by stating, and expressing with

[1] John Holt, *How Children Fail* (Pitman, 1965), pp. 92-4
[2] Quoted in Report by Virginia Makins, "The School I'd Like," *Observer Colour Supplement* (10 December, 1967), p. 35

every kind of non-verbal sign also, that the child will in his own good time overcome this difficulty and there is nothing to fear. Similarly, if we add to Holt's hypothesis of the destructive effects of fear a hypothesis that we are all of us "ego hungry,"[1] needing to have the ego fed by recognition and acknowledgement before we can do our best work, teachers can do a great deal to give positive recognition that will ease this hunger.

But why should teachers not share these tasks with students? If they take on themselves all the appraisal of success, together with the setting of an optimistic tone to the classroom and the provision of emotional security, in addition to their concern for developing cognitive skills, they not only take on themselves too much, they also reduce the chances of the young to enjoy the mutual support that they can achieve by creating a society based on personal caring as well as competent working. In fact the adult is at a disadvantage in both tasks. Even if he is seeking to free the young of their fears, he may in fact create new dependencies and so lead to the continuation in the next generation of a need for large paternalistic or bureaucratic systems. Again, if he keeps in his own hands the reward of success, success becomes not the recognition by the group of the individual's contribution nor his own delight in growth but pleasure at pleasing teacher or getting good marks. This is not the way to learn to enjoy intrinsic satisfactions or to depend less on the externals of status to satisfy ego hunger.

Teachers who retain in their own hands the meetings of expressive needs through the working life of the school greatly diminish their hope of influencing attitudes as well as behaviour. There is divergent evidence as to the degree to which schools are successful in establishing attitudes which contravene the traditions of the sub-culture to which pupils belong. It may seem impertinent to suppose that they should try. Nevertheless Josephine Klein's description of English

[1] To use the phrase of Dr. Florence Roane, U.S. Visiting Professor, Goldsmiths' College, 1965-6

traditional attitudes certainly seems to justify us in assisting this cultural change from "traditional *social attitudes: moralistic, punitive, anti-outgroup*. English traditional attitudes, for our purpose, are nineteenth-century attitudes. They include such beliefs about people as that women are not the equals of men, that coloured people are inferior, and that criminals should be dealt with harshly."[1] At the opposite pole she describes as counter-traditional attitudes which are "moralistic, anti-punitive and pro–out–group." These are not much better adapted to creating a flexible, adaptive society, for they, too are based on stereotypes, not on a patient attention to actual human behaviour.

The process of evolving a more appropriate ethic, which is neither traditional nor counter-traditional, and moreover is based neither on an appeal to authoritative middle-class codes of behaviour nor to authoritarian working-class assumptions, must be a group process, and for two reasons, one intrinsic and one extrinsic. First, by its nature such an ethic can be learned only in process and cannot be imposed. Secondly, the task is so difficult that one might say that only the warmth engendered by collective ferment can make it possible.

Where pupils participate in decision-making, teachers can become enablers. Where pupils concern themselves with meeting each other's and their own personal needs, and hence become increasingly responsible and responsive persons, teachers are freed to be persons also. The teacher cannot of course dissolve himself entirely into membership of the pupil group. He is required to act as catalyst,[2] to bring into being situations in which truthful perceptions can emerge through creative work, through appreciation of the arts, through the scientific study of behaviour, or simply through seizing on an opportune event. He has the task always of recognizing, although in a non-judgmental way, where genuine human problems arise now. In particular, it is one of his most import-

---

[1] J. Klein *Samples from English Cultures* (Routledge and Kegan Paul, 1965), vol. II, p. 538
[2] I use this analogy, but it must not be pressed too far; cf. p. 233.

ant functions to give undivided attention to an individual, and that regularly. Teachers become increasingly assured in letting groups proceed with team work while these essential private exchanges are maintained. One of the tasks of a focus-group is to ensure that each pupil has regular opportunities for them. A student has not of course, this continuing over-riding responsibility for the well-being of each individual. This is part of the pastoral role of the adult, which collaborative learning should enhance, not limit.

In this context the teacher's pastoral role is far more closely integrated in his day-by-day classroom work than it has in fact been in most secondary schools. For in the past the classroom has been the place where conformity has been required, where competition has flourished, where the value expressed has been that of power, and this has not accorded well with the teacher's pastoral care or the emphasis on responsibility, loving-kindness, and virtue being its own reward, which are the precepts of most schools. Nor does the occasional kindness in a cool climate reverse this. "We must all be kind to Jane today because . . ." Have we not heard such phrases as if kindness should be rarely shown, or needs special "reasons," whereas hardness or impersonality does not?

The teacher's pastoral role comes in fact to consist more and more in sponsoring within the classroom an environment which makes loving a little easier, and in which the teacher also becomes able to be more honestly himself, to reveal his weaknesses as well as his strengths.

> We cannot ask that all teachers be emotionally mature, but they do need the maturity and honesty to recognize and admit to their own immaturity. Truthfulness and personal acceptance are what young people need, and since the teacher can no longer know all the answers, intellectual or personal, he must not pretend to. His feet are of human clay, like everyone else's, and once he admits it he is free to use them to keep moving on, with pupils and colleagues, in their search for greater understanding of people and conditions in a changing world.[1]

[1] C. M. James in Fifth Report, pp. 63-4

The teacher's concern for the individual remains paramount even though he now recognizes that the well-being of the student is likely to be served best by the support of a collaborative group. His greater sociological and psychological understanding, and his broader experiences of life make him the right person not only to give direct support to the individual in private consultation and the informal counselling that are so much part of the good English teacher's day, but also to ensure that the social norms of the group are not towards an arid conformity, but are based on the need to respect and elicit diversity. We need not doubt the potential tyranny of the group if it is not based on this respect. It is the teacher who is charged with setting the scene for a collaboration of equals. His greatest hope lies in being as truly himself in his personal relationships with individual and groups as he is able. "The teacher may need to reveal some of his quite ordinary human responses such as his own apathies and annoyances even. These emotional minutiae will prove the reality of the encounter."[1] The teacher must not dissolve into his role, leaving much of his real self behind, when he comes into the school grounds, for if he does so he denies to the groups with whom he works the possibility of having as a social norm the acceptance of people in the round, which a truthful relationship requires. He reduces the possibility of genuine conflict of opinion and personality which young people need to experience, within a context of good-will.

There are great dangers in attempting to create a conflict-free society in school, especially when at home the small family is so tight-knit and carries such a load of anxiety and suppressed emotion as many do today. A school which uses the powerful forces of group process to establish unauthentic norms does double damage to its members. It denies them the experience of coming to terms with their own violence and that of others; and it sets official school norms which, being unrealistic to living, breathing, hating, loving human beings,

[1] W. L. Johnson in *Second Report*

are norms for school only, and do not carry over into other living. It may be hypothesized that much of the failure of schools to counteract or modify home values, where these are damaging, has been due to the cool authority of the school, which cannot match the profound influences of early formative experiences. Honest human relationships in ordinary groups provide the most powerful therapeutic experiences that public as opposed to private home life, can offer. This is true of people who are emotionally damaged but not to the extent of requiring psychiatric help in psychiatric groups or individually (a kind of help which it is of course quite out of the realm of teachers and fellow-pupils to attempt). If schools now offer this kind of experience and then the tone set is too moral to be true, it invites confusion and rejection.

It follows, then, that if we are not going to attempt the undesirable and dangerous task of setting up a rival set of moral *rules*, the task of the teacher is to hold the ring, ensuring that what is encountered is not a learning of such rules but a climate in which people can without danger voice their thoughts and others will expect to pay attention to them. For this purpose the teacher's acknowledgement of his own fallibility is a necessity.

In this context, many of the teacher's difficulties about expressing a point of view on a controversial topic fade away: he offers himself, failings and all, as evidence not as example—except in so far as he exemplifies truthfulness, concern, and a willingness to change his view if the evidence is against it.

Group work that values the well-being of each of the members of the group and is not merely the effective teamwork of Model B, becomes itself exploratory. It becomes creative, in that students are creating a climate, creating their own individual interpretation of values. It is dialogue of profound importance. Since *enquiry*, *making*, and *dialogue* are the fundamental human behaviours on which, I believe, the whole curriculum ought to be founded, it will be manifest that if I move into a new chapter headed "curriculum" I am not crossing a frontier into different territory. In the unity of the collaborative school it is the simple truth that curriculum is all that goes on in the school.

It is a commonplace among English teachers to say that they don't teach subjects, they teach children. By the same token, in today's situation children learn teachers. "What did you learn in school today?" "Oh, I learned Mr A and Mrs B and Miss D"—add four more initials and you have a pretty good answer to describe the digital incoherence of many a secondary-school day. It is often said with awe that children are remarkably astute judges of their teachers. They have need to be, and certainly they have opportunity.

In talking about the *context* of collaborative learning I have also been talking about its *content*. I have been suggesting that this content includes the persons in the school and also its whole value-structure. I have been suggesting that the persons who are learned are too few, and that we should be learning not only the teachers but our peers and ourselves, and each in many relationships to other. I have been suggesting also that the values that are learned should be very different from the values that are learned today, and should include caring, tenderness, optimism for self and others, trust of circumstance instead of wariness, collaboration instead of competitiveness, "social self-realization"[1] as the basis of our individual well-being rather than anti-social self-realization as the source of egotistic advantage.

When I think nowadays of a secondary school I have the mental image of the kind of schools I visit. Here children work in clusters, moving off on the advice of a teacher to a more detailed study of some special aspect of a common problem, consulting teachers and each other, sharing their findings, and using mathematics no less than verbal language, the arts no less than discursive language to do so. If a reader goes on into the next section, in which I discuss curriculum, bringing with him a picture of an authoritarian adult teaching a didactic class lesson in a dust storm of chalk and talk we shall soon lose each other.

[1] cf. Theodore Brameld, *Education as Power* (Holt, Rinehart and Winston, 1965)

Chapter 4

Rationale of Curriculum

HERE I SHALL distinguish four questions, which can be used as the basis for building curriculum:
1. *When to teach what?* or in its more refined form, *When to teach what to whom?*
2. *What are the values*, social, cultural, and individual, which are the reference points *for curriculum; and what are its objectives?*
3. *What are the social trends which indicate guiding lines for curriculum?*
4. *What is human living like and how can we make schooling more like living?*

I believe that there is a place for the first three questions, but only if they are perceived from a different standpoint from what is usual, that is to say, if their hidden assumptions have been called into question.

1. WHEN TO TEACH WHAT?

This is still the most usual question asked in English schools, for when English teachers think of curriculum, most think of syllabuses. When they think of syllabuses they have often in mind the requirements of external examinations. Even when they are not teaching students who are likely to take such examinations their expectations tend to be set in these terms, and many syllabuses are pale imitations of the courses of study taken by higher streams. This is not to say that the presentation is always dull. Although evidence would be hard to come by I would suppose that the amount of well-planned and attractive presentation of traditional material that goes on in English schools is at least as high as anywhere in the world.

But to ask the question "When to teach what?" in its conventional setting, which invites the picture of class lessons, individual or team-based, is to ask a misleading question. For it rests on the false assumption that there is an optimum route for progressing through a fixed area of knowledge, which is suitable for all members of given squads of children provided their I.Q. or previous progress on this route suggests that they can be taught together. This stems from thinking of students as the objects of the teaching process, the done-to people. "I don't teach subjects, I teach children": children in the dative or children in the accusative. Once we learn to think of students as the subjects of their own sentences, we free them. For it becomes clear that each must have the freedom to follow routes that are appropriate to him: what for him may be a short cut, a closure readily achieved, may well for others seem roundabout—and vice versa, for how often have we seen in "good" class teaching the child's leap forward denied and him returned to the orderly progress of the class? Students move in their own directions and they arrive by different routes.

"This book tells me more about penguins than I care to know." Adults may have a marvellous cornucopia of cultural riches, but it is no good pouring them on the heads of the young, if they do not care to know, or not at that moment, or in that phase of their development. They will not care to know if they are not apperceptively ready, if they are otherwise preoccupied, if the material in some way threatens them. This does not mean that we should tuck our cornucopias under our arms and retire from the field of the curriculum. It is to insist that if we are to avoid recourse to extrinsic incentives, manipulation by immediate rewards and threats or by appeal to future status, we have to find a way of life that allows the dynamism of the young to explode in self-directed ventures. There will always be a place for an occasional lesson by a teacher enthralled with his own self-directed delight in his subject-matter, but that cannot, and extrinsic incentives should not, be the basis of curriculum planning.

When one refines "When to teach what?" into "When to teach what *to whom*?[1], if the refinement is to have its proper significance, one is asking questions about individuals, and a further rephrasing is necessary: "When should this child learn what?" The answer then lies in a very subtle accommodation between the child's introspective knowledge of himself and of what he cares to know and the teacher's equally subjective though less direct perception of what the child is like and what he might care to know.

This is not anti-curriculum. We have an obligation as agents of our pupils to enable them to direct their own interests in ways which we see could be profitable for them. In practice, this guidance does not consist nearly so much of heading them off from food they could not digest as of raising their expectancies. Children do not come out of the everywhere into the classroom. They come from homes and neighbourhoods, bringing with them personal histories and experiences of mass media, all of which are constantly affecting their palate. If over a period we trust two-year-olds in a cafeteria they choose a balanced physical diet. If in the field of learning young people choose narrowly it is likely to be the result of cultural deprivation which suggests to them that the learning equivalent of chocolate ice-cream on the menu is not for them.

Teachers have told me that even in the most culturally deprived school, if the environment is rich, most young children need far less guidance than anxious adults would suppose. But in secondary schools, the guidance given by a teacher in client-centred discussion with an adolescent may be expected to involve more support of his hopes for himself,

---

[1] Ole Sands in *Role of Supervision and Curriculum Direction*, ed., Robert R. Leeper (Washington, Association for Supervision and Curriculum Development, 1966)

because of the anxieties that puberty creates. His sights will be raised:

* By our showing that his concerns, with who and what he is, with living in a technological society and how that affects him, and with human relationships can be the basis for studies.
* By our discussing his work frankly with him, in a context of complete acceptance of him as a person, which alone entitles the teacher to say "I like this part of your work; I am more doubtful about that."
* By our suggesting to him that if he wants to progress further in self-directed ploys he will find it useful to work through such-and-such an assignment or programme in order to grasp more fully the significance of a certain concept, or to read more widely in some relevant field.
* Occasionally, but with caution and far less frequently than one might suppose, by our suggesting a substantial change of diet. One of the purposes of the Fourfold Curriculum is to make it easy for students to pick up skills and study in new fields as and when they find they "care to know," so that such changes do not disrupt a child's schooling (see later, pages 129f.).

2. WHAT ARE THE VALUES AND OBJECTIVES for curriculum?

Even in this subtle form, which is of course not what would be generally understood by "When to teach what?" there is a likelihood of over-emphasizing content. The question provides no basis for selecting the criteria on which the teacher can plan his advice. The approach through values and objectives is an attempt to ask a more fundamental kind of question about schooling. In discussing it, I shall use as a basis the UNESCO Report on Curriculum Revision and Research,[1] although this is now ten years old, since it sets out as clearly and

---
[1] *Education Studies and Documents*, No. 28, UNESCO, 1958.

authoritatively as any statement this approach to rational planning of curriculum.

In a phased programme of planning, the Report suggests, the first four requirements are to recognize the need for curriculum change, to mobilize resources for making change possible, to study the problems and needs of society, and to study the characteristics and needs of children (a brisk and perfunctory section, this last). It goes on:

> The next step is a reformulation of objectives for the various courses and at the various levels and grades. The following criteria have been found helpful: (a) objectives should be based on three types of studies—studies of the needs of society, of the characteristics of learners, and of subject content; (b) objectives should guide the selection of content; (c) objectives must, besides pointing out the essential elements of each learning situation, indicate whether they are facts to be memorized, methods to be applied in solving problems, etc.; (d) the components of general objectives should be shown, as for example, learning to think effectively will involve learning to interpret facts accurately, to detect assumptions, to distinguish facts from opinion, etc.; (e) to avoid confusion, objectives should be grouped under appropriate headings, such as adjustment to home life, appreciation of aesthetic values, etc.; (f) objectives must be comprehensive as well as clear and specific.

THE MERITS OF THE MODEL

Let us look first at the merits of a model which has remained *à la mode* in many parts of the world for over a decade. These are:

* It is a dynamic model, whereas conventional content-based proposals are retrospective, and provide no criteria for choice.
* It does not beg the question of intra-disciplinary versus inter-disciplinary studies, whereas conventional English proposals are primly subject-based.
* It is a comprehensive model, presenting a complex of the

main facts and values on which a country might base its educational proposals.

* It goes behind the separate pieces of knowledge that the subjects are concerned with to the behaviours of pupils, permitting a movement towards developing cognitive skills rather than covering a syllabus.
* It is streamlined and purposeful and straightforward, providing reference points to which educational planners can turn whenever brows are furrowed.

The model is so forceful, so inviting, and so much *de rigueur* that it requires an act of courage to look at it sceptically and to ask, "Underneath all those beautiful, internationally admired clothes, is there really an emperor there at all?"

There is a dangerous intellectual tendency in a period of mass education for such simple, forceful ways of organizing material, easily understood, to become the pieties of the day. They are written down in thousands of students' notebooks all over the world, and handed down as received truth, so that it becomes a necessary part of one's documentation, like a passport to respectability to show acquaintance with them. By accepting or denying the dogma a writer or lecturer or student is forced into the same situation that I described in team-teaching: everyone is pressed into thinking in the same routine, even if with the idea of rejecting it, and thereby our own personal vision is distorted and new developments delayed. This is true not just of education but of most learned studies. This situation is the world of Scholarship, as Whitehead criticized it, in contrast with the free-ranging intellectual activity of Speculation.[1] It encourages people to see certain ways of thought as obvious, which is a fundamentally anti-scientific attitude. To some of us this model is by no means obvious. It has grave weaknesses, weaknesses closely allied to its strengths.

---

[1] A. N. Whitehead, *Adventures of Ideas* (Cambridge University Press, 1933).

THE WEAKNESSES OF THE MODEL

The first two points are unexceptionable: it is admirable to have a dynamic model and it is good that it is not narrowly conceived in terms of specialist subject-disciplines alone, but can be variously interpreted. Nevertheless its faults are fundamental:

1. On *values* it is so comprehensive that it ignores the facts of living, which are that choices have to be made. It is not always possible to create a design for living so accommodating that each member of the eternal triangle it poses—society, learners, and subject content—can flourish. When you are in a classroom, when you are planning work with colleagues, you will often have to chose. Which will you favour—for this is where the crisis of choice usually centres—the person? adult society? or the serial development of the subject? This is the most fundamental choice of every teacher. It is here that he asserts his true priorities.

The model moves on to the planning of objectives without any by-your-leave, simply begging the question of the value of such planning. On what grounds is it assumed that we should plan curriculum in terms of objectives? This assumption needs to be very carefully examined. I believe it has its uses—but this emperor is small and wizened and should not rule the world by default.

2. (*a*). My first objection to planning by *objectives* is the simplest. Even for evaluation purposes, when it comes down to the brass tacks of an evaluation scheme, even Bloom's *Taxonomy of Educational Objectives*[1], the most subtle and distinguished enterprize in this field, is not very helpful. It is a useful piece of analysis, no doubt, to distinguish which of two behaviours a student is evincing but it is easier said than done. Moreover

---

[1] Benjamin S. Bloom and D. R. Krathwohl, *Taxonomy of Educational Objectives*, Book 1, *Cognitive Domain* (1956), Book 2 (D. R. Krathwohl et al.) *Affective Domain* (1964). I assume in this section that the reader is familiar with the concept of "behavioural objectives" developed by Dr. Bloom and his colleagues.

in any one situation of evaluation it is impossible to know whether for instance, a pupil has engaged in a complex act of synthesis or has displayed a feat of memory-recall. A whole superstructure of theory has been built up, which is not, I suspect, in practice greatly used.

My other objections are less subjective.

(b). This kind of analysis traps the educator in something similar to the analysis of symptoms that has proved so damaging in medicine whenever the complex interweaving of characteristics, behaviours, and experiences which make up the complete human individual in his setting is ignored. Despite all the sincere and cautious safeguards in the Bloom taxonomy about the dangers of dividing affective from cognitive aspects of behaviour great damage has been done by these two dimensions being examined in separate volumes published eight years apart. And the whole scheme is handicapped by the absence of the psychometer Handbook, which has not limped on to the field thirteen years after the cognitive. Of course it is possible to concern oneself with affective questions in one group of experiments under research conditions and with cognitive in another. But in the classroom, at home, at work, at leisure, we are living-breathing-thinking-feeling human beings, and we behave in a complex of felt thoughts, thought feelings, and physical doing, which both expresses and influences these thoughts and feelings.

It is much easier to analyse Humpty Dumpty than to put him together again, and this way of looking at pupils is all too apt to blind us to human encounter because we are seeing the child in terms of our objectives.

(c). It is not surprising, in view of the behaviourist backgrounds of much American thinking (and this system stems from the United States) that it should invite the world to focus its attention on observable behaviours rather than on the personal experience of the individual and on his "propriate striving." There is another aspect of the system which reinforces this trend: the desire to have objectives that are operational. In this context an objective is not an objective unless it can be evaluated. The motive is respectable. There has been far too much generalized chat about education, in which the individual's needs have been nominally safeguarded, though he is in fact the victim of the cultural (subject) content of his course.

In England our examinations have not assessed the behaviours the examiner is looking for: the first hint of such an approach came in the Schools Council's statement in its third publication on C.S.E.[1] clearly based on the taxonomy. The whole idea of a grid, with the material listed on one side and the desired behaviours across the top, was a revolutionary clarification of examining which deserves our gratitude. But how interesting that in an era of three-dimensional models, this one is resolutely two-dimensional: the person's coding system, by which he makes sense or no sense of the material, which enables him to achieve certain behaviours regularly and not randomly, this cannot be identified, cannot be evaluated, and is significantly omitted. So is the whole way he sets about his work, which is the key to so much of the teachers' understanding of him. For an examination system this is convenient. For an education system it is to omit the Prince of Denmark. Once more, albeit in a "scientific" guise and avoiding some of the subjectivity of other assessment techniques, evaluation rules supreme.

To plan a curriculum in terms of objectives has two further dangers.

(d). Having taught us to analyse the person into disjecta membra it tempts us also to think of some spendid person of the future whom we might create rather than the adolescent who is trying to communicate with us here and now.

The system makes a distinction between means and end which sets the means apart from the end instead of recognizing that they are intrinsic to it. It is thus that the student's

---

[1] *The Certificate of Secondary Education: An introduction to some techniques of examining*, Secondary Schools Examination Council, Examinations Bulletin No. 3 (H.M.S.O., 1964)

real present is sacrificed to a future we imagine for him. If teachers concentrate on objectives, they undervalue diagnosis and over-estimate their powers of prognosis and prescription, thereby sacrificing Johnny-as-he-is to John-as-we-want-him-to-become. They are tempted also to over-estimate foresight and undervalue opportunism. Opportunities for additional learning may be forgone because they disrupt a schedule. The teacher who notices that a student (or cluster) has chosen a new route, or that an isolate with one kind of learning difficulties has joined a group with different problems, may be disturbed instead of being exhilarated.

(e). My final objection is the specific misuse of objectives in curriculum planning which the UNESCO Report exemplifies. It lies in the nature of the objectives proposed. This may seem an unjust complaint considering that the statement is intended to be non-judgmental, allowing each nation or group of planners to select its own objectives. But once again, an assumption of vital importance has been made without acknowledgment. After discussing "Step Six, Selecting Appropriate Subject Matter and Activities" the Report moves on to:

STEP SEVEN. ORGANIZING LEARNING EXPERIENCE AND PLANNING UNITS OF STUDY.

"... In planning units of study the following steps have been found helpful: (a) survey the ideas and suggestions regarding the needs and problems of life and of the students with particular reference to the field with which the unit deals: (b) explore the experiences appropriate for obtaining these objectives: ... (d) sketch out the learning activities to be included in the unit: (e) check the consistence of the learning activities with the objectives and problems: (f) plan the teaching unit—*arrange the learning experiences in a psychologically effective sequence.*[1]

The last phrase is the most revealing—"psychologically effective": we must ask, for whom? For all the students? One and the same sequence? Who would care to take on that task?

[1] Report on Curriculum Revision and Research (*Education Studies and Documents*, No. 28, UNESCO). My italics.

This is the language of assembly-line processing of products, not of patient observation of students. The setting is one of selecting objectives for a unit of work and then planning the experiences. The underlying image is of the factory rather than the consulting-room or the school.

If a group of teachers were to set as its aims for students a plethora of diverse objectives appropriate to each, this kind of language would be impossible. In the ordinary context in which it is applied, the whole exercise of thinking in terms of block objectives for a unit of work is a system for disregarding individual needs, a system for creating conformity.

We have to avoid these naive simplicities and recognize the complexities of educating very different people, who bring to each situation different conceptual maps, different perceptions, different talents, different (but unknowable) potential, different past traumata, different degrees of optimism, different interests. It is all too clear that in the eternal triangle of society, culture, and persons, society and culture have been allied to oust persons.

CONTENT AND OBJECTIVES IN AN OPEN CURRICULUM

Neither the When to teach What? question nor the study of objectives provides the safeguard for the learner that curriculum planning should ensure. Nevertheless there is a place for both, provided they are not crudely used.

A. *Thinking about when to teach what* is a serious question: when the "what" is taken seriously because the obsolescence of knowledge is recognized. Too often the speed of obsolescence is forgotten, or it is referred to but not analysed sufficiently to bring it home to the individual teacher in the classroom. Some supposed knowledge is found to be mistaken, particularly in rapidly moving sciences, because generalizations have been too narrow to account for new data. Some supposed knowledge is for the moment unchallenged, but has become far less important in the light of new data and no longer earns its place in the school. Some traditional uses of knowledge (such as a dedication to computation) are time-wasters because social conditions no longer require them or there are technological aids to hand. Some areas of knowledge which have been thought to be too advanced for pre-University students have now become so important that the school cannot deny access to them (even though teachers may not know much about them). Some new generalizing notions are found to be so fruitful that they should replace less fruitful ways of studying.

Behind all this lies the fundamental truth that the notion of "coverage" is out of date. One can have priorities about what one suggests as content of school curricula, but essentialist fiats or unilateral diktats for the curriculum can no longer be issued.

—*Thinking about when to teach what* is a useful question: when the "when" is treated with imagination, to raise our expectancies of what the curriculum might offer to children and if it reminds us how much time is wasted in school on repetitive studies.

—*Thinking about when to teach what* TO WHOM is an important question: when the "to whom" is added and is used to remind us that we can, if we think out curriculum afresh, give answers very different from many of the traditional ones, so that they relate to the concerns and interests, the life-tasks and the intellectual development of the young. Too few teachers in England have recognized this point. In too many schools traditional assumptions continue, and the curriculum becomes more and more crowded. A headmaster with experience of the way the time-table becomes over-crowded as new needs develop described the present situation:

> ... Any enquiry resulting from a keen interest shown by children in a section of the work they are doing in a subject inevitably takes them over the boundaries of that subject into another, perhaps several others. Good teachers would like to encourage this evidence of

interests, but they simply cannot afford the time, especially if the syllabus is geared to external examinations.

This situation is likely to get worse. The body of knowledge is constantly increasing, and advances in knowledge take place along the interfaces of subjects; new subjects or sub-divisions of subjects seek their place in an over-full curriculum. Competing for time also are matters of pressing social concern, e.g. sex education, road safety, international crises.

Where these responsibilities are taken most seriously the pressure on children become unreasonable and unproductive. At one end of the scale the universities and training colleges complain that their first year students have been crammed to such an extent that they have not developed their powers of reasoning and questioning; at the other end adolescents are manifestly ill-equipped to adjust to adult society or to know how to change it to meet new needs.[1]

Thinking about content is an element in all curriculum planning. It is not its ground plan.

B. *Thinking about the objectives of education* is useful if it is seen as a safeguard for the students against the excessive reverence for cultural content (subject matter). But it, too, must be used in a context of a habitually attending to what each child is like now. If used in the following limited ways it may help teachers and students to feel that their work is purposive:

—*In thinking* ABOUT PUPILS it should be seen as a checklist of possible behaviours which children might exemplify and which teachers should be looking out for. It has positive value (and the Bloom taxonomy should be given all possible credit for this) in drawing attention away from the lower mental processes of information-gathering and memorizing to critical thinking and synthesis.

—*In thinking* ABOUT PUPILS it should be seen as one means of identifying a student's relative strengths so that these can be encouraged, and that working through them he, too, can come to be optimistic. In this way it can be used to ensure experience of success.

—*In thinking* ABOUT PUPILS it can be particularly useful in helping an interdisciplinary focus-group of teachers and the

[1] P. G. Mauger, in Second Report, p. 4

teachers concerned with other aspects of the curriculum to X-ray the learning of a child and see the vertebrae that lie below the obvious flesh of content. We may remember Whitehead's familiar dictum about the rhythms of learning: romance, precision, and generalization. Demonstrably, most children in most secondary schools spend most of their time on precision. This would be ameliorated if teachers focusing together on a child remembered that many cognitive objectives are common to several disciplines, although of course each discipline involves certain ways of behaving of its own. If a child's powers of evaluating complex material, for instance, are by agreement with him stressed in part of his day there can be reference to this in other parts of the curriculum to reinforce that learning, but he will not have his attention narrowed to this all week long, as can happen when all teachers independently have recognized a need but have not consulted together.

—*In thinking* ABOUT PLANNING PHASES OF WORK it is useful because it gives teachers confidence that they are being purposeful and effective.

—*In thinking* ABOUT PLANNING PHASES OF WORK it will be useful to teachers provided their thinking is individualized by constant reference to the needs and progress of individuals. This will mean that in addition to asking what kinds of questions might arise within a proposed area of investigation, they will be reminded to ask also, what kinds of expectations might we have of this phase for *each* student considered separately? And then they must allow him the chance, daily, to surprise them.

—*In thinking* WITH PUPILS about their own work it is valuable.

In fact, far the best use of this kind of thinking is to see it not as a taxonomy but as a toxophily. Children cannot be fitted into a taxonomy, but they can be invited to think in terms of a range of targets that they could aim at. In this way, if, in consultation with teachers, a student can come to see the kinds of behaviours he could be aiming at, he is becoming more truly a partner in his own education than if the targets he sets himself are ones concerned with content, or with getting 10 out of 10 for memorizing. Then there can be a true feedback for him. He is, in fact, being invited to learn something of the grammar of thinking, and to know that he is learning it.

Having said this I recognize that I may, even after protests, be submitting too much to fashion. I have known a number of outstanding teachers, original people deeply concerned with their students' learning and general well-being, who have found it totally impossible to use the concept of working towards objectives. One final comment must therefore be made: if any teacher genuinely believes that he has worked freely and imaginatively with students and that he has no need of a rescue operation to free him from the domination of content and syllabus, then, if he finds himself hampered by thinking of objectives, he should have no truck with them.

It may well be that his deep intuition about his pupils is the emperor whom we have learned to despise just because our concern with evaluation makes his clothes unfashionable. The whole press towards objectives, even modified and minimized in the ways I have proposed, may well be one of the foolish fashions that dominate the educational world from time to time. It is certainly a temptation to people engaged in education to reassure themselves that they are men of action, and abreast the times with techniques that are approved in industrial undertakings. But teaching is not an industry.

It may seem that in discussing content questions and objectives I have gone into greater detail than is appropriate to a section on the rationale of curriculum planning. I have done so deliberately because my view of curriculum demands a recognition that the kinds of enterprises in which individual students are engaged (including their relationship with teachers) are what matters in a curriculum.

When to teach what? is a tactical question quite clearly; *planning towards objectives* makes a spurious claim to strategic status by ignoring all the complexities of the situation it proposes. In moving on to the third and fourth questions which I want to study in relation to curriculum we move more deeply into the problem.

3. WHAT SOCIAL TRENDS SHOULD INFLUENCE CURRICULUM PLANNING?

Some American writers[1] are now asking what tasks are facing public education owing to changing social trends. This can be to take an important step of choosing priorities, of drawing our attention towards the needs of persons living in our rapidly changing world. William Van Thil, for instance suggests[2] the kinds of priorities with which we should be concerned:

1. Helping children and youth to come to grips with the international problems of their times.
2. Developing democratic human relationships among young people of varied races, religions, nationality backgrounds and social classes.
3. Teaching young people to participate as intelligent citizens in the great human issues of our times.
4. Educating young people for a society in which the unskilled and undereducated are obsolete.
5. Developing young people who are unique individuals, characterized by individuals differences and a variety of needs and interests.
6. Helping each and every boy and girl to develop into the best he or she is capable of becoming.
7. Encouraging young people to cultivate reflective thought, to use maximally the method of intelligence.
8. Answering the fundamental question as to human knowledge, "Knowledge for what?"

The difficulty with this list is its curiously random character, for it moves back and forth without acknowledgment between the things that adults think that the young ought to be able to *do* (albeit in terms of values which most of us would readily

[1] e.g. Richard I. Miller, *Education in a Changing Society*, Project for the Instructional Program of the Public Schools (National Educational Association, Washington D.C., 1953), pp. 122-130
[2] William Van Thil in *Role of Supervisor and Curriculum Director in a Climate of Change*, ed., Robert R. Leeper (Washington Association for Supervision and Curriculum Development, 1965)

accept as likely to be of great importance) and the kinds of persons that they ought to be *becoming*. Thus the fifth and sixth requirements are not in the same category as the rest, but this is not recognized. Is not our problem how to help pupils to become the kinds of persons envisaged in 5 and 6, from which the rest would follow?

It is of course perfectly right that we should as educated persons examine social trends, but if once we draw from this examination a list of things that young people ought to be able to do we draw attention away from the greater question, What, if we gave them the chance, might they be able to be? For, as the Chinese proverb reminds us, the best way to *do* is to *be*. It might happen that as they grow to full stature they will find that they no longer think of social responsibility, but rather of opportunities for shared enjoyments, mind less about "the method of intelligence" and more about the development of contemplation, pay less attention to democratic relationships and more to personal perceptiveness. We cannot both prescribe the values of the future and also liberate the young to develop their own.

Moreover to think in terms of scanning social trends suggests that they are inevitable, that the environment is something fixed, within which human beings operate, whereas in fact "man creates and re-creates his culture." There is a touch of fatalism here. There is also a lingering belief that if by instruction or habituation we can train young people to behave in certain ways they will spontaneously and in quite different conditions apply the principles we have formulated for them. We are still trying to do their living for them.

4. WHAT IS LIVING LIKE AND HOW CAN SCHOOLING BE LIVING?

I propose this as the fundamental question to be asked in creating curriculum. I mean by it that we can engage with the environment in three different modes, and in each mode there is a continuum of possible engagements:

A. The first mode is *Enquiry*.

Alone or with others we may seek to find out more about the material, the objects, the creatures, the persons, or the ideas surrounding us. The continuum of possibility in the mode of Enquiry ranges

> *from* —asking questions
> *through*—receiving answers to questions we have not asked
> *to* —apathy.

B. The second mode is *Making*.

Alone or with others we may set out to alter the material, the objects, the creatures, the persons, or the ideas surrounding us so as to make something new. The continuum of possibility in the mode of Making ranges

> *from*—changing what is given according to one's own invention or design
> *through*—changing what is given but on pre-ordained lines which one has not chosen
> *to*—passivity.

C. The third mode is *Dialogue*.

Alone or with others we may be open to and respond to the material, the objects, the creatures, the persons, or the ideas surrounding us and invite them (where appropriate) to respond to us. This is an engagement with the other that is distinguished from enquiry and making by being non-purposive, although one may well be aware that out of it growth or creation may come. The continuum of possibility in the mode of Dialogue ranges:

> *from*—habitual loving acceptance and generous giving to what is other
> *through*—spasmodic openness and response
> *to*—oblivion.

The most important criterion for creating a curriculum is that it should ensure that the whole process of learning approaches the living poles of these continua, and not those of apathy, passivity, and oblivion. It is through the kinds of engagement that we experience with the many aspects of the environment that we become the kind of people we are. Thus, when I speak of the need for schooling to be *living* my language is deliberately value-laden. I believe that the living behaviours are to explore, to make, and to enter into dialogue, and that these are the ways members of a school should engage themselves. I believe also that if we expect young people to spend their youth taking an in-between path (it is not a middle path, but is close to the negative pole), permitting them only to answer questions we have formulated for them, to "do" (see below, pp. 106-8) what we have invented or designed for them or have accepted from others, to be preoccupied with self crudely understood at the expense of other, then much of their subsequent lifetime is likely to be spent in apathy, passivity, and oblivion.

It is through the fully personal kinds of engagement with their environment that the young are likely to become capable of that same kind of engagement in the future. It is true that living in this full sense is not permitted to all of us much of the time in adult life, but this is because of the sickness of our society, not because of the necessary hazards of living. If school is supposed to be, as we are told by the Crowther Report (para. 167) "an environment that is designed for" the young then it is improper for us to diminish its vitality in order to prepare the young for that sickness. It is a remarkable comment on our expectations of schools that many people feel so deep a sympathy for workers engaged on the assembly line, where at least talk is usually possible, and spare so little thought for the young set in their lines, processing identical data, and in silence.

SUMMARY OF VALUE ASSUMPTIONS

I have criticized "when to teach what" questions in so far as they prize subject content above the diverse concerns of learners.

I have criticized objectives in so far as they prize the aims of the teacher above the diverse purposes of learners.

I have criticized the scanning of social trends in so far as this is an attempt to prescribe what the learner in an unknown future may do.

My value assumptions, the requirements that I make of curriculum, are thereby made clear enough.

In analysing my value assumptions (pp. 61-2, above) for the context of collaborative learning I said: "My value assumptions . . . are thereby made clear enough. I am seeking an education in which young people are actively *engaged* . . . . in which they are decision-makers . . . and in which their perception of each other and of themselves . . . is a major concern of the collaborative process."

I have now formulated, by implication in my criticism of other criteria for curriculum building and explicitly in my assertion of the fundamental importance of enquiry, making, and dialogue, the modes of active engagement with the environment which I then had in mind. I now propose to examine these ideas in more detail in the next chapter.

Chapter 5

Enquiry, Making, and Dialogue

ENQUIRY

These are the three kinds of enterprises in school which could enable children to acquire the tools of our culture without absorbing its failings of restless anxiety, self-deprecation, centrifugal activities—the reader is free to project on to society whichever seems to him the most damaging, secure in the knowledge that what he disregards others will choose, for there is ample choice.

If I speak first of *enquiry* it is because it was this concept that in our studies in the Curriculum Laboratory we came first to see as fundamental; and our work is primarily associated with it in many people's minds, in particular, of course with interdisciplinary enquiry. The first phase of our thinking about curriculum was to speak in terms of working on a common theme with a "problem-solving approach." However, in practice, there was a tendency for the problem-solving to be forgotten and for teachers simply to collaborate in teaching through "thematic studies." Hence the need to formulate a more specific concept, which I named Interdisciplinary Enquiry (IDE)[1] with the intention of emphasizing the central importance of exploration. A further difficulty remained: how was the relation of the arts to enquiry to be explicated? It was clear that the arts have their own autonomy and must

[1] Second Report, p. 2

not be submerged in academic processes of enquiry.[1] My argument was:

> Self-creation through the arts is at the very heart of our thinking about creative learning and we see its relations to IDE as manifold. There will be times when the arts are used consciously to communicate and thereby to explore more deeply and personally the findings of other studies or the feelings of anger, delight, and so on which these findings have aroused. But we are not given to the heresy of social realism and the subjections of the arts to commonly understood social purposes. Writing, dance, pottery, and the rest are ways in which pupils can express, discover, and order many areas of concern and enjoyment which have little or nothing to do with their enquiries in IDE. Some of these arise from the material of the arts itself. Sometimes the arts will illuminate IDE, sometimes they will initiate it. Sometimes they will be quite independent. The relationship will vary from time to time and from person to person.[2]

Later, in process of writing this book, I came to believe that I had been asking the wrong question. I had asked, If enquiry is fundamental what is the place of the arts? I could have asked, If making is fundamental what is the place of enquiry? I began to see enquiry as always preliminary to making, a part of the process of making, or a kind of making. I suspect now that one's choice as to whether enquiry or making is the more fundamental mode of human engagement with the environment is (like most important choices) a function of personality. It is characteristic of the person who is at heart a scientist, relishing discovery, to underline enquiry, and of the person more akin to the artist, concerned with creation, to emphasize making. This difference of emphasis is perhaps the only fundamental difference between two groups of creative exploratory people traditionally sharply distinguished, for each process involves exploration and each is creative.

---

[1] cf. *IDEAS*, No. 11.
[2] ibid., p. 3

STYLES OF ENQUIRY: EXPLORATION, EXPERIMENT, EXPLANATION

It is useful to distinguish three styles of enquiry, based respectively on a desire to explore, to experiment, and to explain. The concept of *exploration* is familiar and quite properly a major source of interest in the junior school curriculum. "An unexpected snail appearing on a classroom floor, for example, kept many children fascinated for days. They threw up questions concerning movement, time and speed, problems of food and shelter; they became aware of subtleties of colour and the fascinating floor patterns it made."[1] Here is a typical exploratory enquiry. Its field is biological but might well have been the properties of a substance, or mathematical concepts, or the social behaviours of human beings. *Experiment* as a basis for enquiry (as opposed to its being part of an exploratory process) is less frequently formulated, but is the distinctive feature of all enquiry which starts with the question, What would happen if I/we did such-and-such? It is most clearly manifested in science "tinkering"[2] but of course underlies experimental biology also. It is the basis of action research in adult life, and with a little imagination could be extended from the natural sciences to children's researches into, for instance, the life of the school or their own processes of collaboration, and could also contribute to more formal planning and recording than is usual of a school's contribution to the community.[3] The search for *explanation* is the search to understand relationships, between facts, between concepts, between theories. It is the basic search for a conceptual struc-

---

[1] B. Mogford, "IDEAS on Primary Education," *IDEAS, no. 6.*
[2] Cooley and Reed in their *Measurement of Science Interests*, made a useful distinction between three types of science interest, over and above general keenness in the classroom: a "woodsy-birdsy" factor, study of animals, etc.; a "science tinkerer" factor, "investigating electric appliances ... devising new inventions" and a "wonderer ... including activities such as finding out about space travel, exploring the meaning of concepts like time, gravity, space and energy". (*Science Education*, 1961, 45, pp. 324/5). If one disregards the content of interest, these factors are good descriptions of exploration, experiment and explanation respectively.
[3] More informally, it is also the basis of processes of disorientation referred to in the section of phases of work later in this book p. 166.

ture by which to interpret perceptions of the environment; and it is fundamental to a living curriculum.

Whatever style of enquiry is in process, the kinds of questions do not vary greatly. Any enquiry is likely to involve a wide range of factual questions: who, where, how many; what will happen if; how, why; and many also involve value questions, is it important, good, pleasant and so on.[1] Children doubtless prodded the snail, for instance, to see what would happen, and asked why it had a shell, for exploration normally involves such experiment and explanation. Similarly experiment and explanation involve each other and involve explanation also.

Granted these complex interweavings, it may seem that to distinguish these three styles of enquiry is to split hairs. But the distinction is important because it differentiates between three human purposes which underly human curiosity, and are negated in human apathy. Basically, the aim of exploration is "finding out", its success lies in finding answers to one's questions, its growth in noticing more questions to which answers might be sought. Basically, the aim of experiment is to discover the potentialities for planned change in the environment, its success lies in successful testing of hypotheses, its growth in refining and adding to them. The fundamental drive underlying explanatory enquiry is different: it is our need to make sense of our environment, to create a complex conceptual system, and its success lies in striving at an interpretation which works, its growth in making our system more comprehensive, and incidentally more tentative.

It is worth while distinguishing these three styles, if only to ensure that there shall be opportunities in the curriculum for explanation, that is to say for the continuing testing of one's conceptual map against changing reality, the continuing refinement of the map and its continuing extension, so that more and more of the blooming, buzzing confusion which William James attributed to the infant can be ordered

[1] Questions as to whether people think something important, good or pleasant are, of course, fact questions, not value questions.

and synthesized. There is not much danger, in a curriculum that values enquiry and making, of omitting exploration and experiment, but with adolescents explanation may go by default. With young children the inaccuracies of their map are charmingly obvious: a child refuses his prunes, is sent to another room, there is a thunderstorm and the child is found looking out of the window, disgruntled: "What a fuss," he says, "to make about a couple of prunes." We can all see that his map is that of the most primitive conceptual navigator. But adolescents often have complex strategies for hiding their ignorance and confusion about the world, and their sophisticated cultural patter can successfully deceive us and themselves. Each one of us has only to look back to adolescence to recall yawning gaps in his system of explaining the world. Yet to aid this process has certainly not been a conscious purpose of curriculum in the secondary school; if it had been, we would surely have done better than our present school day. Of all the styles of enquiry, explanation is the one we can least afford to omit, for it is an essential part of the inner growth of the individual. To retreat from exploration of new problems, or to stop having a tentative, experimental attitude to the environment, will make the individual less lively and less competent than he might have been. But to cease the search for explanation is more serious, for it is to retreat into irrationality and stereotyped thinking. A state of alienation from a world which is conceived as meaningless is most dangerous to democratic process. More fundamental still, disillusionment of this kind involves at heart a negation of self and of other selves. If we are concerned to ensure that explanatory enquiry plays its part in the curriculum we shall not thereby confine the curriculum to any one area, for children's interests range widely. But we shall surely find, as is not the case at the moment, even in some schools which respect the concept of enquiry, that the need to observe and explain human behaviour and human society will be recognized and welcomed. We shall find it natural then to include in an environmental study a study of people, to treat social change, growing up, the world of work, and study of personality as important areas of investigation, within which the subject-disciplines (including the arts) can contribute to the child's insight.[1]

ENQUIRY SKILLS

Traditional curricula, designed to give the young a broad agreed body of knowledge, are successful in so far as pupils show themselves competent in apprehending, recalling and evaluating the information proffered to them. In this context, the basic literacy skills are important too. But we often fail to notice that children are not acquiring effective skills of identifying and solving problems or any other kind of self-directed activity. An essential feature of an enquiry-based curriculum must be that children learn to use and to understand good processes and techniques of enquiry. Each discipline has indeed its own acknowledged processes of operation, and this is fully acknowledged in the Fourfold Curriculum. But whatever the discipline or disciplines involved, there are a number of strategies and tactics common to all enquiry. Basically, for instance, children need to identify problems; to understand that enquiries can have more than one shape—in some, it is necessary to pre-plan precisely, whereas in others there is a possibility of serendipity which would be lost through an inflexible adherence to an initial formulation of the questions; to learn to be content with the necessary tentativeness of all human knowledge, while appreciating the kinds of verification that are appropriate to the enquiry in hand; and so on.

There are also useful techniques of enquiry, and children need to acquire a repertoire of these, as for instance to set up a theoretical model which will generate a variety of well

---

[1] For rather more specific proposals see below pages 153ff. We shall begin also to create that continuum of understanding which is vital to an inclusive culture, for undoubtedly concepts that are engaging the attention of research teams or have been found valuable as explanatory summaries in the behavioural sciences—concepts such as conflict, aggression, role; relativity, systems—will be found useful in explanatory enquiry in the classroom also.

categorized questions; to recognize the value of summarizing the stage a study has reached and thereby discover the gaps which could be the basis of further enquiry if they so wished; to control variables in an experimental situation. There are psychological techniques also, for breaking log-jams, by brain-storming and then categorizing the specific proposals that emerge, or by trying to look at a problem from a different point of view. And each individual needs to learn his own simple tips for self-management, which acknowledge his strengths and difficulties in the enquiry process, and thereby his most effective tactics. As teachers come more and more effectively to formulate the enquiry skills that children find useful, they will have to negotiate a route between authoritarian didacticness, which can easily make enquiry as boring a lesson to be learned as any other, and laissez-faire chaos, which is equally disenchanting to the learner. For enquiry in itself is not enough: involvement and competence are required too, and each supports and feeds the other.

In stressing the importance of logical enquiry skills, I do not suggest that they should be pursued with puritanical dedication. It is all too easy for teachers to "consider science and scientific thinking" (and I would add any investigation) "as an intellectual activity of a specialized kind, logical above all things, upon which intrude from time to time those flashes of inspiration or unreason which are responsible for discoveries. For everyone knows that discoveries are not made scientifically, in this sense, at all. They are 'seizing upon some happy idea', 'some sort of inspiration', 'bridging a logical gap'."[1] We must allow and welcome the continuing presence of the non-logical in the processes of enquiry. "Science and poetry, mathematics and words, intellect and imagination, mind and body: [these antitheses] are old, they are tidy, they are mistaken."[2]

---

[1] Elizabeth Sewell, *The Orphic Voice: Poetry and Natural History*, Routledge and Kegan Paul, 1961, p. 18. The quotations are from Max Planck, Fred Hoyle, and Michael Polanyi.
[2] ibid., p. 19

ENQUIRY AND PERSISTENCE

In the traditional curriculum, not only competence but persistence in the acquisition of what may literally be unwanted knowledge is highly valued. The persistent pupil, whether or not he has a high I.Q., is likely to be the successful pupil. It is often suggested that children who have what might be summed up as a "progressive" education are flighty and lack the habit of persistence. Where progressiveness has meant laissez-faire messiness this may well be so. But the contrast should not be between flighty messiness and ordered perseverance, but between two different kinds of failure on the one hand—messiness and spoonfeeding—and two different kinds of success on the other—involvement in work which one has come to see as an extension of one's proprium, and obedience in performing tasks which one's elders and soi-disant betters require. In both situations, habits of persistence are needed and rewarded. All serious students need to buckle down to hard work. It is only the motivation and the rewards that are different.

MAKING

The importance of a heuristic basis for education is familiar and withdrawal from answering questions and a move towards helping the young to ask good questions of their own is a feature of all modern proposals for science teaching, one that we may hope will increasingly spread to all aspects of the curriculum even in a traditional kind of schooling. The case for paying respect to *making* is less familiar and I must argue it more fully. I believe that educators need a new categorization of making which disregards differences in the purposes of the maker and also differences in the nature of what he alters. We need to concentrate instead on what is common to all creative behaviour. This will help us to recognize that not all making is creative. In fact we may suspect that much so-called creative work in schools is not creative at all.

For convenience I draw a distinction between four kinds of making, distinguished by the nature of the maker's contribution to what is made. They are:

1. *Inventing*, which I use to mean envisaging a new possibility, such as identifying a new problem in any subject material, formulating a new hypothesis (subjectively new, that is, to the learner), creating an object according to the maker's personal conception.

2. *Designing*, which I use to mean indicating, and perhaps putting into practice, the way in which an invention can be realized. The designer is a co-creator, even if he is a creator after the fact, and in this broad sense I use designing to cover performance of known works "invented" by others, as in the performance of plays or music, as well as to describe the cooperative work of bringing a technical invention into production.

3. *Maintaining*, which I use to mean looking after for what already exists, including the tools of a discipline, with an eye not only to its past and present condition but its possible future development. Scholars who keep the culture trim are maintainers in this sense.

All these are creative in varying degrees because the maker contributes something of his own to the alteration of the materials, ideas and so on in the environment.

4. *Doing*, on the other hand, I use to mean bringing someone else's inventions or design into being, without in any way contributing to it. Doing is not creative for this reason, it is copying. It is good or bad in so far as it fulfils the requirements of other people.

This rough categorizing is proposed only as a matter of convenience. Clearly, the inter-relationships of inventing and designing are complex and much *making* is an alternation between the one and the other by the same person; quite possibly the comparison of the designer of a product with an executant artist is altogether too arbitrary. Nevertheless the distinction will have served a purpose for curriculum if it articulates a difference between creative making and "doing." The person "doing" contributes nothing to the alteration of the environment except in so far as his skill or lack of it affects the accuracy with which he carries out a pre-ordained plan. He is a non-creative functionary, not far removed from a "living tool."

THE RIGOUR OF MAKING

In the conventional school day much of the academic work, and much of the practical work also, lies very close to mere *doing*. The child is kept at work going over the accepted culture, sometimes exercising "productive thinking" in the narrow sense of drawing correct conclusions from material in which only one form of closure is correct, occasionally contributing his own evaluation of given information, but doing so only as part of the teacher's pre-ordained plan for him, in which he is not a partner and which he often does not grasp. How much more profitable productive and critical thinking would be if it were demanded by the nature of the child's engagement, that is if the need for rigour arose from the creative purpose rather than the apparently arbitrary decision of the teacher; if the answer to the question, "Why are you doing that?" were not, "Because I was told to," or "Because we always do," but "Because I need to," whether the need is to test a hypothesis, to make one's dancing more skilful and expressive, or to get a pot ready for firing.

MAKING AND COLLABORATION

Invention and design remind us of the variety of activities that students can contribute to creatively, since making is not confined to divergent thinking: the purposeful convergence in the process of designing is an important part of carrying out creative work. Hence within this rough categorization there is a place for the contribution made to collaborative creative work of those whose strength lies in creative criticism, in not being deceived by the obvious at this practical level, rather than in conceiving new ideas. A valuable contribution can even take the form of a flexible optimism about process, a willingness to continue to cast round until others come up with new ideas.

MAKING AS REALISTIC

Making is essentially realistic, for it involves an essential continuing engagement between the possible and the actual (man's ideas and the reality situation). It is therefore an aspect of living now and acts as a counterpoise to that tendency to see all real living as happening in the future which can lay waste our lives. "To our boys and girls" says the Newsom Report (para 321), meaning thereby those young people of so-called average and less than average ability, which it equates with early leavers, " 'realistic' means belonging to the real world, that is to the world of men and women, not of school children"; and the remark is quoted with approval in the Schools Council's first proposals for Science for the Young School Leaver (Working Paper No. 10.) If this is so, and for many it probably is, it suggests a massive failure of our schools. It is likely that one of the reasons the schools have failed to provide the required counterpoise to the pressures of some parents and many peers is the emphasis on uncreative "doing." It is something that belongs to the special enclosed moated grange of school, which becomes a preliminary to living rather than living itself.

Making, whatever the material may be—whether the product is an elegant mathematical formula or a handtoy—demands a specific understanding of the material, of how it can be used and what it will and will not do, a realistic understanding of the cooperativeness and yet autonomy of the *other*; so it gives experience of the necessity to accept frustration. But it also does so in a way that is a challenge to flexibility and ingenuity. When the world around us is painful and we have no hope of altering it, we spend much of our time, especially when young, in the kind of phantasy that is no more than an escape from an oppressive environment. The opportunity for real making, with help available to make real success possible, is an essential part of the counterpoise we need; and it has the advantage that the autonomy of the material provides frustration, but does so in an impersonal form. Knowing that the young need experience of frustration, we still are merely punitive if we make the process of growing up harsher than it already is. In the context of making, the unalterable can be distinguished from the mutable, and the scope of what is mutable perhaps extended. The experience of purposefully refining hypotheses, the increased ability to envisage more clearly in process what the outcome might be, and the increased power of discriminating what is essential to a design and what is peripheral—all these are valuable exercises in a realistic engagement with the outside world.

MAKING, ART AND TECHNOLOGY

If I have emphasized making as a process rather than differentiating its material products, I have done so in order to try to counteract a tendency damaging to the young, our habit of giving them imposed tasks in all fields of study, when they would obtain the virtues of accuracy, rigour, and realism, as by-products of a more autonomous kind of education. I do not want thereby to add strength to a hierarchy of values quite opposed to my own, which see knowledge *about* as superior to knowledge *how*. On the contrary, in my view one of the most serious weaknesses of our present education is the denigration of the practical. I have already put up as a possibility the idea that the popularity of pure science might be enhanced by more opportunity for *making* in the workshops (see page 34) but work in the workshops is important in its own right. The ability to come and go in a technological world, and not as a stranger, is an essential part of the process of identification today, as Erik Erikson has suggested. Writing of new roles and competence today ... "to fit into and take active charge of technological and scientific development, learning thereby to identify with a life style of testing, inventing and producing" he warns us that "Youth which is eager for such experience but unable to find access to it will feel estranged from society, upset in its sexuality, and unable to apply its aggression constructively."[1]

This is perhaps most obviously true for boys, but schools which have given more chance to girls to work in the workshops have in my experience been greatly surprised by their enthusiasm. We do not want to reinforce a division of sexual roles which diminishes the self-concepts of members of both sexes. "He for tools only, she for tools as his" is just about as silly a slogan as its holier predecessor and is all too likely to be complemented by "she for home only, he for her at home," and a sex-based distinction between a world of things and a world of persons which is as damaging as the caste-based distinction between the world of things and the world of ideas.

Far too many people in our society feel they have a psychological block as regards the manual skills through which the technical arts can be approached. Yet if we are to hope for a continuum of experience in which all members of a modern society feel that technical advances enhance rather than threaten them, and none feels himself excluded from a mysterious world, it is through the opportunity of this kind of making, perhaps simply through taking quite a minor part in a shared venture, that we may find people most easily become self-confident and self-possessed also, in the sense of not being possessed by machine or other projections of inner fears. It is out of a general respect for craftsmanship and technical studies, which does not see the crafts or industrial arts as peripheral to education (as they are today for all those capable of what are thought to be higher kinds of work) that this confidence should emerge, and with it a strengthening perhaps of the advanced technology group, the "theoretical-

---

[1] Erik Erikson, "The Negro American," in *Daedalus*, XCV (1966), 145-171

practical" students whom adult society would greatly welcome for their economic importance.

COMMUNICATION IN ENQUIRY AND MAKING

Throughout any process of enquiry or making we have to look to the quality and diversity of communication. Learners need to acquire good habits and techniques of communicating with each other the plans, data required, or present state of a study, and this is allowed for in sharing or reporting back sessions as in the primary school. What is less frequently noticed is the value of communicating clearly with oneself. The bonding of action and description is important in all learning. Young children tend to describe their actions to themselves as they go along; it is usually considered an advance in socialisation when they stop doing so, as the silence imposed in many secondary classrooms bears witness. But if they have not learned silent speech we are denying them the habit of identifying precisely what they are aiming at and how they are proceeding, an identification which helps understanding of process and of self. (The precise statement may not be a description of a precise state of mind: to learn to say, I am now in a muddle is important, leading as it will either to identifying the evidence that is lacking or to leaving the problem aside until one's ideas sort themselves out.)

Communication is not equivalent to verbalisation. There is value in not only making use of the symbolic descriptions of speech or mathematical language, but deliberately acquiring and retaining a repertoire of enactive and iconic representation.[1] Our early "symbolical gorgings"[2] have made us overvalue the statement that is divorced from action and imagery. Children, and adults too for that matter, need to build into their processes of enquiry a flexible use both of sketches, flow diagrams and so on and also particularly of structural models, actual and imaginary, which they can manipulate; another

---

[1] J. Bruner, *Toward a Theory of Instruction* (Harvard, 1966) pp. 10-21, 66-8.
[2] G. D. Phillips in First Report.

application of the same principle is to use movement as well as pictorial representations to interpret and articulate a mood or a human situation, or even a problem of design, and to treat this as an expected part of classroom behaviour.

DIALOGUE

The value fundamental to enquiry is curiosity, its aim discovery or explanation. The value fundamental to making is originality, its outcome change (including the change of materials into new products). The value fundamental to dialogue in the sense that I use the word is wonder. Any outcome that it has is a by-product, since its essence is that it is non-purposive. An exploratory, creative education with no place for *dialogue* would rapidly become exploitative and manipulative.

There is great danger that as advanced nations develop greater skill in discovering and encouraging creative talents of all kinds the tendency to exploit and manipulate all the resources of the environment, including human resources, will become more ruthless. Schools have an over-riding obligation today to provide a counterpoise to these trends in Western culture. There is probably less opportunity for reverence of the *other*, material or personal, in our secondary schools than there is even for exploration and making. Schools through their social climate and their curriculum are conveying a use-morality and a use-aesthetic. One outcome of this is that much of the exploratory and creative work that does take place is shallow. Open, patient observation alternating with periods of relaxation when the conscious mind is withdrawn from the work in hand, or when it plays around an idea—this is the rhythm that worthwhile discovery and making demand. The quality of much of our pupils' work in school is necessarily impoverished because we are impatient and exploitative and allow them quite simply too little time to brood and too little time to discover to their own satisfaction their personal cycles of withdrawal and involvement. But dialogue would be important to the curriculum even if no discovery or product resulted from it. It is self-justifying, the essential non-purposeful component of spending one's youth well, in which end and means cannot even for the purpose of analysis by distinguished.

In saying that the man who did not pause to wonder at the world was as good as dead, Einstein commended the well-being of the animal that functions well. But he also implied that the world merits our "wonder," and thereby expressed his acknowledgment of value outside human process. The formulations of the world religions and also the personal affirmations of many individuals, some believers, some agnostics, have borne witness to their acceptance of this value. Its claim to our attention cannot be strengthened by any count of heads or by pointing to the contentment of those who accept it, for that would be to justify the self-justifying by reference to other values. It is to be affirmed or denied by each individual on his own account. But to those who affirm it, the gift of wonder must be itself a source of wonder, and fundamental to the quality of living for a school.

DIALOGUE WITH MATERIAL, OBJECTS, AND CREATURES

Adolescence may well be a period when young people's capacity for dialogue is at risk in our society, and special efforts need to be made to sustain it. It is a period, after all, when they are inevitably and rightly concerned with their own personal development, including the physical changes they experience in puberty. It is also likely that as they become increasingly at home with more elaborate formal operations, to use Piaget's terminology, the increasing freedom with which they can manipulate complex data without reference to objects may draw their attention away from the externally existent world. And if they are inclined to see only the future, not the present, as the "real world," (page 108, above) their phantasy life instead of being fruitful and explanatory may have less and less basis in the rich commonplace observations of the day-to-day.

It may be simply that from about eleven or twelve onwards the young become more aware of other people's values. Certainly those who share something of Einstein's delight and wonder in experience should recognize the need to provide in school a basis in experience for resisting a powerful environmental press. In comparing Mexican village children up to ten years old and twelve to thirteen with Mexican and United States urban children, Michael Maccoby and Nancy Modiano showed the trend in the modern culture:

> A city child coming from an industrial society starts by dealing with objects in terms of their perceptible, concrete characteristics. He soon comes to consider them in the light of what he can do with them. In time, he is led to more abstract formulations as to how things are, how they are alike and how different. Some go so far that they lose the sense of the concreteness of things and become buried in a dry nominalism. They are like people who see a painting immediately in terms of its style, period and influences, but with no sense of its uniqueness.

In summing up the contrast with the more primitive culture of the villagers, they state:

> If the peasant child is not dulled by village life, he will experience the uniqueness of events, objects, and people. But as the city child grows older, he may end by exchanging a spontaneous, less alienated relationship to the world for a more sophisticated outlook which concentrates on using, exchanging, or cataloguing. What industrialized, urban man gains in an increased ability to formulate, to reason, and to code the ever more numerous bits of complex information he acquires, he may lose in a decreased sensitivity to people and events.[1]

It is alarming to find this tendency to overvalue use and the product at the expense of openness to experience actually praised as part of an advance in maturity appropriate to the secondary phase of education; yet this is bluntly stated by the Newsom Report. Under the heading "What should 'secondary' imply?" we find:

---

[1] Michael Maccoby and Nancy Modiano, "On Culture and Equivalence: I," in Bruner, Olver and Greenfield et al., *Studies in Cognitive Growth* (John Wiley & Sons, 1966), pp. 268-9

> To make a pottery bowl involves considerable experience of handling clay: in getting to know empirically how clay behaves . . . and gradually acquiring skill of hand and eye in making it obey the potter's will. All this gathering of experience is learning of a primary kind whether the pupil is ten, twenty, or forty years old. But the purposeful employment of this skill to produce a bowl *which will serve a special purpose and look right in a particular place*—and to be right in one's judgement nine times out of ten: this is a secondary education.[1]

Here the elevation of the functional is explicit. In fact, if for "pot" you "read "person" you have an apt picture of our functional attitude to people. which naturally spills over into a functional view of their creative lives. This is the shared disaster of our age.

People sometimes speak of "experienced-based education" as if it were something anybody could have, and the only question was whether it was worth having. These cross-cultural studies remind us that to maintain at the secondary age this aspect of dialogue at the very simplest level of being aware of objects through the senses, is an achievement to be hoped for, not something to be had just for the asking.

In describing enquiry, making, and dialogue, I implied that the ranges of behaviour were roughly comparable (page 95). But a distinction is now necessary. Answering others' questions and "doing" according to others' designs are not satisfactory ways of spending one's youth, because they ignore the child's need for participation and tend to make him apathetic and passive; but they do acknowledge the values of curiosity and originality even though they deny to the child the opportunity to exercise them. The range of relationships in the mode of dialogue is different, and the comparison though convenient was in this sense misleading: between being in dialogue and being oblivious there is no middle way. One is either in dialogue or one is not: the supposed continuum is simply a matter of a frequency count, of how often one is aware, how often blocked, and of the extent to which we are preoccupied with concerns that we would really wish to have

---

[1] ibid. p. 312; my italics.

priority or are simply trapped in habits of self-regard or anxiety.

Dialogues with objects, creatures and persons should be a continuing value underlying all of a school's work, and it is more important to identify ways in which it is often blocked than to offer a few necessarily limited examples from the vast range of possibilities of expressing this value in the life of a school, which will often be evinced simply in a richer enjoyment of what one would be doing anyway. However, this is not to ignore the importance of enterprises specially offered with this value in mind. One for example was a pilot study which the Curriculum Laboratory undertook in collaboration with the Victoria and Albert Museum of which the whole purpose was the personal involvement of young people with a variety of objects displayed in a special room which they were asked to look at and handle, write about, but above all draw or choose between.[1] The quality of involvement in this simple exercise in dialogue was quite remarkable. It led to a more effective use of the museum, to a greater personal understanding of themselves in relation to things, and to some greater mutual understanding also. But it was the personal absorption that mattered to all of us who experienced it with them.

Absorption is not necessarily awe-struck. In fact we should hope also for desire to play with and manipulate things in the search for a full dialogue with them; and we should be pleased too when we find a positive search for empathy with the people who originally created them, for this is in keeping with the mood of a creative society which is less inclined to look back at the wonders of past ages, more interested in making imaginary contact with the interests, needs and problems of their makers, for we might become like them. The essential characteristic of wonder is not so much awe as love. "The loving man is one who grasps non-relatively each thing he grasps. He does not think of inserting the experienced thing into relations to other things; at the moment of experience

---

[1] This study is described by R. Marcouse in "Personal Response," *Museums Journal*, 1968.

nothing else exists, nothing save this beloved thing, filling out the world and indistinguishably coinciding with it. . . . What you extract and combine is always only the passivity of things. But their activity, their effective reality, reveals itself only to the loving man who knows them. And thus he knows the world.[1] And so too in his awareness of creatures, of other people, and of himself, and also of those who made the treasures he enjoys.

DIALOGUE WITH OBJECTS

Dialogue with objects can be blocked by our ulterior motives towards the environment:

—Observing in order to classify according to a pre-ordained plan: the equivalent of going round a gallery talent-spotting, attributing works of art to Picasso or Braque and leaving it well satisfied, with no sense of the uniqueness of each object. Even at infant school classification sometimes drives out observation and enjoyment because of teachers' desire to move children rapidly on to cognitive skills that are thought to be superior.

—Observing in order to use, which concentrates on separate aspects of an object and denies its integrative system.

—Observing with the purpose of judging according to pre-determined criteria. This often leads to a halo effect: you approve or disapprove one aspect and fail to notice others.

—Observing for choice and decision making.

All these have their value, of course, but if we do not *also* experience a quite simple non-purposive openness our attitude becomes rapacious. Hence we miss vast areas of enjoyment, of enrichment, and also of cognitive growth,[2] and will in the

---

[1] Martin Buber, *Pointing the Way*, Collected Essays, tr. and ed. by Maurice Friedman, Harper and Rowe 1957, pp 28ff.
[2] cf. J. Bruner, *Towards a Theory of Instruction*, p. 84.

long run, for that matter, be less effective in our instrumental confrontations with the environment.

Dialogue with objects can also be blocked by previous failures in personal development, inadequacies in the self which we offer to the dialogue, as for instance by:

—Lack of adequate sensuous experience in earlier phases, in some cases stretching back to earliest infancy where there has been too little experience of physical handling and being handled.

—Lack of experience of learning to concentrate on sense experience. Pupils are constantly required to concentrate on cerebral activities, far too rarely to listen acutely and selectively, to explore through touch, to look and look again, to savour smells and tastes.

—Lack of consciousness of self as having personal worth. Trained observation enhances a sense of coherent identity. If you do not think you have worth you do not offer yourself to the environment. Anxiety traps us in ourselves.

—Lack of ranges of appropriate symbolism in which at times, when the moment is apt, to crystallize experience.

Dialogue with creatures presents no problems of motivation. Wherever opportunity is given in school to have living creatures to tend, observe, and enjoy the young welcome it. The need is only to remind ourselves that this is not something we grow out of as we leave primary school. It is of continuing importance, particularly since for many families this experience is denied by rules of tenancy.

DIALOGUE WITH PERSONS

The same obstacles as reduce our observation of objects operate equally powerfully in our attending to each other. In "games people play"[1] people are not in dialogue with others: they are exploiting and manipulating figures in their phantasy

---

[1] cf. Eric Berne, *Games People Play* (Grove, 1964)

world, to whom they deny identity as self-subsistent systems, deserving wonder just because they are.

In the day-to-day experience of working in groups, the habit of living openly to persons can grow, through listening to them, seeing them, imagining the possibility of being as they are, but only if this is recognized as a social norm of the greatest importance, part of an experience of caring that is essential to human growth. Adolescence in its developing consciousness of self could be a critical stage for the development of consciousness of others. We need not expect this dialogue always to be comfortable. Often it will involve confrontation[1] of a strenuous kind, and this is probably necessary for personal growth, as in confronting others in genuine dialogue we confront ourselves. This experience of reality needs to take place in an environment where the worst will not happen, where the wounded will be rescued, yet where truth prevails (see page 69ff, above).

An important feature of secondary school curriculum will therefore be to encourage an understanding of the wide range of human behaviours that are possible, and this will be achieved only in rhythm with a growing consciousness of self. Here is one of the reasons why schools must be "porous" institutions, not insulated from the rest of the world.

INTERNAL DIALOGUE

It is here also that the arts are seen to be central to a reformed curriculum. They provide both the language and the opportunity for self-discovery and self-creation, and do so rather in the quality of living they make possible than through any products, such as exhibitions or school theatrical productions. Brian Way explains this process:

This consciousness of self forms the foundation (a rock-like founda-

---

[1] cf. Clark E. Moustakas, *Creativity and Conformity* (D. Van Nostrand, 1967), p. 45: "The confrontation is a meeting between persons who are involved in a conflict or controversy and who remain together, face-to-face, until their feelings of divisiveness and alienation are resolved."

tion, if the growth is slow and organic rather than swift and imposed) of living in harmony with oneself, aware of and able to use all one's resources in each aspect of life, unenvious of others whose birthright may include the endowment of particular gifts that are denied to us, perceptive of both inner and external forces of living.... Consciousness of self is wholly positive, and springs from an intuitive awareness of the uniqueness of individual personality.[1]

All the arts contribute to this growing consciousness of self and relief from a self-consciousness "which is responsible for many acts which are as false and unreal for the doer as they are for the observer."[2] Perhaps the contribution of drama and dance-drama is most direct and unassailable, although that, too, is enriched by collaboration with other modes of expression which involve more external play with the environment. For in dramatic improvization the material used and explored is the person's own physical being, own experiences, and own emotions, some of which he may have had no awareness of. In drama we do more than play out our hidden feelings, expressing our hates, fears, love, joy, or detachment in ways which may help us to behave better in "real" situations. That is to treat drama simply as therapy, which is an important by-product but not its function. Far more important is the increase in sensitivity to ourselves and others and the truthful exploration of what it is to be that improvized dance and drama expresses and promotes. If this is combined with other forms of expression and exploration in interdisciplinary (including undifferentiated arts) sessions, it will be still more enriching.

There is another aspect to dialogue in the sense I use the word, and this is the internal dialogue that continues in every human being unless we silence it by refusing it a hearing. Many people deny all that is not rational and purposeful and so reduce internal dialogue to mere internal argument, as they consciously work out decisions, solve problems, sort out

---

[1] Brian Way, *Development Through Drama* (Longmans Green, 1967), pp. 157-8. The detailed proposals in this book are valuable for all teachers, not only for drama specialists.
[2] ibid.

experiences. But if we are to be truly in dialogue with ourselves we need to be open also to those other configurations of experiences and ideas which emerge through the symbolism of dreams and are perhaps most directly expressed in poetry, in doodling, and again in drama. If we can only allow our minds to drift, we arrive at rich insights, powerfully expressed. There is a whole skill of relaxation and trust in experience which is easily lost in the clatter of urban living, in the busyness of rational behaviour, in a life which has little place for silence or meditation or just *being with*.

One of the features of schools most unfriendly to this secret dialogue is the tendency always to analyse, dissect, and discuss experiences, and in particular of the literature and the other arts which should so richly feed us. We do positive damage to development if we always recall ourselves and our students from their hidden imaginative lives to discuss an art-form or bring our rationalizing intellects to bear on the social significance of what we have experienced together. It is possible to "have *an* experience" (see page 121) simply by allowing time for it to sink in.

Schools dominated by the three Rs or parsing Latin, which had no place for the affective, left the universe of private discourse untapped but also undespoiled. They did not sow seeds and then rake over ground where roots were tentatively groping into depth. Frivolous invitations to engage in expressive or creative work in circumstances where persons are not cared for or where children's offerings are judged according to some predetermined criteria of excellence, not simply welcomed as dialogue, are a great danger of the more fully personal education we attempt today. We need ourselves to be in dialogue with our pupils and with our own inner selves if we are to dare to attempt it. We need also to have retained our capacity to play.

EDUCATION FOR A WELL-SPENT YOUTH

"It was remarked to me," said Herbert Spencer, "by the late Mr. Charles Roupell ... that to play billiards well was a sign of 'an ill-spent youth'." What might be the signs of a well-spent youth today?

In drawing attention to the quality of our engagement with the environment as the key to the quality of curriculum, I have by implication, although with a different starting-point and in different terms, allied myself to those who place the well-being of persons at the centre of their requirements for schooling. Often they put forward as their criterion for curriculum choice that it should meet the needs of adolescents. I prefer to be rather more specific and to see needs as life-tasks and as concerns. Needs are life-tasks when seen by the eyes of adults, who are aware of the tasks laid on us by the society in which we live (for the character of life-tasks is culturally determined even if they are closely related to phases of development). To the young themselves, life-tasks are their fundamental concerns, their felt needs. A curriculum should assist the young with their life-tasks, recognize and help them to cope well with their concerns.

To accomplish a life-task is not, however, to do something in the future, setting oneself an aim and finding the best means towards it. We do endless damage to ourselves by bringing into living (of which education is a phase) the terminology of industrial production and of wars, in which means and ends can be distinguished because the quality of life is not the prime concern of the businesses and armies concerned with them: not only the quality of life but life itself may be sacrificed there in the determination to achieve objectives.

Accomplishing a life-task is not something *achieved* by living appropriately to one's stage of growth now; it *is* living appropriately to one's stage of growth now. Loving, working, finding identity—these are processes which do not require us to move on from one task to another, but simply to love, to work, to be ourselves and be recognized as such, as we are now, changing as we grow older the forms of love and the ways we express it, the kinds of work and the skills with which we do it, the scope of our identity and the kinds of recognition we welcome and can offer.

Beneath the passing interests of the young are their shared concerns: they are preoccupied with problems of identity, of relatedness, and their ability to control their environment.[1] Their fears are (though the categorization should not be taken as exactly matching) of apathy, withdrawal into oblivion, and passivity in the face of persons and circumstances, all aspects of a deprived and hollow existence.

An education which concentrates on positive kinds of engagement with the environment is of its nature enriching to persons. The rationale I propose for curriculum construction gives priority to what young people can *be* (even though we shall never know precisely what that is), not what they might *do*; and to what they can be *now*, not what they might do *later*. It is proposed in the belief that if young people spend their youth well they will have the best hope of being effective and at ease in future roles and of cooperating to create a less meagre culture than our own, one for persons to grow in. This is not its justification: it requires no justification other than that they spend this period of living in living as well as we and they can make it possible. Nevertheless it is fair to extrapolate to some of the kinds of behaviour which we can hope might emerge later on.

SOME SIGNS OF A WELL-SPENT YOUTH

I would not dare attempt a final list, even for myself, of my hopes for the young, and each person, of whatever age, will set his priorities rather differently, but today my own hopes would be that through their lives they would be affectionate

---

[1] cf. G. Weinstein et al., *A Strategy for Developing Relevant Content for Disadvantaged Children*, Report of the Elementary School Teaching Project of the Ford Foundation (Fund for Advancement of Knowledge) 1964-7; mimeographed document.

towards self—past, present, and becoming; that they would respect and cherish their own relative strengths and those of others, rather than worrying about their weaknesses or assuming that they have to deny and seek to change what is unique in themselves because the culture is not friendly to it; that they would be able to enjoy themselves and know that they were doing so. I would hope that they would be able to cope with a variety of roles without threat to their sense of selfhood, and hence to support others in doing so also; that they would be equally ready, as was appropriate to the occasion, to take a leading or a subsidiary part in any situation: that they would wish to continue to explore the possibilities of processes, situation, institutions, and values (and would so do with well-developed enquiry skills and on a complex scale); as a first requirement they would simply be observant. I would hope also that they would be able to live at ease in uncertainty, looking neither up to authority nor back to tradition for nostrums or tranquillizers, but trusting themselves to experience, being on the way to learning to distinguish a confidence that "all shall be well" from infantile magic. It is perhaps too much to hope that they would be so free as to be able to "love God and do what they wish" (or its agnostic equivalent) in the confidence that they could not then fail to act well; but we could have every expectation that they would be more sensitive to the good in others, and to their needs, and less dependent on stereotyped codes of behaviour, more inclusive and less demanding in their affections than we were taught to be, more free to offer themselves and accept others in mutual empathy, unjudging.

If even part of this were to happen, actual genocide might be averted and also its spiritual equivalent, passive acceptance of dictatorial or bureaucratic fiats. Lives might be *lived*, by people who were good at being their own selves and at acknowledging in a growing mutuality the diverse selfhood of their fellows.

Chapter 6

The Organization of the Curriculum

THE FOURFOLD CURRICULUM

The study I have made of the modes of our engagement with the environment may have seemed very general and far removed from the planning of a school's working day, but the implications are practical and demand radical re-thinking of everyday practice. The kinds of questions and answers that I move on to in this section are less general and are more open to change and development. I would not suggest that the Fourfold Curriculum is any final answer to our requirements of school, but it seems to me at the moment to be the most sensible way of meeting them.

If we look at the implications of what has gone before, certain requirements clearly emerge, fundamental to curriculum planning:

1. The school environment must be sufficiently diversified to allow different children to arrive at different points by different routes and at different times; this is what is involved in caring for individual well-being, and in thinking big about talent (see above, page 29), and it is one way in which development through the acknowledgement of a child's relative strengths will be made possible

It follows that any tight fitting of children into courses, and any idea that late or eccentric developers can never catch up, never belong, because they have missed certain fixed requirements, are unacceptable. Despite all difficulties the aim must be to accommodate the school to the needs of all.

2. Since curriculum is seen in terms of the quality of the engagement with the environment, the emphasis has moved from learning subject-matter to becoming at home with a subject-discipline. This is a fundamental point which I shall discuss in detail later. For the moment it is enough to say that there needs to be experience both of inter-disciplinary and intra-disciplinary studies, but that integration of subject-matter by teachers has no particular merit.

3. If motivation is to be intrinsic, bases of intrinsic motivation need to be identified. I see these as:

(*a*) Partaking in active engagement with the environment in ways to which students can make a personal contribution.

Answering other people's questions and working to other people's design have their place if the context of exploratory and creative study requires them. Within that context they may be extremely valuable, as are for instance assignments and programmes designed to help individuals or clusters to acquire skills or concepts that they need. Writ small, this occurs in IDE/M; writ large it is the function of a whole cell of the Fourfold Curriculum, the "remedial" section (see pages 129f).

(*b*) Not only the manner but the matter of the engagement being seen by the child to have relevance to his *concerns*; and this means not merely a relevance to passing fancies that he can enjoy and leave, although this is important, but relevance to matters that have his long-term respect and commitment.

(*c*) The tasks which any student undertakes being appropriate to his level of achievement now. This aspect of motivation is sometimes ignored, but the feedback to him is fundamental: he must have sufficient challenge, but he must also have sufficient experience of success. Only teachers in close touch with pupils can know what success each individual requires, but we can expect that greater support is needed by those whose performance is not high than by the gifted. Teachers sometimes suppose that in a situation permitting more exploratory and creative work than is usual today their skill in diagnosing and guiding pupils will not be called on. On the contrary, to ensure that he maintains the dynamic that comes from work intrinsically interesting to him and at the same time to ensure that the level of challenge is just right for him and to assign the right work at the right moment, an appropriate programme, for instance when he most needs this, demands a high degree of professionalism.

4. Not only will active enquiry, making, and dialogue be the foundation of the curriculum, but the areas of investigation agreed on will have to have a certain amplitude of scale, especially as students grow into mid-adolescence. There is a place for precision in any work, but minutiae have to be justified by being essential to some larger system. Hence much of the skill of the teacher will lie in guiding the young to tasks which serve their purpose but at an appropriate level of competence.

It is to meet these kinds of requirements that I have formulated the proposal of a Fourfold Curriculum.

The elements in the Fourfold Curriculum, which are of course to be seen as four cells of activity, not four quarters, are these:
1. Interdisciplinary Studies: IDE (Interdisciplinary Enquiry) and IDM (Interdisciplinary Making)
2. Autonomous Studies (intra-disciplinary studies)
3. Remedial Education or "Clinic" (education related to special needs)
4. Special-interest Studies or "Orbital Studies"

1. INTERDISCIPLINARY STUDIES

In introducing IDE in 1965 I wrote:

> We stand for a policy unique in English education. The essence of our work is the belief that if people are to live well in a creative, flexible society the human gift of enquiry and exploration must be fostered throughout school and later life, and that it is the special

feature of a democratic society that all its aspects are open to investigation by all its members. Our first pillar is therefore ENQUIRY, enquiry which is active in process and often leads to action. Secondly we believe that once one starts to enquire into and attempt to solve fundamental problems, the barriers between subjects, which seem formidable when they are dividing up a fixed body of knowledge, seem less relevant, and the work necessarily becomes INTERDISCIPLINARY: we have to use a variety of disciplines in formulating the problem, creating hypotheses as to its solution, working on and communicating our findings. It is no accident that in the knowledge explosion it is in the areas between subjects that the great advances are being made, and it does no service to learners at any level to suggest that subject boundaries are important when they cease to be convenient. On the other hand it does them no service either to suggest that the great disciplines which the human mind has created are trivial; on the contrary, as pupils move out of childhood and are co-opted into the adult world they need the chance to become aware of some of the key concepts, the great general ideas that have emerged in these disciplines and to understand, by using them, the theoretical structures which embody these ideas. Our concern can therefore be identified as being with INTERDISCIPLINARY ENQUIRY IN THE SECONDARY SCHOOL, which we shorten into IDE.[1]

I would now add the concept of INTERDISCIPLINARY MAKING, and I am hesitant of using the phrase 'interdisciplinary studies' lest these shall be supposed to be integrated teacher-directed studies, where teachers plan an integrated course by combining subject-matter. It is safer therefore to refer to this section as IDE/M. In IDE/M, clusters of children with "the provocative assistance of focus-groups of teachers"[2] that is to say interdisciplinary groups of teachers, concern themselves with important areas of investigation or undertake creative enterprises of a scale which call on a number of disciplines.

2. AUTONOMOUS STUDIES

Edwin Mason has outlined the other cells of the curriculum so succinctly that I welcome the opportunity to quote him:

[1] C. M. James in Second Report, p. 2
[2] A. E. Mason, Fifth Report, p. 32

ORGANIZATION OF THE CURRICULUM

Autonomous Studies, in subjects which demand linear treatment, which are not "coming through" in interdisciplinary enquiry, and which are nevertheless deemed necessary at the time. All subjects are likely to be appropriate for autonomous study at some time: the case is not that some subjects are appropriate for IDE and others not. It is rather that in all areas attention to the discipline of a subject will be called for some time, and in some subjects this kind of attention may need to be regular and persistent, so that it will need to be timetabled. Autonomous studies need not be conducted in classes and should be heuristically and creatively taught, within the framework of the discipline. Here again clustering is individual or paired work on programmes (anything from job-cards to "structured programmed learning"[1] with sophisticated machinery). Expressive arts need also at times to be autonomous, enjoyed for their own sake and not bent to the ends of a given enquiry.

Autonomous studies in this sense are of course not to be confused with the independent study by individuals, which can take place at any time.

The composition of this group of autonomous studies will vary a good deal from one school to another, since it would be against the ethos of the collaborative school to demand interdisciplinary teaching of a teacher who did not approve of it. Thus already in some schools mathematics is at the heart of IDE (although not confined to it), whereas at others the mathematicians prefer to do all their work independently, and this is accepted. As a rule teachers emerge who do not at first wish to engage in the experiments of the first focus-groups but who rapidly recognize the increased involvement, the developing powers of observation, and other valuable characteristics of pupils undertaking IDE/M, which carry over to their autonomous studies; and these teachers are ready then to work in interdisciplinary studies. On the other hand schools working in IDE/M are still in the earliest stages, and we may well come to a time, therefore, when new and more theoretical bases can be evolved for distinguishing autonomous from

---

[1] For an outline of "Structural Programming" as devised by the centre for Structural Communication, see Anthony Hodgson, "A Communication Technique for the Future," *IDEAS*, No. 7

interdisciplinary studies, and achieve a greatly increased flexibility as children pass from one to the other. In the end autonomous studies may melt into the Remedial and Special Interests sections, in so far as they cannot be accommodated in IDE/M. For the moment their autonomy is vital.

It is important, too, to recognize that there is a danger that IDE/M, if it were diminished into an element in the administrative routine of a mechanical school, would soon be used to steam roller individuality, and would thereby immediately lose its collaborative, creative, exploratory character.

3. REMEDIAL EDUCATION

"It is never too late" should be the rallying cry of the collaborative school, and the remedial section or *clinic* is the organizational expression of this faith.

> Every adolescent needs to receive expert specific remedial help with any learning or skill technique which is holding him back from achieving an immediate, subjectively-important learning-objective. (This does apply to all: it matters as much to the "bright" thirteen-year-old inventor of a hovercraft as it does to the "dull" fifteen-year-old who cannot read his instruction-manual for servicing an engine, and we assert that "remedial education" must be thought of in the same way for all students); . . . .
>
> Hence the remedial element is designed specifically to give rapid and massive support where specific weaknesses are identified as blocking progress either in IDE or in autonomous studies. This again may be offered in groups of any size; but it is here that the most expert possible diagnosis of individual constellations of difficulties is needed, and quite individual support is most likely to be profitable. The setting of children in "rag-bag groups" of the "generally weak" is damaging to them and defeats its own ends; so it is here that the development of a greatly varied store of individual remedial programmes is an urgent task for schools to undertake, as well as for research-institutes and publishers.[1]

---

[1] A. E. Mason, Fifth Report, pp. 32-3. For proposals for the free use of this "clinic" in the later years of schooling see C. M. James, "The Raising of the School Leaving Age and the Fourfold Curriculum," *IDEAS*, No. 4, 1967

Some "remedial work" is best done by using members of staff as peripatetic teachers, some by students going to teachers in their specialist accommodation, but much of it will best be accomplished by a school having an extremely well-indexed supply of programmes, concept loops, and so on, which should be seen as appropriate for meeting the needs of small groups and of individuals rather than as a medium for mass instruction.

4. SPECIAL-INTEREST STUDIES

The fourth cell is devoted to:

> *Special-interest Studies*: time in which the young can follow as deeply as they wish strong personal interests, individually or in any kind of group which helps them . . . . This should not be organized as a forced-choice from a variety of possible interests envisaged by the staff, but entirely open. Many special interests may prove ephemeral, but they have none the less value for that.

In proposing this Special-interest cell I was introducing into the Fourfold Curriculum an element which had been an integral part of the work of another colleague, Leslie Smith, as headmaster of an East London school —his concept of "orbit":

> Examples of orbital arrangements include remedial language, remedial mathematics, advanced engineering, extra lathe practice, office practice, certain aspects of commercial studies, advanced art, stagecraft for purposes of school productions, life-saving and advanced swimming, various aspects of athletic training and games coaching, various outdoor pursuits like canoeing, construction work on school projects, individual and group project work of all kinds, field work, motor vehicle maintenance, advanced joinery, television and radio maintenance, community services and dozens more besides . . . .
> The organization of the orbital scheme is complicated, but possible. Teachers are placed outside the normal time-tabled programme— in orbit —with powers to extract children from their normal lessons provided the pupils concerned are likely to benefit from such orbital activity. Sometimes, it is possible to place a teacher in orbit on two or

three sessions each week—a lot depends on staffing ratios—so that a number of children can follow a course for, say, six weeks or a term.[1]

The Fourfold Curriculum provides a diverse environment in which very different children can find what they need. It is in my view the direction in which comprehensive schools must move if they are to provide comprehensive education for diverse children without divisiveness.[2]

A NOTE ON THE STATUS OF INTERDISCIPLINARY STUDIES

The concept of interdisciplinary studies requires further elaboration partly because it is often misunderstood, partly because to suggest that these studies are a fundamental part of any curriculum which attempts to meet the requirements of young people on a scale worthy of their acceptance involves English curriculum in a controversy that has been powerfully argued in the United States.

The readiness with which many teachers all over the United Kingdom have studied our curriculum proposals and the growth of IDE/M to which this readiness has led has been, to me, remarkable and unexpected. The concept has been examined quite naturally, in the way in which people always try to sort out new information, by seeking to assess the new idea in relation to what is already familiar, identifying in what respects it is different and in what respects similar. Some people have of course played the game people always do when their real purpose is to deny to themselves the possibility of accepting a new idea: they oscillate between saying it is too novel to be practicable and that it is so familiar as to be old-fashioned. It is sometimes necessary to say, "I can listen if you say it is outlandishly new and I can listen if you say it has been tried

---

[1] L. A. Smith, "Non-streaming in a Secondary School," *The Essex Teacher*, No. 36 (November, 1964), p. 27
[2] For proposals as to use of these cells, and in particular the grouping of children within them see below pp. 148ff. For suggestions as to time-tabling, see L. A. Smith, Supplement No. 1, to IDEAS.

and found wanting, but if you say both no dialogue is possible."

Since the comparison that is usually made is with the work in social studies of the late '40s and '50s it is worth having a look at that movement (which deserves a research study).[1] This was a movement towards integrated social studies that grew up in secondary modern (non-selective) schools after the concept of secondary education for all had been established by the 1944 Act. It was a serious effort by teachers to help young school leavers (who were not engaged in an academic education leading to public examinations) to find their way about the world they live in. It was not at all dissimilar from the Schools Council's recent proposals[2] for a modest integration of geography, history, English, and religious instruction, as a basic element in the last two years of education of pupils who, with the raising of the school leaving age in 1972, will be staying on at school until they are sixteen. There is no doubt that there was some excellent teaching of integrated subject matter at this time. Yet within ten or fifteen years the movement had fallen into disregard, if not disrepute. It is worth looking at some possible reasons. This will show that the work was as a rule very different from IDE/M; and analysing the differences should help to clarify what IDE/M really is, and how it may survive—altering and developing, of course, but not sinking almost without trace as the social studies movement can be said to have done.

THE SOCIAL STUDIES MOVEMENT AFTER 1944

The first reason for its failure was extrinsic to it, though central to the nature of much English educational thinking. It may be described as the murder of a beautiful hypothesis by an ugly fact, the fact of examinations. When the movement was at its height the schools which offered it were not permitted to present their pupils for public examinations (on the grounds originally that this would distort the pupils' school-

[1] cf. also Denis Lawton, "*Social Studies and the Social Sciences,*" *IDEAS*, No. 4
[2] Working Paper No. 2 (H.M.S.O., 1965)

ing). Social Studies was, therefore, something special for the non-examination pupil. When the rules were changed and examinations permitted in these schools much of the impetus was lost. It is perhaps unfair to blame teachers for too readily abandoning the study of society and joining the new trend to examinations; for these were essential hurdles in the meritocratic stakes, and it would have been wrong to deny children their opportunity. Nevertheless the fate of the movement is a reminder that the country needs units such as the Goldsmiths' Curriculum Laboratory which can explore with Examination Boards ways in which it may be possible to limit the damage done by certification at 16, and work done in this respect in consort with a progressive examination board is tactically of vital importance (see page 24n.).

A far more fundamental lesson in this, however, is that so long as two assumptions survive there is a continuing danger of important educational developments being abortive (for with IDE, too, the future is uncertain). The first assumption is that we are educating two kinds of children, the academic and the non-academic. This bedevils all our educational planning. It was officially sponsored in the Norwood Report of 1943[1] as justification for selective schools. Despite having been flayed by Sir Cyril Burt[2], it emerges relatively unscathed in the Crowther Report[3]. And it dominates the Newsom Report, which accepted a remit to discuss the education of children of "average and less than average ability" in isolation from that of seemingly superior children; any Committee prepared to submerge into waters darkened by that squid was bound to

---

[1] *Curriculum and Examinations in Secondary Schools*, Report of the Norwood Committee (H.M.S.O., 1943)
[2] In "Symposium on the Selection of Pupils for Different Types of Secondary Schools," *Brit. Jour. of Ed. Psych.* (June, 1947), et seq.
[3] For instance, while eschewing the "false idea" that the less competent performer is especially good at crafts, the Report proposes "Crafts as the backbone of his education," basing this on "the fact that it is through making things and through doing things, that this interest is best aroused and his capacity to reason trained" (para 228), stating without evidence that this is true of all poor performers and implying that it is not true of good performers. It is true that in another part of this admirable compendium of viewpoints a rather different line is taken (569-71)

blind itself and us to the urgent needs of *all* children in secondary schools. For this is the second assumption: that children who (owing to a natural interest in learning, perhaps accompanied by a talent which takes examination syllabuses in its stride, perhaps led on by ambition for future success towards which this is the first hurdle, sometimes bearing witness to a marked docility in the face of parents or teachers) are prepared to stomach a traditional secondary education have no need of anything better.

Perhaps the most important breakthrough of the Pilot Courses, from whom I have so often quoted, was the immediate recognition that these assumptions are false:

> To anyone reading our report it may seem surprising that we have not limited ourselves to those referred to as the "Newsom children," the pupils of "average and less than average ability" between 13 and 16 whose prospects were to be our first concern. We found such narrow reference insufficient: the common concern we discovered among ourselves . . . was dissatisfaction at the present situation in which we felt that not only the "least able" but *all* children are in some sense hurt by the limited personal educational opportunity offered to them at all stages of secondary education.[1]

One of the most paradoxical of our conventions in secondary education is that the study of society, often described as "social education," is not required by those whom a divisive society through a divisive education destines to be leaders; it is required only by those doomed to be led. Thus the first lesson of the death of the social studies movement is that until that point of view is changed other liberalizing movements will fail also.

The other causes of its failure were intrinsic weaknesses although of course it would not be fair to suggest that all teaching was ineffectual.

The first intrinsic weakness, as seen by one who as a headmistress was intimately concerned with the movement, was that teachers had not adequately analysed their purposes or

[1] J. Clark in Second Report, p.62

clarified the contribution that they, as teachers, should make:

> For example, the survey is probably one of the most useful techniques for interdisciplinary study and was used extensively in the forties and early fifties. It ceased to be employed because teachers were mainly concerned to collect and classify information, but were unable to, or did not realise the need to, evaluate and interpret the findings of a survey. The work thus remained at the descriptive level and did not lead to the formation of concepts. There was, therefore, little transfer and the children's learning tended to be unrelated and patchy. Since no concepts were formed no frame of reference was built; neither teachers nor children felt a sense of progress or mastery. I believe teachers confuse "facts" and concepts and mistake the amassing of information for concept-building, which they assume just happens.[1]

If we conceive of enquiry as collaborative learning, this kind of confusion stems from the teacher's failure to contribute his share. We should not, of course, expect to know beforehand all the findings of a genuine enquiry, but we need pre-planning to foresee the range of skills which are offered to students (in this case the skill offered would be a more confident, refined and purposeful use of survey techniques) and the concepts which might emerge from it and summarize it, while fully recognizing the diverse uses to which different children will put a phase of work.

If the teacher does not make this contribution, the result can be a kind of scrabbling futility hard to describe but unmistakable in the classroom, perhaps similar to the conditions of the laissez-faire group in the classic Lippitt and White experiments. John Dewey's well known distinction between "having *an* experience" and undifferentiated experiencing is pertinent as a reminder of the pitfalls of unplanned and unreflective enquiry:

> .... we have *an* experience when the material experienced runs its course of fulfilment. Then and then only is it integrated within and demarcated in the general stream of experience from other experiences. A piece of work is finished in a way that is satisfactory; a prob-

[1] Miss J. A. M. Davis, University of London Institute of Education, in an informal letter to the Nuffield Foundation Feasibility Study in the Humanities (1965)

lem receives its solution; a game is played through; a situation, whether that of eating a meal, playing a game of chess, carrying on a conversation, writing a book, or taking part in a political campaign, is so rounded out that its close is a consummation and not a cessation. Such an experience is a whole and carries with it its own individualizing quality and self-sufficiency. It is *an* experience.[1]

Too few teachers in secondary education have the skill to ensure that each pupil has *an* experience. An education which fails in this respect does its own form of damage, inviting children to undertake serious ventures and yet allowing the ventures to have meagre outcomes which lead them to have meagre self-concepts and low expectations. It pretends to increase their coping powers, but does not help them to do so. If some pupils engage in this kind of ineffectual "social education" while a superior group is working in a neat and tidy "academic" way (which has status although it is intrinsically less demanding than enquiry) then they will never believe that they are being properly educated.

Dewey's comments remind us that the teacher's task becomes increasingly complex as pupils become ready to move from the more or less straight-forward collection and classification of facts in the relatively short-term enterprises appropriate to younger pupils to the more elaborate hypothetical schemes of IDE/M that are possible in adolescence. Yet Whitehead has indicated why this task of looking back on what has happened and identifying it is a fundamental requirement of all education: "From the very beginning of his education, the child should experience the joy of discovery. The discovery which he has to make, is that general ideas give an understanding of that stream of events which pours through his life, which is his life."[1]

The way through is to achieve a relationship of teacher to pupil less didactic than that implied by Dewey: as pupils themselves progress they can explain and summarize more and

---

[1] John Dewey, *Art as Experience* (Minton Balch and Co., New York, 1934, Capricorn Books, 1958), p. 35
[2] A. N. Whitehead, *Aims of Education* (Benn, 1929), p. 3

more fruitfully their own experiences (for the group experience is a complex of individual experiences, shared so far as possible through many kinds of communication). It is in this process that they come increasingly to see gaps in their enquiry and its outcomes and learn to propose additional spurs of growth. This is perhaps the most important outcome of all.

In effect the kind of study described by Miss Davis failed because the teacher did not recognize either his responsibility or the nature of intellectual disciplines. Unless there is a rhythm of openness to ideas with short-term closure, if the teacher makes the mistake of "staying locked in an open position,"[1] the learning is neither disciplinary nor collaborative, and the social context is one of insecurity without assurance of worthwhile success.

The third weakness of the social studies movement as it was generally understood is significant to those who believe in IDE/M, because IDE/M is precisely designed to enable young people to concern themselves with problems of fundamental importance which range beyond the limits of any one subject-discipline without their work being marred by this failing. This was the weakness of any scheme where the teachers are creative, the students are merely taught. It is the weakness built into any scheme which relies on the integration of subject-*matter*, rather than the collaboration of subject-*disciplines*.

"To put it simply," says a teacher working in this "integrated" way today, "I used to teach a subject. Now we teach a theme." In an integrated curriculum, large carefully planned syllabuses are created, covering "fields of study." This is an attempt to overcome the manifest weaknesses of totally separate subject-teaching. Very often, an integrated syllabus is taught by class-teaching methods, and in its most primitive form teachers retain even the conventional 40 minutes whistle-stop time-table, merely agreeing that the material of one lesson shall dovetail with another given by another teacher later in

[1] James Macdonald and Esther Zarat, *Study of Openness in Classroom Interactions*, (mimeographed paper, University of Milwaukee-Winconsin, 1966)

the day or week. In a more sophisticated form the integrated curriculum is one way in which team-teaching is employed (above, pp. 57-9). If this technical advance makes teachers with different subject specialisms meet each other and work together with greater understanding the gain is important. It will be damaging, however, if they fail to notice that the enthusiasm and inventiveness comes from them. For this is no more than workmanlike joinery, fashioning a neat coop which pupils can least realize that they are in, as opposed to gazing at an incoherent world through different peep-holes, as they usually are required to do. The teachers have been exploratory and creative, not the students.

Listening to integrated lessons is no substitute for roughage in a curriculum, as the listlessness of pupils in some social studies courses indicated. We may expect a similar disenchantment among their sons and daughters today if teachers fail to realize that the Schools Council's proposals for the Humanities programme for the Raising of the School Leaving Age exhibit identical failings.[1] One of the difficulties in gauging the pros and cons of "projects" (and even of "centres of interest" which are sounder theoretically, as their name implies) is that they can range from complete manipulation of an authoritarian kind, as is the case with the four "Areas of Enquiry" in the projects proposed by the Schools Council document, to something very similar to IDE/M. This is where the key to curriculum planning must be seen to be the quality of the engagement with the environment not the subject content, nor a teaching technique.

As with all the names we have evolved,[2] the name Interdisciplinary Enquiry and Making is no gimmick, but indicates as clearly as possible the precise nature of what we seek to promote. IDE and IDE/M are interdisciplinary processes which require the active use of a number of different disciplines. Disciplines are complex tools for exploring and changing the

---

[1] Schools Council Working Paper No. 11, *Society and the Young School Leaver* (H.M.S.O., 1967((see p. 64)

[2] e.g. "focus groups", "clusters", "collaborative School"

environment. They are not areas of study and they are not "bodies of knowledge," although each discipline is limited to its chosen area and each acquires in the process of its engagement with the environment a body of knowledge which is constantly changing as the discipline explores more deeply.

THE UNITED STATES: THE SPIRAL CURRICULUM

We now come to the second reason for examining Interdisciplinary Studies more closely. The rise and fall of the social studies movement of the '40s and '50s traces in miniature and belatedly the grand battle that has dominated the American educational scene for two-thirds of a century. Professor Alice Miel's summary in her account of the spiral development of the curriculum reminds us how thoughtful and enterprising American concern with the curriculum has been:

> For the greater part of our educational history the separate subject has been the only known way to organise the curriculum. It was not until the end of the last century that there was any real attempt to grope toward other patterns or organization. The first proposal was to correlate subjects similar in content, while maintaining the boundaries around each subject. After 1915 came the suggestion to break down barriers between allied subjects and to create broad fields such as social studies; general mathematics and general science. By the 1930s the unit of work cutting across subject boundaries was being highly recommended . . . . During the period when curriculum integration was the keynote of the day, the separate, logically organized subject was in ill repute. Teachers were urged to draw on the various subjects for material "to solve the problem of the unit."[1]

Two of the difficulties experienced were similar to the two internal weaknesses I have imputed to the social studies movement, together with a lack of suitable supportive material for teachers that was also familiar to English teachers: "First, knowledge was not organized in such a way that it was easy to draw upon it for problem solving. Second, skills of helping

---

[1] Alice Miel, "Reassessment of the Curriculum—Why?" in D. Huebner, ed., *A Reassessment of the Curriculum* (New York, Teachers' College, Columbia University, 1964)

young people to build order and system out of scattered knowledge were not well developed."

And Dr. Miel goes on: "One of the most important gains from this period was the insight that the individual can deal with many separate experiences and put them together into meaningful and orderly wholes *if he has the right kind of help*. Educators could return to consideration of the separate subject without feeling extreme guilt."[1]

These last two sentences are suggestive of the difference between our experience and that of an educational system where the total curriculum is a matter of serious concern. Educators in this country have barely questioned the separate subject, far less felt guilty about it; and how many staffs in how many schools have set themselves to think what kinds of help students need in order to put their experiences into meaningful and orderly wholes at the end of a day, or a week, or a year? Analysis, not synthesis, preoccupies us (cf. p. 102).

IDE/M AN ADVANCE, NOT A THROWBACK

Dr. Miel goes on to say that at present American educationists are "as it were on the 'separateness' side of the spiral once more" but that "the concerns are not the same as at the lower level," "when the separate subject was in favour." It is here that our work is a contribution to this dialogue, for Interdisciplinary Enquiry and Interdisciplinary Making are an advance, not a throwback to old ways that have been rightly abandoned. We may even be laying the foundations for the "new stage, as yet unnamed" to which she looks forward "which will represent new attempts in a curriculum synthesis."[2]

There are two important aspects of our proposals towards this next stage. The first is the necessary recognition of the disciplines as tools with their own systematic character. The second is more fundamental. It is our acknowledgement of the

---
[1] ibid.; my italics
[2] ibid.

tentative, creative, exploratory, and interdependent nature of human knowledge. This enables us to see that our task as teachers is not to induct young people into known certainties but to invite them to collaborate with us into explorations of the unknown. We are concerned together to create the future, not merely to reproduce the past. The acknowledgement of uncertainty must be implicit in all our engagements; it will be expressed in the attitudes of all teachers and does not present technical paedagogic problems. It is therefore around the status of the disciplines that argument properly centres at this stage.

The movement towards integration of subject matter could properly be described as anti-intellectual, as an intellectual mish-mash, and my purpose in introducing the concept of IDE was to dissociate it from such stereotypes and to acknowledge the systematic nature of the disciplines.

The school is the institution charged by society with assisting the cognitive growth of the young, and this occurs in advanced societies through an increasing ability to recognize and use abstract concepts. But these are not part of the natural scenery, they are lenses through which human beings have learned that it is helpful to view the environment. A discipline is a system which makes certain assumptions as to the nature of the area with which it is concerned, the sources of verification it will accept, and the degrees of probability it requires before giving tentative acceptance to an hypothesis. Its hypotheses are expressed in and summarized by concepts, and it is these to which children should have access, not as given truths but as useful ways of interpreting and explaining experience. There is undoubtedly a place in the school for learning to use disciplines in a way which stresses their autonomy: it is a convenient simplification, a deliberate narrowing of focus which can help students to become accomplished in manipulating its concepts and its intrinsic techniques of communication. This is the function of Autonomous Studies.

Even within Autonomous Studies there is need to recognize

two points, often ignored, one related to children's learning, the other to the disciplines.

First, we have to remind ourselves that children arrive at concepts through individual processes, and learning situations must include a whole variety of occasions and opportunities which are denied to children by a rigorously linear course of instruction. The young need us to think far more in terms of "shuffling the pack" rather than dealing it out in the way teacher finds most satisfying.

Secondly, we need to think a good deal more deeply than before about what is meant by the fashionable term "the structure of a discipline." It might be said that this is one of the grounds on which the long-drawn-out battle between what Whitehead called Speculation and Scholarship[1] is now being waged. For people appear to envisage structures according to their own personality structures. To some, the structure of a discipline is comparable to sub-atomic structure or molecular structure; it is a complex of hypotheses which do not require a hard edge to hold them together since they are mutually relative and mutually supportive. On this view, which is the one to which I am drawn, the "system" of a discipline would be a less damaging term than "structure." For the term structure is ambiguous. By others, the notion of the structure of a discipline is spoken of as if it were a brick-by-brick construction, which must be built up in a certain necessary order; there easily follows, by a familiar false analogy, the argument that if one brick is missed out the whole edifice will be endangered.

As ever, the scholars (in Whitehead's sense) are at it again, making the scholarly sound respectable, the speculative a little shady. Because of a mental set towards the pre-ordained (which incidentally has helped them to function effectively within a traditional system and so to become persons of considerable influence) they use the concept of structure to

---

[1] A. N. Whitehead, *Adventures of Ideas* (Cambridge University Press, 1933) Ch. 7. The need is of course for an alliance between these two tendencies, each of which is, in isolation from the other, "useless." "The proper balance of the two factors in progressive learning depends on the character of the epoch in question and on the capacities of particular individuals." (p. 138)

persuade us to see the teaching of a subject as an unalterable process of initiation into an unassailable bureaucracy of knowledge.

Dr. Bruner, to whom we owe the salience of the notion of structure today and the insights which it can give, has presented it in forms which have made this ambiguity possible. However, in his latest reference to structure he is unequivocally concerned with so structuring knowledge "that it can be most readily grasped by the learner"[1] and has said: " ... since the merit of a structure depends upon its power for *simplifying information*, for *generating new propositions*, and for *increasing the manipulability of a body of knowledge*, structure must always be related to the status and gifts of the learner. Viewed in this way, the optimal structure of a body of knowledge is not absolute but relative."[2]

When structure is seen as relative, consideration for learners is once more admitted into planning of the curriculum and we move into a different universe of values. It then becomes possible to see that methodological problems are subsidiary questions and that our answers must accommodate in the first place the differing needs of persons and only secondarily the differing characteristics of the systems human beings have created. We then discover that much of the talk of an essential order of development in the teaching of a subject-discipline refers not to any internal requirements but to what has been assumed to be the most effective way of teaching an imaginary modal child. Much traditional ordering of syllabuses, as the recent revolution in language teaching demonstrates, has been found to be inefficacious, even modally.

We can come back now to look at the proposals for Interdisciplinary Studies as an element essential to satisfactory emotional and also cognitive growth:

1. A discipline deliberately narrows its field of vision. This

[1] J. S. Bruner, *Toward a Theory of Instruction* (Harvard Univ. Press, 1966), p. 41
[2] ibid.

ORGANIZATION OF THE CURRICULUM

is legitimate and necessary to our advances at the frontiers of knowledge. But to limit schooling to intra-disciplinary studies is to deny to students the hope of obtaining a synoptic view of the world. It would be possible to conceive a schooling in which all the earlier years were spent in autonomous studies and the inter-disciplinary studies were purely retrospective, helping the sixth-former perhaps to make sense of what he had been doing over ten or twelve years. But this is to admit the importance of systematic thinking but to deny the experience of it; after that length of time students accustomed to disjecta membra may very well have lost the wish to reconstruct the bodies.

2. Although the highest advances have required this narrowing of focus, our everyday living is inter-disciplinary, and nearly all the kinds of questions which match with the fundamental concerns of youngsters require more than one discipline for their answers. It is familiar to all good teachers that questions raised by pupils even in a class-lesson range far beyond the competence of an individual teacher or the scope of his autonomous sphere, and the more heuristic the techniques the more frequently (and properly) this occurs:

> "Enquiry" as a motivating force is essential in the building up of a discipline, since, without the stimulus of the interrogative, relationships cannot properly be assimilated . . . an enthusiastic teacher can often induce the desire of his pupils to know, and then lure them to the brink of understanding for themselves. But in life what people "want to know" rarely falls into the neat "subject" divisions purveyed in schools.[1]

There is small wonder that this is so since, as the same writer affirmed, disciplines "should be seen as multi-dimensional interpenetrating patterns and not as compartments of knowledge with poorly demarcated boundaries." We spend much of our time inducting students into demarcation disputes rather than inviting them to "build up characteristic

[1] N. Spearing in Second Report, p. 10
Y.L.S.

modes of thought or trains of relationships."[1] In fact, it is only honest to admit that far too much of our conventional teaching is not an education in disciplines at all, but is itself a mish-mash of unexamined tradition, demanding little more than memory-recall.

3. The most fundamental reason in my view for introducing inter-disciplinary enquiry is that it helps the young to live in a world which has some coherence for them because they have had opportunities to investigate important areas of human concern; for this they must draw on different disciplines in formulating their questions and proposing and testing and communicating possible answers. But in terms of responsibility for assisting their intellectual development and their introduction to the disciplines there is another point to be made: it is partly because of the importance of grasping the nature of the major disciplines that I suggest that they should be studied in concert. One of the most important ways in which we learn to identify the nature of any tool is to use it; and perhaps the most important way to learn to distinguish a tool, an object, a way of thought or anything else in the environment is to compare and contrast it with others. If pupils spend a good deal of their time in school learning with teachers who can say, "Well, as a historian I see the problem in this way," or "as a biologist," and so on, or with mathematicians who can use quantified language to clarify and communicate complex material, they will be coming into relationship with disciplines by experience of their comparative use. They will be learning not only what is different in the disciplines, notably the degree of probability that they demand and their bank of concepts, but also the broad general characteristics of all adventurous learning, its necessary tentativeness, the importance of identifying gaps which invite new enquiries. They should also be achieving a most important quality of thinking for modern life, a cognitive flexibility which will enable them to "see round" a problem because they have

[1] ibid.

learned to see problems in the round. They will have an armoury of possible symbolic systems both for formulating their problems and for communicating their findings. Furthermore, their powers of systemic thinking should grow through such complex holistic studies. Finally, and quite simply, (although it is true that this might be managed in an intra-disciplinary education albeit to a lesser extent) they will be constantly required to have a "deep-end philosophy," that is, to use the highest mental processes of which they are capable.[1] Memory recall will just not do for this kind of work.

4. Thus in inter-disciplinary investigations students should learn to think effectively about important problems, and they and their teachers will in the latter years of secondary school increasingly come to see, from the nature of their own work, that the "subjects" we now recognize are not a final list, but require newly emerging disciplines to amplify our knowledge.

This is perhaps particularly important for the growth of teachers (and thereby of students though less directly). Too many see the entry into the school of newer disciplines, however well extablished outside school, as a threat. Many historians, for instance, fight a rearguard action against the sociologist, biologists do not welcome the new importance ascribed to ethology, and so on. Such teachers therefore introduce a divisive element into education which may well affect the outlook of the advanced student who faces quite new developments in later life. It is after all no matter for shame for a teacher to be associated with one discipline only. To deny access to others because they had no place in the fixed body of knowledge of one's youth is to show that too many teachers have been conditioned to see themselves as prisoners of their early qualifications, not as people themselves growing and learning.

---

[1] cf. Z. P. Dienes and M. A. Jeeves, *Thinking in Structures* (Hutchinson, 1965)

CURRICULUM 11-18

The proposal that Inter-disciplinary studies should form a substantial element in secondary education is a hypothesis to be tested by action research. Its theoretical structure is sound, because it recognizes the nature of children, of learning, of the culture, and of *living*. There may prove to be difficulties in practice which will make it untenable. We have not met them. On the contrary, teachers who have initiated IDE/M are confident that despite their own difficulties and weaknesses their students are learning more, are more observant, more perceptive, more articulate, organize their ideas better. For the moment we are right to accept the subjective impression of experienced professionals, although looking to research in due course to confirm or deny its correctness. In the absence of new evidence that calls into question its theoretical structure we should concentrate at national and international level a great deal of research on seeing how the Fourfold Curriculum might operate most effectively.

There is a multitude of tasks to be done. If we really want young people to have the tools to understand themselves and their environment, and the heart to enjoy them, we are calling for a revolutionary reappraisal of practically all that goes on in school. The kinds of ventures which have been thought adequate in recent years are by this standard simply patching: thus admirable as the Nuffield proposals for improving science teaching in secondary schools may be, all but one[1] assumed in the first instance the propriety of having separate science teaching of the three familiar sciences; they assumed that the basis of their work should be preparation for external examination at 16 and 18; they assumed that there should be a marked divergence at secondary stage between the science studied by those likely to leave school at the statutory age

---

[1] The exception is the project for Science for the Young School Leaver (see Schools Council Working Paper No. 1). This is holistic but its terms of reference are limited to the non-G.C.E. candidate, a divisive concept. It is true that, subsequently, a "mixed" Chemistry, Physics, and Biology programme for the first two years of a five year O-Level course has been vouchsafed, and a new look at Science, 9-13.

and the examination pupils; and the idea of collaboration between the natural sciences and any other disciplines (again except perhaps for the Young School Leaver) does not even appear on the horizon. The proposals for both the science and the humanities programme for the statutory leaver (and the latter leaves much to be desired) assumed that this is some special education for special children, so that no study has been undertaken of political socialization of all children, nor of the study of society as it might be undertaken by all students throughout secondary school. National thinking has been so traditional and restricted that no study save our own has been undertaken of the education appropriate to the eleven to thirteen-year-olds.

It certainly cannot be assumed that a simple extension of primary educational techniques and attitudes will solve their problems: indeed in the light of the fourfold curriculum the primary curriculum itself needs a re-examination far more profound than the perfunctory acknowledgement it received in the otherwise useful Plowden Report. For although the organization into four cells is no more than the separation necessary for more advanced studies of kinds of activity that may take place in one classroom in the junior school, the notion of collaborative learning and of inter-disciplinary studies based on enquiry, making, and dialogue calls into question much that goes on even in a "progressive" primary school. My own experience of seeing teachers with primary experience working with these older children is that they are more manipulative than we would hope, and also that they are not aware of the support that students need at this age in developing formal operational thinking. Primary and secondary teachers should advance together now in a shared investigation of the learning of those pupils most neglected today by our education system, the students of ten to fourteen or so. It is there possibly that the most concentrated damage is done.

The kinds of tasks which will have to be undertaken include studies of ways in which the social sciences and the natural sciences may best come together in inter-disciplinary studies and may best be learned autonomously; this is perhaps the most urgent need. For although for a time we may accept the teacher's personality as being the best basis a school can have for determining what disciplines are studied in isolation at what stages of the students' development, it would be helpful if the teacher had information as well as hunch to go on in making his decision. But they will include also studies of the bases on which to offer a learning programme: is it, for instance, helpful to children to go behind the idea of the area of investigation and to concentrate on the idea of a grammar of thinking, using for instance such concepts as identity and difference (and therefore classification cf. pp. 152, 169) as the *material* for exploration and not just part of its outcome; and if so to what proportion of what children at what ages? Again, granted that dialogue and self-discovery are part of the school's way of life, how can the curriculum itself (as against the actual social context of of collaborative learning) best support their development? What kinds of learning can the behavioural sciences best contribute—what is the place of social psychology, for instance, and are concepts such as those of aggression or role seen by adolescents to be relevant; and if they are, what good ideas can we produce to help teachers and students to work on these and other fundamental tools of analysis?

We have so much more to learn about a curriculum of this kind that anything I can say about practical proposals for planning is offered in an entirely tentative way. Some of the suggestions that follow I made two years ago in consultation with teachers,[1] and these have been used as a basis for classroom experiment since then, but these also are given only as examples, and I would hope that many schools would improve on them. For it goes without saying that it is for teachers, knowing their own personal and communal resources, to come to their own best proposals in considering their own situation.

It would be sensible for any school serving children of 11-18

[1] In Second Report, pp. 12-21,

to have in mind a rough picture of the school as consisting of three main stages, the last sub-divided:

A. The Preparatory Stage, roughly the first two years, 11-13
B. The Transitional Stage, the third year, 13-14
C. The Mid-adolescent Phase, (i) fourth and fifth years, 14-16
                          (ii) sixth forms, 16-18[1]

These should not be seen as cast-iron divisions, of course, for not only do youngsters of all ages meet in *clinic* and in *orbit*, but regular collaborative ventures within IDE/M, as well as occasional explosions of learning and making which involve a whole school or schools, are a feature of the collaborative school.[2]

A. THE PREPARATORY STAGE

At this stage, in the process of acclimatization to a different school, the need for security and recognition is paramount. The cultural shock of moving from a school where most (perhaps too much) of the day has been spent under the wing of a single teacher to the divided school-day of the secondary school must be averted, and for this reason, if for no other, it is a good idea for some 50 per cent. of the time-table to be spent in the stable though not static atmosphere of IDE/M. This makes it possible for an inter-disciplinary focus-group of teachers to have something of the same close knowledge of pupils that their single class-teacher had in their junior school and yet to provide the stimulus of specialist experience and differing temperaments that most young people of this age can be expected to cope with and enjoy; in fact, some are already well and truly disenchanted with the single teacher before they leave their junior school.

---

[1] These were stages proposed by our fifth group of experienced teachers; cf. Fifth Report, pp. 43-55, in which the needs of students at these different stages of growth are examined in greater detail.
[2] cf. John Jones, "Idea in Action," *IDEAS*, No. 3; Jessica James, "Underneath the Lake: a Venture," *IDEAS*, No. 5

In thinking of the kinds of enquiries which might be engaged in at this stage it is important to recognize and establish what is valuable in their childhood perceptions of the world around them and ways of handling it. We have already seen (page 114) the loss of specificity of observations that occurs in urban children vis-à-vis members of more primitive cultures. At this stage, therefore, the possibility of immediate response to the "Use-me-ness" of tools, a spontaneous interest in objects in their own right, the wish to be able to describe them through various languages (the arts, words, figures) is to be encouraged; as is the interest in identification and classification which should be an expression of acute recognition of individual characteristics. Psychologically, many are still in the way of making collections, and this boosts the ego and helps observation at one stroke. This may well be a good stage, too, for helping children to recognize and chart processes of arguments visually through such techniques as flow diagrams and relatively elaborate visual models of their own making. If it turns out that a habit of using models purposefully can be established successfully by pupils of 11-13, it should be of great importance to them as they move on to relatively large-scale abstract enquiry.

In sum, the preparatory stage of secondary schooling, or the senior years of middle school, in L.E.A.s where that is the system on which schools are organized, is a time when we should hope to involve children deeply though not necessarily for long periods at a time in concrete operations which recognize their increasing ability to cope with complexity. At the same time it is essential to be preparing for two approaching developmental tendencies.

The first of these is that of undertaking increasingly abstract hypothetical thinking ("formal operations"). In the latter years of junior school some pupils are already showing bursts of this kind of thinking; it is not to be hurried, but clearly there should be many opportunities. For this purpose again, IDE/M is a good context since it will not invite children to get trapped in schemes of thought they will need to abandon,

ORGANIZATION OF THE CURRICULUM

whereas immediate movement into special-interest groups might demand of them greater continuity of application than they are ready for.

The second is often thought of as quite separate, since a study of the mutual support given by Piaget and Freud is still awaited. This is the growing ability to stand outside oneself and imagine what it might be like to be someone else. This stage of developing sensitivity, which should in due course emerge into the altruism of mid-adolescence and adult loving, can be observed and greeted by teachers, and can become a basis for dialogue through literature and drama; but it can also be looked to as a launching-pad for a study of ways of life, of exploration of man's achievements—we are nearing a stage where history can have some meaning for their understanding of changing processes of human living— or for studies of what it might be like to grow up in a quite different culture.

It is very much a time, too, for establishing personal identity by recalling earlier childhood, checking up by reference to others that one has reached this age satisfactorily, rather than matching self against unknown future possibilities. For the more mature girls, who reached puberty in primary school, this concern with the self of the future may be more important, and this adds another dimension to the same interest in the growth of young humans and other creatures. Contact with young children should not be limited to older students.

It was for reasons of this kind that I proposed in 1965, as two possible Areas of investigation worth considering for this age-group, "Man the Explorer" and "Growing up;" both ideas have been welcomed and used. At that time I suggested that first-year work should be "a large scale study but with short-term goals and exploration beyond the scope of the environmental study, which is likely to have been well worked in the junior school."[1] Today, despite the welcome and the use, I would have some reservations about my first proposal, although supporting the second as a reasonable suggestion for

[1] Second Report, pp. 16ff.

practical testing, as it deals with a fundamental concern in terms of a wide range of geographical, cultural, historical, and biological studies, and for some provides a rehearsal of the approaching changes in relationships at home and with peers.

I believe that futher experience may show that in planning secondary education, the notion of a major Area of Investigation which, though broken down into many different "phases," (see page 165) may occupy upwards of a year's study, is probably an important advance on the short-term centre of interest; for the centre of interest often results in studies which are related only by coincidence, not conceptually, and this may lead to all sorts of fascinating minutiae with no mutual relevance, and therefore no feedback from one cluster-group's work to another. Or a project based on a child's question may be made by the teacher to carry a greater load of learning than its passing interest for children merits. I suspect, however, that in proposing a large-scale study, even with short-term goals, I may have been trying to commend a scale of systemic thinking that was inappropriate for newcomers to secondary schools. Only free experiment in schools will show whether more sporadic forays are more appropriate.

At this age, also, we should perhaps look especially to symbols of archetypal importance rather than purely intellectual themes: Seonaid Robertson identified and described the concentrated interest archetypes such as water, caves or journeys can arouse;[1] and sometimes by chance, sometimes intuitively, sometimes in full understanding other teachers have discovered how powerful a unifying factor and stimulus to sustained discovery they can be.[2] Of their nature, these cannot be asked to fit into any large-scale thinking discursively planned, since they generate their own power to fascinate.

One tradition of the best primary schools that we should absorb into secondary school is to look less to events and more to the total environment as "starters" for this age-group. We may work hard to imagine what would be good stimuli

[1] In *Rosegarden and Labyrinth: A Study in Art Education* (Routledge and Kegan Paul, 1964)
[2] e.g. Jessica James, *IDEAS*, No. 5; E. J. Margerison, "An Island," *IDEAS* Nos. 8/9.

for students' learning and still miss something quite simple that children need. The concept of the stimulating and diversified environment is especially important for coeducational schools, at this stage, when we may expect a divergence of interests between girls and boys. (Wallach's study of the disadvantages of the creative girl at this stage is a reminder of the support she needs.[1]) Perhaps more important still is an acknowledgement of the need to be able to alter the environment, and this in itself might prove to be an important basis for studies in the early years at a new school.

B. THE TRANSITIONAL STAGE

Even to speak of stages is dangerous for it suggests norms of expectation and unvaried provision, and Edwin Mason's description of the kinds of problems the thirteen-year-old experiences would be relevant also, of course, to many a year or so later or sooner. But there is evidence that at this age it is especially important to be allowed to be irresponsible, to be provided, that is to say, with a firm context of learning but not to have moralistic demands made; and he indicates how this may be:

> At the same time, worries about the range of one's competences, about self-control, and about one's status vis-à-vis adults (at thirteen one does not claim to *be* adult as one may at sixteen) all provoke a moodiness and inconsistency of behaviour that make some regularity in the environment extremely desirable: one needs many fixed points of reference. Yet this regularity is very difficult to cope with. In this stage, the young can hardly be expected—or expect themselves—to show consistency of success in anything. Because both the need to experiment and the fear of failure are very acute, interests fluctuate greatly, and perseverance towards chosen objectives tends to be difficult. Daydreaming occupies much of the day, enthusiasms proliferate but may soon wane. One does not wish to be locked into one's choices; so we would not recommend that stress on choice which must certainly operate in the upper school. And yet the third-year

---

[1] Wallach and Kogan, *Modes of Thinking in Young Children*. See p. 31 above.

pupils must be prepared as well as they can for the choices that they will be making.[1]

We can expect a gradually increasing interest in special-interest or orbital work, as long as we do not spoil that with ideas of a moral obligation to have sustained interests. We can expect also that, owing to the greater individuation that is taking place, more "remedial" help in the *clinic* section will be needed, especially by those students who suddenly develop new interests and ambitions, as can happen at this stage, as they become more forward-looking and more aware of employment requirements or find they need to improve their competence in some subject that they have not done well in until now. It may be found by schools that some of the time given to IDE/M will be better spent in this remedial work, and there is a possibility that autonomous studies will increase in scope. Nevertheless I would hope that at least some 35 or 40 per cent of students' studies would continue to be the clustered collaborative work with students one has come to know and be known by pretty well, which IDE/M provides.

Too often the school tags along after the youngster's developing interests, if it acknowledges them at all. I suggest that as students move towards mid-adolescence, during which they will be coming to establish adult identity-patterns and matching themselves against adult roles, teachers should be helping them to lay the groundwork for this advance.

It is around this age that the growing ability to cope with "formal operations" begins to be more common and more sustained. Now surely (and possibly a year or so earlier) enough young people will be able to take advantage of large-scale studies to justify a full commitment to a major Area of Investigation. It was with these two suppositions in mind that I suggested that the third year in an 11-18 school is

> an admirable opportunity to formulate questions about the place that work and leisure will have in their future lives. We emphatically do not have in mind a course in job-hunting, but rather to involve

[1] A. E. Mason in Fifth Report

the growing interest in adult life and the more discriminating time-sense that we can expect at this stage in a study of the economic aspects of our society, in terms of economic and social history and of anticipated trends.... It should .... openly recognize that the third year pupil will shortly be a young adult and probably associates adult status with work status. But beyond this, we hope that if vocational interest is accepted and shared by the school at this stage it need not dominate the enquiries of the 4th and 5th years, when other less obvious aspects of adult status can be canvassed. Finally if an important part of our task is to encourage self-understanding leading to good decision-making, enquiry which leads many to match themselves in imagination against possible kinds of work can trigger off good self-appraisal. For others the process of making a decision about work may be less conscious: we are giving these an opportunity to gather evidence to use in their own way.[1]

Here at least is one strand of adult living that might be one strand (or if desired by students and teachers the ground-plan) of IDE/M for thirteen-year-olds. One significant advantage is that it is essentially outgoing, involving educational visits and invitations to local representatives of industry and commerce.

Another investigation which was undertaken with great success was far more general. This was a study of change in the environment described by a Bristol schoolteacher, Tom Lewis.[2] The two are not of course mutually exclusive, and it may well be that the very breadth of Mr Lewis's investigation made it more valuable than my narrower proposal. To begin to understand the processes of change demands something approaching an adult time-scale. At the age when young people are well aware of their own changing circumstances and of their physical changes this could be a study to which many could become committed.

---

[1] Second Report
[2] Tom Lewis, "Third Year Grown-Ups," *IDEAS*, No. 4, 1967

C. UPPER SCHOOL

It is usual in English schools to make very sharp divisions between sixth formers (17 and 18 year olds) and the rest of the students. This had its place in days when education was an induction into authoritative positions, and to be a prefect was to feel only a little lower than the headmaster. With the new freer organic structure of the school, the prefect system and the general grandeur of these older students are outmoded, and their own groping towards symbiosis, rather than the idea of doing things *to* people or *for* people which we understood by "responsibility," makes prefect duties less attractive even to the socially concerned sixth former than they were. Another factor which used to divide the sixth from the rest was that sixth formers had acquired certification at 16 (which was seen as an important staging post in maintained schools) and apart from the "general sixth" which was a feature of some girls' schools few stayed to the sixth form except those who were preparing for A-Level. But today many students stay on into a sixth form with no examination in mind, or just to pick up some extra qualifications at Ordinary level.

It now becomes possible to look at the young in terms of their human development rather than of their potential entry into a school's power system or their examination results. In terms of adolescent development, the ages 14-18, the years of mid-adolescence, are a vitally important unity.[1] In the social life of the school, in the Remedial and Special-interest sections we can expect far more sharing between the younger and older mid-adolescents than has been usual (though younger pupils would not be excluded). This is after all only realistic. The secular trend to earlier puberty means that the fourth and fifth formers are as physically mature as sixth formers were a generation or so ago.

Nevertheless we can expect that IDE/M will be largely undertaken in two groups, and I shall deal with them separately.

[1] For a study of the special needs of this age-group see Fourth Report.

(1) Fourth and Fifth Years (14-16)

The raising of the school leaving age will mean that for the first time we will be educating a whole cohort of pupils up to the age of 16, which we have (however foolishly) selected as the age for public examination. The assumption that non-examination and examination students must be educated separately in 4th and 5th years because many of the former would leave during or at the end of the 4th year becomes out of date, and we are able to envisage unstreamed work at this age, as among younger pupils. This will be possible if interdisciplinary Mode 3 types of examination can be introduced for all or part of a student's G.C.E. O-Level as is already happening in C.S.E. In that case during the 4th and 5th years there may be even an extension of interdisciplinary work, especially as it becomes evident that at this stage freer interdisciplinary work enables pupils to cover more ground in conventional terms as well as developing deeper interests. Then it will be possible to plan a broad general area of investigation for two years with a vertical grouping.[1] On the other hand if these proposals fail we must expect a great reduction in the time that examination pupils can spare for these fundamental studies.

In mid-adolescence we can expect to see a number of important trends—

* The development of a "hierarchy of interests, including the loves and loyalties of adult life," as described by Allport.[2]

* Increasing concern with adult social roles, including home as well as work.

* A more settled and determined sexuality: 16 is after all not only the age at which 'O' level is undertaken; it is also the age of maximum sexual potency for males and the age of consent.

---

[1] C. M. James, "The Raising of the School Leaving Age and the Fourfold Curriculum," *IDEAS*, No. 4, 1967
[2] *Becoming* p. 29

* An important mood of Utopianism which I see as perhaps a result of the confluence of trends recognized in depth psychology and by Piaget: altruism connected with the newly powerful sexuality and the ability to undertake major systems of hypothetical thinking. It is the age for thinking. What could life be like if we were all loving to one another?—a critical moment that we shamefully ignore as we drive the young on to competitive acquisition of status tokens.

These trends must be recognized in a person-centred school in the 4th and 5th years, and for all students. Since Pilot Course schools deliberately concentrated attention on the earlier years of schooling we have as yet less experience of what might be done at this stage, although we can learn something from the work done by a few pioneers with today's early leavers (fifteen-year-olds). My hope would be to see developments on roughly these lines:

1. An increasing recognition of the importance of Special Interest studies. These could include out-of-the-way O-Levels if desired. They would also undoubtedly include pre-vocational studies for those students to whom it seems quite unreasonable to be required to stay on at school unless vocational interests are met. They would include also the many interests such as typing, motor-maintenance, domestic science, child care, rural studies, which are vocationally useful for some but personally useful to all young people who find them interesting—and I have in mind, of course, provision for both boys and girls in all these fields.

By setting pre-vocational studies in the context of Special Interests we acknowledge the validity of any interests that genuinely involve the young; there is no need for any aspect of life to be eschewed by a school except the practice of vice or crime. At the same time, we are taking a necessary step of liberating school from the special responsibility it was engaged in for preparations for jobs. With the setting up of the Industrial Training Boards, which are charged with this function and can fulfil it effectively, the national requirement that society makes of schools has been clearly de-limited. We know now, both from the findings of the Crowther Report and from those concerned with the Industrial Training Act, as well as from conversation with good employers, that for young school leavers the most important qualification is a sound general education.

One of the difficulties in the past has been that two sets of sub-cultural values have combined to trap young people in vocational courses, sometimes of a narrowly conceived kind: these are the belief of working-class boys (and to a lesser extent girls) that adult status consists of going to work and earning a living and the middle-class dedication to notions of personal vocation and of the virtue of work for its own sake. Often the courses proposed have been of little value since for some higher levels of skills the machines available have been far too old-fashioned, and for many young school leavers the whole notion of pre-vocational studies is inappropriate anyway, as their work does not require such skills.

It is important to recognize the sacrifice that we demand of working-class boys in requiring them to stay at school to sixteen. There they are, physically competent, sexually mature, ready to earn. And we may recall the moving comment of the girl quoted years ago by an investigator that between leaving school, collecting a wardrobe, and getting married at 19 so as not to be on the shelf "you only have one year to live."

Her situation will seem to her to be worse than ever. There is food for serious thought in Edwin Mason's proposal: "Especially when the school-leaving age is raised, and earning-opportunities are in that way diminished, it may become important for a secondary school to establish some sort of agency to find its senior members part-time employment worth having (in terms of reward as well as learning)... work out of school hours, of course, not "work experience" which is seen simply as a learning situation."[1]

[1] Fifth Report, p. 51

2. I do not think it will be necessary to have any special *kind* of school work at this stage, although there may be scope for increased privileges. There should certainly be growing emphasis on independent study and easy access to Remedial programmes for those who suddenly come to and want to prepare for more ambitious kinds of employment than they had earlier believed possible—an outcome we should expect from an experience of success through early puberty. This is after all the "never-too-late" cell of the Curriculum.

3. What I do believe to be important is that at this stage, even more than before, Enquiry should lead on to Making, and that this should (if the young wish it) include creative contributions to the community life on a greater and more sustained scale than can easily be made by younger pupils. This has two important justifications: first that it makes good use of the growing altruism I have spoken of, secondly that it is education in the competencies required of an expert electorate. Seeing the many gaps in a way of life where community is so sadly inadequate, students move on to explore new possibilities of action, to make schemes for positive contributions to the world around them—and they learn "know-how," how to use the local government services to good ends, how to meet and talk with the officers and elected representatives who are accountable to their parents and teachers and very shortly will be to them.

If some students have to be stashed away working for "O" levels, they should not be denied access to this kind of experience of giving. It would be eminently appropriate if it were organized by those free of examination commitments on behalf of all. One does not require success in a public examination to be an active citizen; on the other hand, no-one should be deprived of the opportunity. Schools which limit "social education" to the so-called "Newsom child" have their values askew.

(ii) The Sixth Forms (16-18)

It is not within the scope of this book to discuss the question of early specialization, to which English insistence on élitist education (and that on the cheap) has led us; nor can I do more than mention the known inadequacies of A-Level as a predictor of University success. My task seems rather to be to put forward general theoretical propositions about the form education ought to take, but in discussing the immediate future to do so in terms of probability, of what can be managed now, today, by any school without reference to other institutions.

IDE/M has an important part to play in the so-called "minority" time, which is intended to broaden the scope of sixth form work. Similarly it is indispensable for the new general sixth form, as students continue their general education or make good the gaps in their previous qualifications. Here again the flexibility of the Fourfold Curriculum is valuable in providing occasions when small groups of students or individuals working independently can make use of the consultative services of teachers in the Remedial and Special-interest sections. This is the kind of service which is provided already by many schools at sixth form level, and one might say that these two aspects of the Fourfold Curriculum are an extension to younger pupils of the same kinds of advantage.

It is in proposing IDE/M as a basis for "minority time," which is intended to broaden the scope of the sixth form for A-Level students, that our work has its most significant contribution to make to sixth form studies. It is a highly appropriate central feature of the work of the general sixth forms which are increasingly emerging in the relatively prosperous South of England, where students who do not expect to go on to University (or higher professional courses requiring similar qualifications) stay on at schools to establish their general education at a more mature level and to pick up perhaps some qualifications previously missed. Bearing in mind the importance of stable experiences in mid-adolescence this trend is one that should be encouraged.

School could be the ground-base for a week spent largely on individual studies inside or outside the grounds, and on Enquiries undertaken at greater depth—and distance from school—than before.

In terms of minority time for early specialists there is room for the development of a different mode of approach to IDE/M, one which recognizes their increasingly specialized studies but asks them to collaborate in using their specialisms. To some students, those with personal leanings toward synoptic, synthesizing ways of looking at problems, or with special interests quite outside their school specialism, minority time is welcome; but to others it is merely a requirement of the school and so much waste of time. To these latter sixth-formers it has as little significance, and therefore as little value, as enforced "liberal studies" have for temperamentally similar students in technical colleges. People learn in so far as they set new knowledge, skills, and interests into a context of what already has value for them. If adult society accepts narrow and easy specialization as adequate, then the context of knowledge, skills and interests of many students will be narrow. It is better to accept this fact and ask them to direct their specialism into shared investigation, acting as the consultants in that field specially concerned with its contribution to the common study. To puff up the corpse of liberal education by artificial injections of formaldehyde does little good for students of this kind. On the other hand, no student should be confined against his will to the contribution of his specialism to IDE/M: that would of course be quite contrary to its purpose, which is to broaden the scope of the person's engagement with the environment, thereby helping him to become more fully and consciously himself, and to move at ease in a complex culture.

PHASING IDE/M

Pre-planning of "Phases" of IDE/M

I have suggested some of the considerations on which teachers might propose Areas of Investigation and Phases of IDE/M. I use the word *phase* to distinguish the process from the typical unit of work in American curricula, since although some units (like some projects) may have the qualities we look for in IDE/M, some are highly structured, didactically presented, and are brought to an abrupt conclusion at the end of a fixed number of weeks. "Phasing" looks to the collaboration of students, to a far freer structuring based on the questions which arise as enquiry proceeds. A phase may last anything from a week to a term or longer, and can be a gradual process, permitting (if desired) some students to linger while others move on to prepare the ground for future studies. A useful model to have in mind for phasing is not the simple single stage rocket which goes on on the basis of its original propulsion until it drops, but the multi-stage rocket.

I do not believe that at the moment our knowledge of learning processes is sufficient to propose that any one kind of *phase* should reign supreme. Indeed, learning should be so diverse that it is inherently unlikely that this would ever be so, though one should hope for much more experimental work which would add to our repertoire, and which would also study the merits or disadvantages of current proposals in relation to young people of different ages, attainments, and cognitive styles. For the moment we may welcome diversity, recognizing incidentally that the "Hawthorne effect," which confirms that variety is indeed the spice of life, is a very important teachers' aid, second only in importance to their foresight and their opportunism. What follows is therefore only an analysis of the basis of some phases which teachers have found or might find useful. Some may be arrived at by students themselves settling on a major Area of Investigation and themselves phasing in the aspects which they want to consider over a year or more; some will be short, to the point, and done with. The essential feature of the process of work is that it should involve and lead to exploration, experiment or explanation which is seen by the young as having value and that what is made is genuinely the outcome of their productive thinking and creative skills. Many topics satisfy none of these criteria.

* Phases may be based on specific stimuli from which enquiry freely develops (a pattern familiar to primary education), as for distance from an object or group of things found by pupils, the use of new equipment as students come into or move up the school, or visits and other school events.

The use of structural games is appropriate here. So also are the "structural programmes" created by the Centre for Structural Communication[1] which draw attention to problems of relationships between ideas. In addition to the accepted notions of providing a diversified environment; one way is to provide a large supply of junk materials, another is to provide excellent tools of a weight and size appropriate to growing children, another to provide easily worked materials ranging from paper to new strong types of board as used by D. L. Burges of Education Development Center. The use of disorienting equipment has its place too, such as masks, coloured or distorting glasses.

* They may be based also on local, national or international events, another familiar form of specific stimulus. It is one of the fortunate traditions of English schools that they have some freedom to work on problems of urgent current interest, however controversial. An inhibiting factor, of not wanting to seem to indoctrinate pupils whose parents' views may be very different from the teacher's, disappears in truly collaborative learning, in which shared enquiry, critical thinking, going to good and varied sources of evidence, and the expression of personal perceptions has been established

[1] cf. A. Hodgson, *A Communication Technique for the Future*; *Ideas*, No. 7; also many articles in *Systematics*

ORGANIZATION OF THE CURRICULUM

and where one of the accepted values of the school culture is that students participate in decision-making.

* Phases may arise from a *mood*, a period of profound interest in some fundamental problem of life or death, of which it is not important to know the origin, only to acknowledge its existence and significance to the young.

* Phases may arise from ideas or experiences in which the fundamental appeal is to the imagination, from symbols of archetypal significance as varied as caves, water, heroes, dangerous journeys. As long as the central imaginative interest is maintained and is not diluted by narrowly conceived discursive thinking, these symbolically significant themes can intensify the quality of exploration and creative work, some of it of a quite "academic" kind (see above, page 154).

* Phases may be based on a continuing narrative created by the pupils, of a "soap opera" kind, which draws on the creative imagination of the young to engage them in serious studies of human beings and societies.[1] This has the additional advantage for anxious students of enabling them to discuss personal problems at one remove.

* In some phases the exploration of problems may fan out from, or follow sequentially from, the presentation of a single fact or idea (as Professor O. R. McGregor has suggested[2] that a comment on the changing sex ratio might lead to studies in public health, in demography, economic history, emigration, literary values, and so on.)

* Phases may be based on the work of one discipline, which is seen for a time as central, acting as a vehicle for others. The discipline may not be represented in IDE/M itself, and the phase is then a way of creating links between IDE/M and autonomous studies, particularly those like languages

---

[1] E. Joseph has described the value of this kind of study with 13-year-olds, many culturally deprived (forthcoming issue of *IDEAS*)
[2] In a lecture at Goldsmiths' College, 1965

and physical education, which are likely to be seen for the most part as autonomous.

* Phases may occasionally be based on *presentations*. There is a case now and then for exploiting the more structured work provided by units such as the American Social Studies Curriculum Program of the Educational Services Inc.,[1] units which are developed "to help teachers by producing the kinds of materials they might like to prepare themselves had they world enough and time."[2] We can expect these multi-media materials to increase (and a gifted focus-group of teachers may well find it possible to create such presentations for themselves also). As occasional relaxation for students from their more creative endeavours these could well be a useful addition to a school's repertoire, partly for their Hawthorne effect, partly to give more time to teachers pre-planning a demanding phase of work. Some of this material is brilliantly produced, providing a great deal of opportunity for games, multiple-role playing and so on, but the freedom is only within a structure too pre-ordained to be appropriate for frequent use in IDE/M.

* A more creative enterprise is to base the phase on work towards a "festival," where the unifying feature is some key concept, but the phase consists of preparing a major "festival" of exhibitions and performances, and is so planned that much of the value lies in the continued analysis and development of understanding of the concept after the festival has taken place.[3]

* Study of an abstract organizing concept can be valuable. It is essential to recognize the very different experiences through which the young come to grasp the significance of concepts and make them their own. Material related to concepts is better seen as reference material available to

---

[1] Now the Education Development Center
[2] Franklin Patterson, *Man and Politics*, Curriculum Models for Junior High School (Social Studies Occasion Paper, No. 4, E.S.I., 1965)
[3] John Jones, "Idea in Action," *IDEAS*, No. 3

ORGANIZATION OF THE CURRICULUM

pupils as they come to need it, and the recognition of concepts as the outcome of an active phase of enquiry which may be hoped for for all children but achieved only by some. However, there is a place for an exploration of new applications of concepts already familiar, such as transaction, growth, change, power, creation—and other generalizing concepts which often have different significance within the theories of different disciplines. Very interesting studies of this kind might emerge in senior forms of schools.

* It might be possible to develop another kind of phase which centred deliberately on concepts relating to the child's manipulation of material for learning, such as: identity and difference (which would be the basis of classifications ranging from those of physics to those of the behavioural sciences) or comparison of the kinds of problem-solving engaged in by different disciplines.[1]

* As older adolescents are enabled to become more open about themselves in school (in a way that lively young school leavers very often are already) the study of personality, of the kinds of choices, attitudes, and behaviours in which it expresses itself, is a basis for much-needed phases. These can draw on experiments (simplified from research experiments) in social psychology; they can draw also on drama and on sharing and perhaps analysing students' and teachers' individual perceptions of, and responses to, objects, visits, and other experiences, for this kind of approach can advance understanding to an extent that discussion very often fails to do. Discussion is invaluable for helping people to formulate and categorize opinions but it is neither as truly exploratory as a more scientific investigation would be nor does it draw sufficiently (as movement and drama signally do) on the rich resources of pre-conscious symbolism.

An essential requirement of all phases of IDE/M is that they

[1] J. T. Padgett describes in *IDEAS*, No. 10 a first-year "phase" based on a different but very interesting application of identity and difference

shall be truly investigatory, not a hidden form of didacticism. This means that although the focus-group of teachers will have pre-planned to the extent of anticipating the kinds of questions that may arise, in the final analysis the phase should be seen only as a starting-point, a launching-pad for enquiry and making, never as processes whose outcome can be surely prophesied. IDE/M is above all an opportunity for free exercise of our fundamental gifts of enquiry and making. Better the most authoritarian system that is overtly so than hidden manipulation by teachers which makes pupils into puppets. On the other hand, teachers may well in an absolutely open atmosphere explain some of their reason for proposing an Area of Investigation, or draw attention to the importance of an aspect that might have been neglected. This will be increasingly possible as students come to have faith in their own capacity to plan major Areas of Investigation, to create with their teachers their own curriculum. Readers who find this comment causes extreme anxiety are reminded that the school offers a safety net for more traditional studies required by examinations and so on in the Remedial Section, and that in any case students belong to the same broad culture as themselves.

Chapter 7

Diversity without Divisiveness

THE DESTRUCTION OF TALENT

It is very easy for teachers to become without knowing it the hired assassins of talent. Teachers risk destroying talent (and since potential talent is part of a person, diminishing the person in the process) whenever they:

(*a*) Assume that there are fixed standards which children should have reached by a certain age.

One of our shames is that children leave secondary school functionally illiterate, and are thereby excluded from opportunity and understanding in our culture, for reading is a threshold skill for much personal enjoyment and social competence, even if its importance is decreasing. The disadvantages of late readers may well be an example of just the destruction I have in mind. Although many able people have been late readers, Joyce Morris's study shows that children who cannot read at the stage we have decided to be correct are unlikely to do well at school.[1] It is a hypothesis worth examining experimentally that there is no place for some of these children to develop at their own rate from the age of eight or so. But this would be only one example of daily damage that is being done by assuming against all the evidence that there are standardized routes and rates of development.

(*b*) Assume that a child's rate of progress in future can be extrapolated from past progress.

[1] Joyce M. Morris, *Standards and Progress in Reading* (National Foundation for Educational Research in England and Wales, 1966)

Children may have different growth rates in intellectual development. They may develop late, but they may also go through long recessive periods, probably from emotional difficulties which may have nothing to do with the school and which even the home may not be aware of either; and even in the most stable child significant learning takes place in spurts that we can recognize but cannot predict. This does not mean that in periods of recession or fallow periods they "are not trying," "could do better"—at that moment they could not do better, are trying their best, or are unable to try.

(c) Have generally low expectations of some children[1].

(d) Give insufficient experience of success.

Becoming a public figure, which is what is required of all of us through childhood and adolescence, is itself a complex test. Adolescence, the second main phase of this emergence, requires the establishment of a personal identity separate from and independent of parents. Massive support is needed at this stage of development. If school does not provide this, one of the results will be a loss of hope about the self as a whole which will be to the detriment of school performance (although teachers who believe in fixed rates of progress may not notice this if progress has always been slow).

(e) Ignore different cognitive styles, requiring the same tasks of all pupils.

This matters particularly to the creative child in a school where expectations and attitudes are not creative.

(f) Assume that children have poor ability, or keep them continually with others who are not doing well, because they have language difficulties.

---

[1] The effect of teachers' expectations on the level of achievement of "low-ability children" (as operationally defined for the purpose of the study) is discussed by C. Burstall in connection with the Junior French Project. High scores on French in all tests are associated with a highly positive attitude on the part of the teacher, and a low score with highly negative attitudes. The effect of attitudes was particularly noticeable in the case of Head Teachers (C. Burstall, "The French Project, an Interim Report," *New Research in Education*, N.F.E.R., 1968, Vol. 1, No. 2)

With immigrants to whom English is a second or third language, this, of course, presents difficulties for a school, but not to tackle them, and to take the easy way out that many schools do of putting them in a low stream or track is nevertheless unforgivable. The damage may well not show at its most extreme except if the child has come from an unstreamed school at home, and is less likely to show among those coming from extremely rigid school systems. If you have seen the havoc it causes with such a child it becomes easy to guess at the damage it may be doing in other cases where the parents themselves may not know the child's true potential.

It is not only the overseas immigrant who can suffer damage of this kind. Basil Bernstein's researches[1] have shown us that for many working-class children the abstract and more formal language used in school is a strange and foreign sort of English, involving strange and foreign modes of thought. These children can be truly immigrants into the middle-class subculture of a school, even if the school is in a twilight area. Add to this the established halo effect[2] which tends to make teachers ascribe intellectual virtues where children behave with the persistence and politeness that middle-class homes encourage, and one has the complete recipe for ignoring and thereby destroying talent in working-class children, except such as is shown exceptionally early in their school lives.

Teachers as "thugs," or "hired assassins," is not a pretty picture and "hired" certainly requires justification. The justification I would offer is the fact that over the years talent has always emerged in the quantities that have been economically convenient. Teachers have been given an entrepreneurial role for the economy, rather than an interpretative one for the community. The whole system of dividing child-

---

[1] e.g. Basil Bernstein, "Social Structure, Language and Learning," *Educational Research* (1961), III, 3, pp. 163-176
[2] cf. J. W. B. Douglas, *The Home and the School* (London, MacGibbon and Kee, 1964), pp. 100ff.; and David H. Hargreaves, *Social Relations in a Secondary School* (Routledge and Kegan Paul, 1967), esp. Chs 5 and 8

ren according to how likely they seem to be to pass examinations and so move on to the next stage of meritocratic success invites teachers to ignore the different latent possibilities in some of them. All the evidence that has been established since 1954[1] that between the first and last years of schooling the proportion of middle-class and working-class children doing well at school is almost exactly reversed, (with the result that a vastly higher proportion of the former are successful in school) suggests that middle-class parents and children overcome learning difficulties through a partnership with teachers of which few members of working-class families are capable. But if the work at school were so planned as to be intrinsically interesting to adolescents rather than being geared to meritocratic success we could hope that more talent might emerge than was needed for employment purposes, and this talent could be expressed in a higher quality of every-day living. The fear of the "rootless intellectual" which is sometimes expressed even by the official liberals of the educational hierarchy has no place in our thinking if we bear in mind that there is leisure to be spent as well as work to be done, local and national decisions to be made with the co-operation of a well-informed and thoughtful electorate, and a continuum of understanding needed about the nature and effects of technological change. There are lives to be lived. There are good grounds for arguing that talent has not been developed because it has been unnecessary economically and perhaps because it has been unwelcome politically. In this sense as teachers, most of us have been, unwittingly, "thugs."

---

[1] In e.g., *Early Leaving* (H.M.S.O., 1954); J E. Floud, ed., A. H. Halsey and F. M. Martin, *Social Class and Educational Opportunity* (Heinemann, 1956); A. H. Halsey et. al., *Education, Economy and Society* (Free Press of Glencoe, 1961); *Higher Education* (The Robbins Report, H.M.S.O., 1961-3), Appendix 1; J. W. B. Douglas, loc. cit.

CRITERIA FOR GROUPING

Until now Sir Herbert Read's melancholy dictum has been justified: "we educate to classify," he has said, "and we classify to divide."[1] Our techniques of divisiveness have been simple to the point of crudity. A far more sophisticated professionalism is required by our new task of encouraging diversity without creating divisiveness. One of the most important problems facing us is to find criteria for grouping students and ways of grouping them that are not damaging. The arrangements a school makes are most likely to fit people of different shapes and sizes through a period of rapid change if they are varied and flexible.

In a book of this kind there can be no fiats. Teachers who accept its basic arguments will feel that these arguments veto certain actions such as streaming, but the kinds of positive decision that they may make should be very varied indeed, being dependent on the members of the school, its situation its buildings, and the priorities that the head and teaching staff recognize for it. Development is bound to be gradual, for the kinds of changes proposed cannot without internal contradiction be arbitrarily imposed. By the time any one school has developed in these directions (but according to its own style), it may well have discovered or learned of better proposals than I could make now. However, it may be useful to offer a survey of possible bases for grouping, and to suggest which seem the most suitable in the present situation of English secondary schooling.

In describing criteria for grouping I am concerned with the basic organization of the school as a whole. Later in this chapter I shall be discussing the organization of "clusters" and larger groups within this system.

Twelve bases for grouping are used or proposed in schools in different parts of the world, although some are more familiar in primary than in secondary schools. These are, in no order of merit or of popularity:

[1] In a lecture at University of London Goldsmiths' College, 1965

A. Interest-grouping.
B. Grouping by teacher-compatibility[1].
C. Friendship grouping.
D. Grouping by neighbourhood.
E. "Family grouping."
F. Grouping by "developmental age."
G. Grouping according to special needs.
H. Grouping by chronological age only.
I. Grouping by chronological age, with sub-grouping by general achievement (streaming and tracking).
J. Grouping by chronological age, with sub-grouping by achievement in some subjects (setting).
K. Grouping by achievement in all subjects without reference to age (grading or vertical streaming).
L. Grouping by achievement in some subjects without reference to age (cross-setting).

A. *Interest-Grouping.* My proposals for a Fourfold Curriculum, to include Interdisciplinary Studies, Autonomous Studies, Remedial Studies, and Interest-based Studies, imply even in their names a belief that interest-grouping has an important place in the curriculum. The relevant point here is that these need have no basis in chronological age. In fact, there are marked advantages in the young spending some of their time with others at different stages of development, and schools may well find parts of the day when students can get on with their work alongside others of different ages who are working at different levels. Some schools already find it valuable for older pupils to spend some of their time informally guiding the younger ones. It is familiar that the best way of learning is by teaching and we should not be deterred by any retrospective fears of a return to the dread monitorial system

---

[1] cf. H. A. Thelen, "Classroom Grouping of Students," *School Review 67*, 1 pp. 60-78; and "Grouping for Teachability," *Theory into Practice*, II (1963) pp. 81-9 abstracted in Alfred Yates, ed., *Grouping in Education* (John Wiley & Sons, 1966)

from suggesting that there is a place for guidance by the older of the younger pupil in IDE or Autonomous Studies. But it is not necessary in interest-grouping or "orbital" work for older to help younger, although in a collaborative climate they are likely to do so, even if only by the occasional hint or by the quality of their own more advanced work; it is the community of interest that is important.

B. *Family Grouping*. Interest-grouping in IDE and other studies can come very close to "family grouping" which is familiar in many progressive primary schools, although "family grouping" is of course not based on community of interest but is simply the free grouping of children over a quite wide age-span. Family grouping could have great advantages, even from the point of view of deployment of specialist staff for IDE; in fact for the small school it may be the only way of obtaining an adequate inter-disciplinary focus-group, and shared IDE for first and second-year pupils is obviously helpful in such circumstances. The larger schools are not at present experimenting with this, although there is some mixing of fourth and fifth years going on, and once schools undertake inter-disciplinary C.S.E. (and G.C.E., perhaps) it is possible to envisage a considerable increase in shared work of this kind.

The psychological advantages are considerable and important. There are great benefits for the first-year entrant to secondary school to come into IDE working alongside second-year pupils with some experience and a sense of security and assurance. In general we should not think of vertical grouping as something for the young child only. The small family of today, nuclear and inward-looking and with only one to three children, and these likely to be very close in age, gives far less experience of sibling relationships than did the extended family, expecially when each sub-unit of the family was numerous. These social changes creep on us so gradually that we are apt not to notice them, and we may quite well be denying to early and mid-adolescents important kinds of experience of their fellows (just as we failed to notice the importance of the avuncular kind of relationship for mid-adolescents until recent studies drew attention to their need for stable adult figures in addition to parents).

This must not be confused with grouping across age by achievement; that does not fulfil the psychological function of interest-grouping or family grouping, for it is based on the supposed similarity between students or different ages who work together, and this can be difficult for the younger academically advanced pupil to maintain. The proposals I make are based on the recognition that there are differences in psychological maturity which may be positively helpful to both older and younger.

C. *Teacher-compatibility*. In practice, much interest-grouping is likely to be arrived at by the young on their estimate of teacher-compatibility. There is a place also for this kind of grouping when teachers are creating class-groups (necessary in present buildings) for Autonomous Studies. Where a number of unstreamed classes are working in parallel, teacher-compatibility can be a good basis for grouping them, if it is convenient. It would not be desirable, in my view, for students to spend too much of their time working with teachers of similar cognitive style to their own, "creative" speaking only to "creative" and "high intelligence" to others similarly disposed, and this is what teacher-compatibility could easily become. But it may well ease the passage of some children if for some of their time compatibility is taken extremely seriously into account. In particular, some disturbed children have a great need for a certain teacher to whom they attach themselves like limpets; to detach them for any arbitrary reason when this need is so strongly expressed would be quite wrong. In IDE, of course, one of the tasks of the focus-group is to see that there is someone readily available for each individual to turn to, and in this fluid situation no special arrangements need to be made, but elsewhere in the curriculum it is something to bear in mind.

D. *Friendship Grouping.* This proves to be one of the bases on which children "cluster," and in so far as buildings necessitate grouping into classes of thirty or so, sociometric grouping for this purpose also is a natural step to take in any unstreamed school.[1]

E. *Neighbourhood Grouping.* This is a good deal practised in some unstreamed secondary schools for first year pupils, in the hope of mitigating the shock of change from the primary school since pupils will still be with others they have known. It has disadvantages. Those children who come from formal old-fashioned primary schools can well do with contact with others more used to self-directed work. Secondly, one of the advantages of the secondary school, with its wider catchment area, should be that young people from different neighbourhoods and quite probably different sub-cultures should be mixed up in class. If other steps are taken to ease the transfer to secondary school, neighbourhood grouping should not be necessary.[2]

F. *Grouping by "Developmental Age."* This was put forward as theoretically desirable by Dr. J. M. Tanner,[3] who argues that chronological age is quite deceptive, owing to the great range in "developmental" age, of which a main aspect is puberty; this can considerably influence intellectual as well as emotional maturity. His point is an important reminder of one of the lenses through which we need to view the differences in any group of young people. After all, there can easily be a difference of five or six maturational years in a year-group in a coeducational school. Late developers are obviously at risk owing to feelings of inadequacy. So too can be early developers. Both may need special help and comfort, as does any child

[1] For a study of friendship grouping in an unstreamed school in the 1950s, see L. A. Smith, *IDEAS,* No. 7
[2] For a list of proposals by experienced secondary teachers and social workers in school, see Fifth Report, pp. 43-8
[3] J. M. Tanner, *Educational and Physical Growth* (University of London Press, 1961), esp. Ch. 8

who is anxious because of feeling different from the imaginary perfect model child they dream of being. But to single out girls for early puberty and boys for late would be as damaging an arrangement as one could well imagine, and this of course would be to go far beyond Dr. Tanner's proposals. We have an argument here, however, in favour of ensuring that we do not stick rigidly throughout the curriculum to year-grouping.

G. *Grouping according to special needs.* This is, of course, the basis for the "Remedial" phase of the Fourfold Curriculum. Such work may well involve an element of grouping by achievement. "Remedial" grouping is, I believe, a section of the curriculum which will become much more important over the next few years. In particular it will be helped by additional technological aids. Much of it should be self-instruction, with the use of programmes appropriate to the needs of students. But programmed work can profitably be done by heterogeneous groups also, as can work with a teacher. Some students will join the "Remedial" section because they are particularly advanced, others because their difficulties cannot economically be met in other cells of the curriculum. When their difficulties or needs are in the same area or of the same style "remedial work," like interest-grouping, can be undertaken in homogeneous groups, in heterogeneous groups, or individually, as seems most appropriate.

H-L. *Grouping by Age or by Achievement.* Until now we have been thinking how greater flexibility might quite readily be provided in many schools. We now move to much more difficult territory in which fundamental choices are demanded. Basically, the question turns out to be how far students should be grouped according to achievement, if at all. The question is difficult, not only because the choice is one which is basic to the school's planning but also because there are so many well-established possibilities to choose from: unstreamed age-grouping, streamed age-grouping, setting within age-groups, grading across age-groups and setting across age-groups.

All grouping by assessed achievement, whether it is used, as in grading, as a main criterion or, as in streaming and setting, as subsidiary to age, rests on certain assumptions, unless we are prepared to state downright that we are looking deliberately for the quickest and easiest results, and are prepared deliberately to waste talent, and diminish personalities in the process. The assumptions are:

(*a*) That present achievement is a good predictor of future achievement.

(*b*) That teachers' estimate of present achievement, as indicated by setting or streaming, does not affect achievement.

(*c*) That from the point of view of achievement children of different levels of achievement do better apart.

(*d*) That the supposed advantages for achievement outweigh any disadvantages of which the system may be accused, such as social divisiveness.

(*e*) That so long as you provide a floor, which is the minimum achievement permissible within a stream or set, it does not matter that you inevitably produce a ceiling for the group immediately below.

(*f*)(As a contributory factor) that subjects are brick-by-brick structures.

None of these assumptions is tenable. The last point (*f*) I have already discussed (pp. 141ff), but the others need to be examined here.

(*a*) The view that present achievement is a good predictor of future achievement is incorrect. It is one of the melancholy facts of English education that streaming which, like selection, is only tolerable if you believe in the fixed I.Q., has so long survived the demolition of that myth. It is true that statistically behaviours are likely to remain constant, but to be a good predictor of future achievement, present achievement would have to be infallible. It is not.

(b) The view that being placed in a stream or set does not affect achievement is untrue also.[1] Achievement is affected by environment, and the expectations teachers (and through them parents) have of children is an important factor in the environment. This is true even in the non-streamed situation, if teachers group pupils according to their estimate of them thus producing intra-class setting or streaming. One of the worst features of streaming on whatever scale is that what starts as a hairline of difference between the bottom of one stream and the top of the next can become a chasm over the years. It is worth recalling that the International Evaluation of Achievement in its study of Achievement in Mathematics stated that "the standard deviation of mathematics test scores in England was found to be greater than any of the other participating countries."[2]

(c) The view that in relation to achievement the young proceed better if they are with others who are at the same level is strongly held; it is the reason why many kindly teachers wish to keep poor achievers away from the others so that they may go at their own speed, as it is said, and not have their weaknesses shown up. And of course it is one of the most favoured arguments for streaming that we must not hold back the bright.[3] This belief is incorrect statistically, as is shown by the only large-scale longitudinal study of streaming and selection as against unstreamed comprehensive education which has been undertaken, the five year compara-

---

[1] J. W. B. Douglas gives incontrovertible evidence as to the improvement and deterioration respectively of children in upper and lower streams from 8-11 years (op. cit. pp. 114-155); cf. p. 172, footnote.

[2] Douglas A. Pidgeon, ed., *Achievement in Mathematics* (N.F.E.R., 1967), p. 144. Unfortunately, it was not possible to investigate the suggestion that this was due to streaming because the unstreamed and unset secondary schools were too few (ibid. pp. 142, 144). Nevertheless, the exceptional stringency with which English schools are streamed made this independent variable an obvious candidate for further investigation.

[3] The view is shared by parents. According to the Plowden Report, vol. II, p. 587, the main perceived advantage of streaming by parents preferring streaming were "slow ones have more attention" (59%), "bright children not held back by slow children" (59%).

tive study of schools in Stockholm in the late '50s.[1] Of course there are difficulties about accepting evidence from another country but those who say that Swedish evidence is not relevant owing to a greater cultural uniformity are in effect saying that we have greater cultural deprivation among more students in England and should therefore confirm their deprivation by having lower expectations of them.

Valuable microcosmic evidence which gives us information of individuals working within a closely observed experimental situation is given by the recent finding of the National Centre for Programmed Learning in Birmingham of 36 ten-year-old children working on a programme: "Comparisons between groups showed that heterogeneous grouping was better both for high and low I.Q. subjects than either homogeneous pairs or individual work."[2]

The significance of this finding and previous research studies from the same unit[3] can be more fully utilized in the context of "clustering" than in the present section on grouping. For

---

[1] Nils-Eric Svensson, *Ability, Grouping and Scholastic Achievement* (Almqvist and Wiksell, 1962) This study showed that over the years there was no significant difference between the attainment, as evidenced by traditional attainment tests within subject-disciplines, of pupils in unstreamed comprehensive schools and those in streamed schools, select-plus and select-minus. The evidence of the N.F.E.R. Report on streamed and unstreamed Junior Schools to the Plowden Committee might seem more relevant than a foreign study. These show a superiority of attainment in streamed schools but the indications "are strongest at 7+ and weakest at 10+." The study is not longitudinal. A good deal of unstreamed teaching is likely to be of a kind which starts slowly but catches up, as Joyce Morris has shown to be true of active as against traditional methods (ibid). For details of this Report see, *Children and Their Primary Schools*, A Report of the Central Advisory Committee of Education (England), vol. II, Appendix 11 (H.M.S.O., 1967), pp. 544-594.

[2] R. Amaria, L. A. Biran, and G.O.M. Leith, *Individual Versus Cooperative Learning in a Secondary School*, Research Report on Programmed Learning, No. 17, University of Birmingham, School of Education (National Centre for Programme Learning, May, 1967; mimeographed), p. 5. More detailed statements are given on pp. 199 and 203. Subsequent studies in secondary schools, which gave similar results, are described by Dr. Amaria in *IDEAS*, No. 7. Her evidence there as to the influence on scoring of personality factors was published too late to be described in this chapter. The nature of tasks is to be examined also: "In the end we may find a case not for streaming or unstreaming but for making up groups to fit the requirements of different tasks"; Dr. R. Amaria, ibid.

[3] e.g., in *Research Reports* Nos. 4 and 10

it draws attention to a challenge which unstreamed secondary schools have so far failed to meet, and which was not met in the Stockholm experiment either, except perhaps for the fact that the unstreamed schools in Stockholm were in some ways less advantageously placed as regards teachers than the streamed and nevertheless showed equally satisfactory results. Properly, an unstreamed school should aim successfully for a *higher* average level of attainment than a streamed school. This must follow from the fact that higher performance groups do as well as under streaming,[1] and that absence of streaming should elicit a better performance from at least some of these who would have been in low streams. For this reason, the current controversy on streaming in England as against non-streaming is fundamentally uninteresting and almost damaging, since it detracts attention from the real problem, which is how best to create a freer situation in the unstreamed classroom, (see page 191ff), and to make positive use of the mixing of "mixed ability groups."

(*d*) The failure of our few unstreamed secondary schools to exceed the mean of secondary school performance may have been offset by their having other purposes for their pupils. Nevertheless, the failure to recognize the challenge has caused the controversy about secondary school streaming to be largely fought out on the boggy terrain of (*d*) above, the question of whether streaming is socially divisive. This suggests in itself an assumption that social and educational considerations are different, which in the context of a wider view of community is not acceptable. It also assumes a false dilemma, that our choice is confined to either setting a priority on the need for a common culture and paying an educational price for this *or* setting a priority on the need for educational "results" and paying a social price for that. Such an attitude unduly narrows the problem, which is not simply one of removing a source of social division that is malign but also of

[1] Svensson, ibid., p. 176

removing an educational technique which is inept. This is the challenge that no school will meet effectively until it stops dividing children into blocks, breaks up the stereotyped visual field, rattles its schemata as in a kaleidoscope, and sets out to consider how best it can perceive the diversified potential and constantly changing needs of persons. Perhaps it may be easier for younger people, brought up on modern mathematics and on relativity and complementarity in twentieth-century physics, to accept the fact of flux, and to learn to meet crises not by setting up tight bureaucratic structures but by a greater flexibility; but this is something we all have to learn.

(e) As to the danger of creating ceilings for achievement it is sometimes suggested that large numbers of individuals nip up or down the back stairs from one group to another, but the evidence is clear that this does not happen nearly so often as teachers suppose, even in their own schools.[1] Streamed or 'set' teaching does create a ceiling.

CHRONOLOGICAL AGE AS THE BASIS FOR IDE AND AUTONOMOUS STUDIES

The most flexible system will necessarily be the least judgmental because judgments can turn out to be self-fulfilling prophecies. It is on these grounds that for IDE and for Autonomous Studies (although not for "Orbit" or "Clinic") I believe that we should continue for some time to plan according to chronological age without reference to achievement. Chronological age is neutral: it is a fact. It may not be a vastly important fact, but to base our planning on it is to show a decent humility before the complexities of human growth. To use it as a base does not, of course, mean that one

---

[1] cf. J. C. Daniels, "The Effects of Streaming in the Primary School: 1. What Teachers Believe," *Brit. Jour. of Ed. Psych.*, XXXI (1961), pp. 69-78. For a recent survey of published material on streaming see Winifred M. Whiteley, *The Uneducated English* (Methuen, 1968), Ch. 8; cf also J. W. B. Douglas, op. cit. ch. 14.

should be bound by it, and I have already suggested the value of experiment in family grouping, and the very great importance of collaborative ventures which go right across age-groups and across divisions in between schools; but totally random grouping for a seven year age-group is not in the realm of physical possibility for a school. For English teachers age-grouping has the advantage of being familiar, and at a time when many other changes are envisaged this is important. Moreover, chronological age has significance to the young themselves. Most of their arguments about privileges and freedoms at home are based on it. For the moment at least it can serve, until better proposals, equally non-judgmental, emerge with experience.

As to the variety of developmental age in a chronological age-group, within a flexible system of "clustering" this could be positively beneficial. Certainly it is disadvantageous if one has in mind class teachings: the difference of tastes in poetry, for instance, between boys and girls in the early years of secondary school has nearly always meant (in my many visits to English lessons) that girls are "doing" narrative poetry when they are ripe for love lyrics. But class teaching is not what we have in mind. Our problem is simply to find a convenient non-judgmental basis for "clustering." In this context there is no need to seek homogeneity, which is impossible to achieve anyway: the differences between members of even the most carefully streamed form are vast, even with the conformity to the mean that constant association and the expectation of teachers are likely to produce.

CLASSES NO LONGER THE BASIC UNIT

Many of our problems have stemmed from a naive acceptance of a simple mathematical formula:

$$\frac{NP}{NS} = F$$

where NP is number of pupils, NS is number of staff, and F is a form or class, and the basic unit of the school.

DIVERSITY WITHOUT DIVISIVENESS

So long as one continues to have the class of thirty or so as the basic unit[1] in thinking about a school then the limit of flexibility is the slotting in and out of thirty or so children. There is a danger too, which the present box-like internal structure of school buildings reinforces, of thinking that the class makes a viable teaching and learning unit, whereas it is too big for effective learning and too small to provide the diversity of mixed ability grouping.

Once one breaks away from the class unit it becomes clear that what is required is the smaller cluster drawn from a larger main unit, changing according to changing needs. Then "mixed ability" grouping becomes something quite different from heterogeneous grouping as it is usually conceived, which is on a basis of I.Q. To work with students of different cognitive styles, different interests, different levels of communication, profoundly different sub-cultural assumptions, different emotional experiences, is to open up a whole new resource for learning, our own human variety.

There is evidence as to the optimum size of "clusters" (pp. 191-2, below), but there is no evidence as to the optimum size of the *Main Group*. Thirty is evidently too small to get the variety one looks for. Most schools have taken a pragmatic decision as to the Main Group. As it happens the first schools experimenting with IDE had an entry of four to six forms (some 120 to 200 pupils) and since we use chronological age as the basic criterion for grouping this was the Main Group chosen. It had the advantage that a focus-group of about 5 or 6 teachers gave a good spread of disciplines and was a manageable size for teachers themselves to "cluster" in. Since then, smaller and larger schools have joined in, and these respectively either use family vertical grouping or divide their year entry into two or more (in a 13-form entry school the requirement would be three focus-groups of teachers with three Main Groups). The decision has been one of convenience. It is to be hoped that large comprehensive schools which wish

---

[1] Even with modifications which allow for smaller numbers in bottom streams

to retain house systems will find it possible to use the house as a basis for the focus-group and Main Group. All this awaits more experience and research.

A PUPIL'S SCHOOL DAY—A FORECAST

We are often asked, What will Johnny do when he comes to school? How will he spend his day? The answer lies in a combination of the concept of the Fourfold Curriculum and the concept of clustering within large Main Groups, although for the moment buildings can make it difficult to provide large open areas and even to put members of a Main Group near each other. Hence in practice the way a child spends his day looks and may in fact be more similar to traditional schooling than one would wish.

When he comes to school in his first year, he is likely to spend about 40-55 per cent of his time on IDE, working in small clusters drawn from a Main Group of some 150 students; as far as possible time will be blocked, a whole morning, afternoon or day. Alternatively, although more rarely, the Main Group will work on an alternating rhythm, at times concentrating for a week or a month almost entirely on IDE, then reverting to the rest of the curriculum. There is a great deal to be said for allowing periods of this kind for three-dimensional studies, for instance. This proportion will change through the years, reducing to some 20 per cent in the sixth form. In the 4th and 5th years the proportion will depend on how far it is possible to introduce interdisciplinary studies in C.S.E. and G.C.E. 'O' level, so long as these remain mandatory for some pupils.

During this part of his day his cluster may move from one room to another, and he is likely to change from one cluster to another; and he will be supervised by a group of teachers with different subjects who can meet most of his needs. At times, for a period or more, one or more of these teachers will be replaced by other specialists, so that if a problem comes up for which he wants help beyond what the other teachers can give he will be able to store it up, and ask their advice. For instance, if the group of teachers in IDE included specialists in English, movement, mathematics, history, and biology, problems relating to geography or foreign literature can be stored up and dealt with for a single or double period when one of the basic group is required elsewhere. Alternatively or additionally he may be told that other teachers are available for special consultation. During IDE times there will always be one teacher whom he knows to be specially concerned with his programme and any personal problems he may have, although all members of the focus-group are concerned with supervision. He can turn to any teacher in the focus-group he wishes, but has extra security in the knowledge that there is one teacher named as having especial responsibility for his programme and his personal well-being. His welfare is thereby doubly ensured.

Although he will do a great deal of the work in clusters, there will be times when a whole Division Group (of some 35 children probably, because of the building) or a whole Main Group (of some 150) will meet together, for a summarizing period, for acting or dancing, for reporting progress to each other, because a teacher has said that there is something he specially wants to address a group about, or for a film or visiting expert. Concept loops, TV discs (when they become available), video-tapes, radio-vision programmes, stills with spoken comments or booklets to which they refer—such aids he is likely to use as he is found to need them within his cluster, since this is an appropriate and flexible use of all equipment that does not have to be ordered for one special occasion. Similarly the cluster may expect to be set to work through an assignment prepared by teachers or to do some special reading in the library. Such work may be done individually, and for this reason we sometimes speak, illogically, of one person as occasionally forming a cluster.

The amount of time he will spend on Autonomous Studies will depend very much on how far the school he goes to has developed the Remedial Section of the Fourfold Curriculum (the "Clinic"). In general if we say around 35-40 per cent in the early years this is probably about right. During Autonomous Studies he will be working on a separate subject discipline, again largely heuristically or creatively, again normally in clusters. In some cases the subject-matter of the Autonomous Studies may relate closely to what he has been doing in IDE. This will depend sometimes on whether the students and teachers feel it desirable or possible to make such cross-references (and this will partly depend on whether the Autonomous Study is thought to be necessarily linear). In others, such as the arts, it will be a matter of his own choice: he may feel in this Autonomous Study that he would rather do something quite different from what engages him in IDE/M.

As schools move into the full programme of Remedial and Interest Work, the amount of time spent on these is likely to depend very greatly on the intensity of the student's own special needs and interests. The remedial phase is of special importance to exceptional children, both those who are retarded in a basic skill, and talented children who need to pick up some extra knowledge because of some special interest that has developed in IDE/M or Orbital periods. Later on one can envisage a great deal of independent work towards special G.C.E. O-Levels (again, so long as these survive) which a student or small group may want to pick up rapidly and informally.

In fact the sooner it becomes recognized that much preparatory work for examinations is best undertaken in "Clinic," the sooner will public examinations take a more modest place in school, being recognized as arbitrary requirements that it is legitimate to "cram" for, working rapidly through assignments and programmes and deliberately learning examination skills, because they deserve no better, and because the important educative processes of the school lie elsewhere, and shall be interfered with as little as possible. In both these sections he will expect to be working individually or in clusters drawn from a number of age-groups. His need or his special interest, not his age, are in these cells the criteria for grouping.[1]

BASES FOR CLUSTERING

Clustering involves friendship grouping, task-oriented grouping, and task-differentiated grouping. For example, it might be found that among a main group of one hundred pupils, a dozen of them are engaged on similar lines of enquiry: these pupils could be grouped in, say, threes, each cluster containing pupils who have chosen to be together. Alternatively, it might be decided by the focus group teachers that it would be beneficial to the work to have some small groups containing pupils who are dealing with similar ploys and some containing pupils who are dealing with dissimilar ploys; and again some degree of friendship grouping might be possible and desirable. In any case it is expected that the groups formed will not be static: IDE creates a dynamic learning situation, and clustering and reclustering, dividing and redividing are fundamental to this situation. Then, of course, IDE must cater for the individual pupil who prefers occasionally to work alone; although even in such cases the individual pupil is always encouraged to share his knowledge, his special skills, with others in his division group or main group.[2]

If we recall the three models I proposed of group work, and the importance of the "collective ferment" of small, dynamic groups in making of a school a vigorous and sensitive social organism, it becomes obvious that the cluster, not the Main Group (100-200), far less the Division Group (30-35) is the most significant unit of the school's life, and much of the skill of teachers becomes that of being good "grouping specialists,"[2] recognizing where pupils working on different aspects of a process can enhance each other's work by being drawn together.

Two up to seven is suggested as a good range of size for a cluster. Berelson and Steiner summarize the evidence available about sizes of working group:

The larger the informal group, from two or three up to fifteen or

---

[1]Examples of time-tabling for a Fourfold Curriculum are given in *IDEAS* Supplement No. 1 by L. A. Smith
[2]L. A. Smith in *IDEAS*, No. 1

twenty, then the greater the demands on the leader and the more he is differentiated from the membership at large; the greater the group's tolerance of direction by the leader and the more centralized the proceedings; the more the active members dominate the interaction within the group; the more the ordinary members inhibit their participation and hence the less exploratory and adventurous the group's discussions; the less intimate the group atmosphere, the more anonymous the actions, and generally the less satisfied the members as a whole; the longer it takes to get to non-verifiable (judgmental) decisions; the more acceptable the unresolved differences; the more the subgroups formed within the membership; and the more formalized the rules and procedures of the group. For most of these tendencies, the watershed seems to be around 5—7.[1]

For task-oriented groups with a learning task or some problem to explore of a relatively non-judgment kind there is a case for the group of less than 5-7, but for other kinds of situation where what is wanted is variety of opinion seven or so is more appropriate. Again for short sharp discussion within a larger group there is plenty of scope for the buzz-group of only three, which can rapidly formulate a question to be asked, or a point to be argued. The work of a school is so varied that it would not be right to formulate a case for one optimum size of cluster; far more important is to recognize that fifteen (and for adolescents probably a dozen) is likely to be too large for basic everyday work, although of course there are phases of planning and types of work where the cluster is itself too small.

Some of the ways in which students can usefully form into clusters are:

* Where several children are carrying out a special aspect of a large scale Enquiry, with the intention of reporting back to a larger group.
* Where they are carrying out by agreement aspects of an Enquiry which the teacher sees will have bearing on each other or are complementary; and so he brings these small clusters together for a time.

[1] Berelson and Steiner, *Human Behaviour, An Inventory of Scientific Findings* (Harcourt, Brace and World, Inc., 1964), p. 358

DIVERSITY WITHOUT DIVISIVENESS

* Where several children together have proposed a more independent line of enquiry which it is practicable for them to follow up.
* Where the teacher has the same hopes, in terms of skills or recognition of a concept, for several children; this can take the form of shared self-directed enquiry by agreement with the teacher, or shared or similar assignments, or use of visual and other aids.
* Where there seems a good case for "pairing" or working in very small clusters of two or three children with very different levels of attainment (see page 183); as our knowledge of grouping grows it may be possible to add personality factors to our bases for "pairing".[1]
* Where the teacher thinks that mutual instruction by a pair will improve a skill, e.g. in throwing a pot, where two students taking turns to tell each other what to do can achieve better results than individuals working separately.
* Where children's aptitudes are complementary, e.g. originality of invention with accurate craftsmanship and manual dexterity.
* For shared creative or expressive work in the arts, e.g. group poetry writing, dramatic or dance improvizations.
* For discussions of all kinds, especially those which involve revelation of feelings or experiences (as most important discussions do).

Friendship grouping is of course likely to underly much of the spontaneous clustering, especially in discussion and creative work. It is there to be encouraged.

THE CLUSTERING OF CLUSTERS

To describe the cluster as the basic cell of the school's life is not to suggest that there is no place for work in Main or Division Groups, as I hope has been clear from all that I have

---

[1] p. 183; Dr. Amaria reports just such a study in *IDEAS*, No. 7

said. If students are to learn to undertake large-scale enquiries, to think big, to recognize complexities rather than settling for the crude and obvious solution, then much of the larger planning will be done by these larger groups, and the coming together of clusters for exchange, for obtaining further information that can usefully be given in a lecture or demonstration to a larger number—all this is patently important.

The kind of large-scale planning by a Main Group of 100 or more students, with work carried out in small clusters, is an advance on what typically goes on in the junior school, where inter-disciplinary collaboration of teachers is also rare. Its very unfamiliarity is another reason why we should so far as possible disengage our minds from the idea of the division group of 30-35, and concentrate on the large Main Group and the tiny cell or cluster.

It may be suggested that belonging to a form with its form-room has justified itself by giving a sense of security for some less mature pupils, and this would if supported by evidence be a strong argument for finding functions for the Division-Group. There are plenty of functions to be found if so desired, such as some aspects of planning of enquiries, of reporting back on these as a screening process before a major "sharing" of the whole year-group, and so on. But the experience of schools working with IDE is that it is difficult to avoid the separatism which the buildings imply, almost enforce, and that tradition has made familiar. We need not set about to create the class-sized group, and one might guess that a failure to overcome the classroom barriers will almost certainly mean that fewer relationships between ideas and pieces of work will be seen by students and by teachers, and that those who will lose most thereby will be the more gifted, who can profit so much by a situation which encourages synthesis (see page 195f., below).

MINORITIES IN THE COLLABORATIVE SCHOOL

How far will the groupings I have proposed meet the needs of minority groups? Such minorities include exceptional children (exceptional in the sense of being at the poles of achievement, and perhaps of talent), children under severe social handicap including the majority of immigrants, and the emotionally disturbed. A related challenge to be met in the life of the collaborative flexible school will be to help those under pressures at home unfavourable to their development, whether in the form of extremes of ambition on the one hand or of low motivation on the other.

This is dangerous ground, for each group has very properly been studied at very great length in expert works. Yet a survey of the possibility of a better kind of secondary schooling which did not acknowledge the existence of their problems would be frivolous.

A. EXCEPTIONAL CHILDREN

Too much English thinking about giftedness is still naive, in that it equates intelligence with high performance at I.Q. tests, or if it has moved on from there it is only to assessing intelligence in terms of a school achievement which makes demands not dissimilar to those of I.Q. tests, in that it tests analytical and convergent thinking. This kind of intelligent behaviour will give a right answer where right or wrong answers are possible, and may be able to adduce good reasons for doing so, and also to criticize other views and evaluate them very effectively. But some children who are extremely talented in these forms of data-processing, which must not be despised, are at a loss to perform the tasks which indicate other kinds of talent, such as ability to propose new hypotheses or new ways of testing an hypothesis, telling stories or improvizing in drama, and so on, which are the province of *making*.

Some of the attempts to establish a dimension "creativity"

as largely independent of "intelligence" have been justifiably criticized on technical grounds.[1] But English educationists have tended not so much to criticize as to ignore. In thinking of intelligence we should always today be aware of the wide variety of excellence towards which we ought to be looking—and to bear in mind also that in all cases it is *tendency* in performance that we should be looking for, and that it may well be that some of those who today languish in low streams would develop "high intelligence" or "high creativity" behaviours but for emotional difficulties. If the school concerns itself primarily with the mental wellbeing of its members and thereby encourages a flowering of talent, it is at least making the best contribution that it can. Although there are of course difficulties too profound for any school arrangements to mitigate, a system which seeks to give experience of success, to note tendencies of cognitive style, and to work through the development of relative strengths works on the right lines for the exceptional child.

(i) *Gifted Children*

(*a*) For the creatively disposed child it is manifest that an education in which exploratory and creative behaviours are welcomed and where there is a concern for personal thinking and authentic feeling makes school a place in which he can richly prosper. Again, the difficulties of the "dominant" child in coping with the class lesson (see page 31) will be removed by the removal of the class lesson. Children with this kind of disposition need release from the closed systems of thinking which predominate in school today.

But there are other kinds of advantage which should accrue for a wide diversity of gifted children:

(*b*) The whole design of the curriculum I propose is that there should be no ceilings set to achievement: the hours of boredom of the quick child, inevitable in class teaching even

---

[1] e.g., by Wallach & Kogan, *Modes of Thinking in Young Children*, esp. Ch. 1

within careful streaming, in order to keep everyone together, are avoided.

(c) Special interests which cannot be sufficiently canvassed in IDE are allowed for in "orbit." It may well be that the very gifted will spend more time in orbital work than others and still make a contribution to the shared studies. For some outstanding pupils with specialized talents orbital work will certainly include spending extra time outside the school. The problem of support for exceptional aptitudes in music or mathematics, for instance, has no established answer. Special boarding schools are one possibility, but within the general run of schooling only plans of the kinds I propose can begin to meet the needs of such children—and they do so without removing them from their fellows.

(d) Giftedness may take the form of an extreme specialism or of a wide synoptic interest. The budding specialist finds his opportunity in gearing IDE, Autonomous Studies, and Special-interest Studies towards his specialism, keeping abreast with the teachers' guidance of other matters, or even falling behind and using the Remedial provision to pick up something he has unduly neglected. The student with broader interests and aptitudes has an opportunity of habitually thinking big, of seeing to an extent greater than most of his peers how different ploys by different clusters of children complement each other. At last he is able to extend himself, and learn greater skill in systemic thinking. This is the talent he offers to the world. At present, in the fragmented, teacher-directed timetable, he has no opportunity to exercise it, to learn to hold a group of variables constant while he examines the implications of varying them, or to see inter-relationships within complex systems. It is the child with this kind of gift also who will most profit by inter-disciplinary studies, for he more than others can become aware of the differences in assumptions, structure, and way of behaving of the various disciplines. This is important not only for him personally; in adult life it should make possible far richer inter-disciplinary and inter-professional exchange than is usual today.

(e) One of the disadvantages of conventional schooling for the talented youngster is that he not only has to jump in the style the others jump but he cannot programme his own hurdles. The opportunities for self-programmed work involved in every phase of the fourfold curriculum are particularly important for the gifted.

(f) Within a situation of collaborative learning many gifted children who are uncomfortably aware of being different from others, who might well be disliked because envied by others as being too good to be true, can be made welcome. The teacher does not expect to know everything. Competition is not encouraged between pupils. The gifted threaten no-one. Many gifted people look back at school as a time not only of boredom but almost of ostracism (unless they were safeguarded by leadership in games, for instance). Either they were too far ahead within an age-group, or under the system of promotion by achievement they were socially too immature for the older people with whom they were placed.

(g) Since one of the tasks of the teacher as grouping specialist is to help pupils to cluster together because their talents are complementary, he can see to it that there is very fruitful cooperation between, for instance, the inventor, the designer, and the "maintainer" or scholar who is quick at research and collecting together material necessary for synthesis; or between the child with new ideas in technical studies and one with manual dexterity; or between the person with an intuitive leap to the outlines of a creative idea and the person with "ideational fluency,"[1] who can put flesh on the bones. This is true "mixed ability grouping."

(h) Similarly, one of the disadvantages of streaming has been that, on the whole, the richer and more imaginative work, though less correct, in creative writing and dramatic improv-

---

[1] To use a term of J. P. Guilford

ization and in discussion of human problems has often been produced by the lower stream. The work of children in upper streams can often be more punctilious in performance but less adventurous, and at times emotionally superficial. Such children will do well to be with pupils who are less academically gifted but have greater emotional resonance, perhaps are less inhibited, and who may be able to encourage them to rest with greater confidence in symbolic, allusive modes of thought instead of the discursive, impersonal style into which the upper streams tend to withdraw. Here again we glimpse a new, more positive interpretation of what heterogenous grouping could stand for.

(i) However, even with conventional criteria for heterogenous grouping it is important to recognize that for children accustomed to group work it is not only the less talented who profit by "pairing" for part of their work—as the work of Dr. Amaria et al. has shown: "Comparisons between groups showed that heterogenous grouping was better both for high and low I.Q. subjects than either homogeneous pairs or individual work."[1]

The explanation appears to be in part at least connected with the more careful analysis that this kind of working demands of the gifted child: " . . . it appears that brighter individuals working alone or in pairs do not give as much attention to the relationships which they need to perceive as those who are 'teaching' the less bright members of the pairs."

(j) It is not only in the major decisions about programming his studies that the gifted child should prosper. Even more important, perhaps, is the opportunity to develop rhythms of work appropriate to him. Almost the most damaging of our present practices is that teachers decide to which grindstone which nose is to be attached at any one time. The more individuated the child the more he needs freedom to heed the rhythm of involvement and withdrawal of creative work and also to develop different dominant motifs in his studies.

[1] Amaria, Biran, and Leith, op. cit., p. 7

(k) Throughout this book I have for simplicity used the masculine pronouns, even though many of the schools with whom we cooperate are girls' schools. Perhaps here the special plight of the "high creative" girls, noted by Wallach and Kogan[1] again deserves a special mention, for it seems that they need especially the support to be got from recognition and acknowledgment of their kinds of gifts.

(ii) *Retarded Learners*

Here again my remarks on a subject which is the study of many experts all over the world must be confined to the broad question of the profit they should draw from the more flexible and less judgmental schooling we propose.

One of the worst dis-services of the Newsom Report[2] was that it confirmed teachers in their tendency to label children, rather than demanding that we diagnose the reasons why individual children do not perform well in school. We are wise, in thinking of retardation, to treat native intelligence or the lack of it as a theoretical construct we should not concern ourselves with. We work more effectively where we see failing children as our failure not theirs. "No failed children, only failed teachers" would be a salutary adaptation of an old cliché.

Whatever the diagnosis may be, one prescription is a prerequisite for the working of any other: all children need a massive experience of success if they are to go confidently through adolescence, and those for whom there is no easy school success to compensate for other difficulties in growing up need it more than any. Difficulties may be expressed in a generalized detachment,[3] likely to stem from early parental deprivation[3] or they may be specific to school learning,

[1] *Modes of Thinking in Young Children*
[2] *Half our Future* (H.M.S.O., 1964)
[3] "Indeed, detachment may be regarded as the cardinal symptom of mental retardation." D. Russell Davis, "The role of Psychiatry—I: Theory and Practice," in M. L. Kellmer Pringle, ed., *Investment in Children* (Longmans Green and Co., 1965), p. 108

taking the form of a dumb hopelessness which may be attributed to previous failure, to settling for low expectations as a way of avoiding future disappointment, as later in seeking a wife or husband. They may on the other hand be due to contempt for a whole system of values which seems meaningless and irrelevant to life on the street corner.[1] Whatever the source of retardation, "a massive area of personal success, subjectively valid"[2] is the schools' first essential prescription. In fact we are in the happy position of doctors of the past with blood-letting or today with antibiotics, who do not require precise analysis of the fever to take the first steps of cure, which in our case is to ensure the reward of success.

Success in the remedial class at the bottom of a vast hierarchy of superior children and teachers above them is not success. Success is being accepted for what you can offer and for what you are in the common collaboration of the school. For this reason, as well as others, it is desirable that the focus-group, at least in the first years of secondary schooling, should include a teacher with experience of remedial teaching, in its conventional sense. This teacher can primarily look after the needs of the weaker performers in the unstreamed work, ensuring success by ensuring that assignments within enquiries are at a suitable level, and giving direct support through difficulties in making choices and planning work. But he will also help, and be seen by these pupils to help, other pupils with their difficulties as they arise. One of the reasons I recommend the use of the term "remedial" for the phase of the curriculum concerned with the special needs of all pupils is to ensure this kind of continuum of experience throughout a school. Moreover, although in theory the occasional difficulties of most children can be met by the separate specialists

---

[1] cf. F. Riessman, *The Culturally Deprived Child* (Harper and Row, New York, 1962). Writing of U.S. culturally deprived families, Riessman says "There is practically no interest in knowledge for its own sake; quite the contrary, a pragmatic anti-intellectualism prevails. Nor is education seen as an opportunity for the development of self-expression, self-realization, growth, and the like; consequently, progressive approaches are opposed.' (p. 12)
[2] Fifth Report, p. 57

in the conventional school, I think we all know that practice is not so satisfactory. The more backward children will *also*, of course, be clients of the Remedial section for part of their school day.

Imaginative "remedial teachers" of the conventional sense will not be surprised to find that a child who is weak in reading, writing, and computation, and who on those grounds has been in a low stream, can often contribute original and sensible ideas to planning and discussion. (I have in the back of my mind as I write this the contrast I saw one afternoon in a thirteen-stream comprehensive school. The top stream of twelve-year-olds were undergoing a formal French grammar lesson into which my graduate student had retreated in panic in her first week of practice and which a lower stream would not have stood for. The bottom stream were engaged in an interesting and important discussion of the concept of mercy.) Weak students become more fully members of a mixed ability group than the over-protective teacher would have thought possible. On the other hand, if they find acceptance and success in spending part of their time on chores that others are glad to have done for them, it is still acceptance and success: minding tape-recorders, mixing paints, is routine work that is much more interesting and useful than much that goes on in lower streams, and should be accepted for itself and also for the by-product of satisfaction that it can bring. If a student makes this offer he should be welcomed. In an unstreamed situation the more backward child is spared the indignity of spending ten vital years of his early experience as an acknowledged outcast. But his contribution in ideas and helpfulness can bring the more positive reward of acceptance. It is no wonder that schools as they unstream report one after the other that the "lower stream type" has "disappeared." (One teacher reported of the unstreaming of first year forms that this had created a good deal of discomfiture among the prefects, an alarming glimpse into the satisfaction they would have derived from knowing whom to despise.)

Moreover writing is not the only form of communication,

nor are words always necessary. The use of tape-recorders and camera work are likewise important and often more appropriate for creative work. This is not to suggest that the literacy skills are unimportant. They may cease to be essential over the years, but for the foreseeable future they are still vital if people are to be able to go on learning, to meet the challenge of retraining and of understanding the world about them. That there should be so much functional illiteracy at the secondary stage is a shocking reflection of the low expectancies that some primary schools have had. The point here is that such difficulties need not cut children off from the exchange of ideas in IDE, and the exchange of ideas may be for some the key to advance in the skills. Moreover, the contact with more able children, which is advantageous to better performers, is significantly valuable for the weaker also:

> [In the heterogeneous pairs] the less bright members . . . profited greatly by the procedure and must have been obliged to grasp the ideas by the persistence of their colleagues. It may be suggested that less intelligent children often suffer in school learning situations not so much from incapacity to learn structures and use them as from an inability to understand or perceive clearly at the input side of learning.[1]

Finally the Special-interests cell of the curriculum may be the route through which a potentially talented child discovers his potential. We all know of occasional cases where an opportunity to play a trumpet or become the agreed expert in some phase of work has been the spring that has released energy and talent none had suspected and has led to advances none would have thought possible. Perhaps if there were more flexibility in the basic planning of the school's life such cases would be more commonplace than they are. All that we know of the effect on progress of environment and expectation, and all we can suppose of the special sensitiveness to environment and expectation of some imaginative children, would lead us to expect just this.

[1] Amaria, Biran, and Leith, op. cit., p. 7

B. CHILDREN UNDER SOCIAL HANDICAP

In racing, we handicap the strong. In education, we handicap the weak. The educational system has been used in this country not to counteract disadvantage, but to confirm it. Selection was a technique for exclusion from true opportunity of those whose language, expectations, and social behaviour put them at an immediate disadvantage. Streaming takes over where selection left off. Another factor, the broken-down schools in slum neighbourhoods, strongly attacked by the Newsom Report in its excellent third chapter, are still with us, although now some action is beginning on a national scale. Even though comprehensive school areas are so planned as to draw on socially mixed districts, primary schools are primarily neighbourhood schools. If in the primary school the battle to compensate for educational disadvantage has been lost, or not even joined, the secondary school will find it difficult to make a fresh start possible. In fact, most of the backward children I have been writing about are socially handicapped.

Many of the problems of a socially divided country with great minorities of wealth and standards of living are beyond the scope of the school to solve. However, there are some additional safeguards that schools can set up (and many do) to ensure that social handicap is ameliorated as far as possible. To identify children with special needs of this kind, a school needs to develop a habit of systematically looking for those children who are likely to be at risk: these will include, for instance, children of large families, who are likely to be near to or below the poverty line[1] but also even in prosperous families are likely to need extra help with language. They will obviously include children of dissolute or non-coping parents and institutionalized children. Truancy needs to be taken very seriously in such a system, not only because of the evidence

---

[1] cf. Brian Abel-Smith and Peter Townsend, *The Poor and the Poorest*, Occasional Papers on Social Administration, No. 17 (G. Bell & Sons, London, 1965), pp. 40-1. The research reported on showed that "about $2\frac{1}{4}$ million or 17 per cent. of all children in the United Kingdom" were in low-income households, also that "over a quarter of the households with six or more persons had low incomes."

that it is likely to lead on to delinquency, but also because it may be the first sign, as indeed is a sudden change of behaviour within the school, of family difficulties which may need the assistance of other social agencies. Lesser disturbances in family life, or the great ones such as being orphaned, can create difficulties which the isolated teacher does not even notice and may therefore greatly accentuate by some unintentional severity which in the circumstances is felt as cruelty.

It is one of the functions of the focus-group and the welfare service of the school, however that service is planned, to look out for changes. They need also to observe the kinds of lifestyle which a child may have set up owing to some much less obvious difficulty such as his rank order in the family, for which steady compensatory support may be needed. One of the valuable pieces of work of the third Pilot Course for Experienced Teachers, which was attended also by two experienced social workers, was to provide from their experience a comprehensive list of social handicaps in this broad sense.[1] Add to this list which includes the kind of difficulty that can come from losing a parent, being a late-comer in a large family, an only child, or one with a thrusting younger sibling, and so on, some more detailed list of environmental variables connected directly with support for intellectual effort (facts which may not always be available, but which can be guessed at in most cases) and the school begins to have an adequate outlook for recognizing social handicap as it affects educational performance. R. M. Wolf's research study lists thirteen such variables:

A. Press for Achievement Motivation.
    1. Nature of intellectual expectations of child.
    2. Nature of intellectual aspirations for child.
    3. Amount of information about child's intellectual development.
    4. Nature of awards for intellectual development.

[1] Third Report, pp. 7-15

B. Press for Language Development.
  5. Emphasis on use of language in a variety of situations.
  6. Opportunities provided for enlarging vocabulary.
  7. Emphasis on correctness of usage.
  8. Quality of language models available.

C. Provision for General Learning.
  9. Opportunities provided for learning in the home.
  10. Opportunities for learning outside the home (excluding school).
  11. Availability of learning supplies.
  12. Availability of books (including reference works), periodicals, and library facilities.
  13. Nature and amount of assistance provided to facilitate learning in a variety of situations.[1]

The provisions of the collaborative school are appropriate for these suffering from social handicap, and so are the attitudes that we have to learn towards all children, a patient attention to the *cues* by which they reveal their real *concerns*, which according to the Elementary Schools Teaching Project undertaken by the Ford Foundation are likely to be anxieties about identity, about their ability to connect with the world about them, about their hope of controlling their environment.[2] These are the concerns of other young people also. The problem of special social handicaps is their intensity and (alas) the justified doubts of these young people as to whether they will ever be able to become themselves, ever be acceptable, ever command their lives. It is not that they require special curriculum, special grouping, but they do require special patience, "a non-judgmental attitude," "for teachers must not feel personally affronted or lose confidence where there is disruption or regression or no sign of immediate results."[3] Their presence in a school must spark off a recognition that:

[1] R. M. Wolf (unpublished dissertation), University of Chicago, quoted in B. S. Bloom, *Stability and Change in Human Characteristics* (John Wiley and Sons, 1964)
[2] G. Weinstein et al., *A Strategy for Developing Relevant Content for Disadvantaged Children*
[3] Third Report, p. 23

a school must be viewed, in some sense, as a social welfare agency:
1. Information about each child should be collected, recorded and known by those working with him.
2. Risk situations of a minor character should be dealt with and support given.
3. There must be an awareness of the necessity to recognize when skilled help is required so that early referral to social agencies outside the school can be made.

Rather than persisting with

> discussion of the latest exploits of certain notorious pupils or of the children from notorious families . . . it can be more helpful if the idea of holding "case conferences" on problem children and their families is accepted in the School. Difficult or unresponsive behaviour is less threatening to the individual teacher if it can be openly discussed, reasons sought, and some policy on treatment be agreed. A record of the proceedings of these meetings should always be kept for review and for reference.[1]

These "case conferences" can well become the basis of cooperation in school with workers in other social agencies where difficulties have arisen or are expected by the other agencies, but they would be only extensions in the school of the regular case conferences which should be held on all students (see page 224). Once a school is concerned with the full wellbeing of all its pupils exceptionally difficult cases do not require a special system, but simply a more intensive use of the basic care system of the school.

It would be good to be able to say that little change would be involved. But there are too many schools where "the Newsom children" are despised and rejected of men, or are the subject of a special benevolence which marks them off no less effectively from those who truly belong in the school and to whom the school accordingly belongs, for us to engage in such easy optimism. Some teachers will undoubtedly find the retreat from judgment to which I have already referred, and which the Third Pilot Course Report emphasizes, gravely difficult. It is partly this, as well as a recognition of the need for

[1] Third Report, pp. 25-6

far better systems of recording and discussion with all teachers if all teachers are to be truly responsible members of a social agency, that leads me to stress here the importance of this kind of orderly professionalism, which by involving the less imaginative and sympathetic in the mechanics of welfare can help them to change their viewpoint gradually and without loss of dignity.

C. THE EDUCATION OF NEWCOMERS

If I suggest that education of first generation immigrants does not present us with new kinds of problems or with problems of a greater degree than we have already (except in the field of basic linguistic competence in English) it is not because I take the difficulties lightly, but because I believe they may blind us to the continuing injustice of our behaviour to other children, also "outsiders" in the established middle-class culture of the school system.

In the centres of some of our cities, previous waves of immigrants, including non-Caucasians, have simply been integrated into the undisturbed deprivation of the lower working class. In other places, it is the size and vigour of the new wave of immigration which makes it difficult for schools and other people to lose them without trace in the convenient maw of our class system. For it seems that this is the most convenient category that most English people, and doubtless many teachers, have of making their arrival comprehensible, if not acceptable. This extension of the class system to absorb coloured immigrants in particular has recently been recognized by references to the dangers of creating a new "underclass." In the context of our cosy satisfaction with social divisiveness, government advice to limit immigrants to 30 per cent of a school population has a faintly ludicrous air.

There are differences, of course, which make the problems of immigrants particularly painful, and may well lead to increasing social unrest, but none of these should be so difficult in the collaborative school as in more conventional institutions. The answers to some key questions arise out of the established ethos of the school:

Should immigrants (mostly of Indian and Pakistani parentage) who have difficulties with the English language be kept in special classes, especially "admission classes"?

—Like other groups with special needs, they should spend as much time as possible in common work, but their special needs should be met, preferably by a full-time or visiting teacher who knows their first language, in the Remedial and Special-interest phases of school. If at all possible a teacher or teacher's aide who knows the language should also be with them in IDE and Autonomous Studies. Any school with imagination and access to a specialist teacher will already have considered offering for C.S.E. or G.C.E. the literature or language which is native to any pupils who take their culture of birth seriously.

Should the curriculum be different for a school with a large number of immigrants?

—A healthy school should examine itself and should use matters that are seen to be relevant for pupils as a basis for their inter-disciplinary studies. It is important for all pupils to learn to see each other in terms of individual recognition, not of stereotype. This is what really matters, and honest group discussion is fundamental to the life of a school which includes immigrants as in any other. A comparative study of the culture, geographical background, and so on, of the countries of origin of all its pupils (including England, Wales, Scotland, and Ireland) might well be central to IDE at any age. Beyond this, a school which recognizes the importance of working through relative strengths will ensure that immigrant children have opportunities to display and exploit their natural or cultural strengths (such as the physical grace and vitality of many West Indians or their dramatic intensity).

Should the school (whether it includes pupils of colour or not) study the concept of race?

—No, and the proposal that they should do so in the Schools

Council document entitled *Society and the Young School Leaver*[1] is a very dangerous one which should not be proceeded with without a great deal of research. There is far too much likelihood that what will happen will be that race and colour will become more salient in the perception of pupils, black or Caucasian pink. What is required is the study of the great problems all human beings share, and within that the recognition that different cultures propose different solutions to them. It is certainly right, too, that native English and other British students should come to understand the part that their ancestors played through enslavement in creating some of the special cultural attitudes of West Indians.

Should the school try to affect the behaviours of immigrant children where these differ from English behaviours?

—Schools are becoming far more well-informed than they were about such cultural differences, and are well aware that a distinction of great importance has to be drawn between those immigrant groups where there is a desire for total integration and those who disapprove of many English institutions, such as our marriage arrangements and the position of women. In helping West Indian children, for instance, to moderate their voices[2] or control their hair in our climate, teachers are helping them to do what they themselves wish—to make themselves more acceptable socially and thereby more at home. On the other hand, where there are important cultural differences, as with Indian, Pakistani, some Jewish, and some Cypriot children, the school has no right to interfere except in so far as a modus vivendi is worth aiming at if pupils from these homes are to have a rather wider experience than might otherwise be possible, as for instance by taking Indian girls on outings where no men or boys will be involved.

Should the school make special efforts to meet parents or guardians of immigrant children?

—As with other parents, the school needs to support parents

---
[1] Working Paper No. 11, p. 77.
[2] Now, of course (1971), many West Indian young people are rediscovering, and therefore wish to preserve, their cultural identity.

by relieving their fears and encouraging them about their children's progress. Always, a partnership between home and school is likely to be beneficial.

The expectations of immigrant families may very well be different from those of most native English families which find it difficult to understand the ethos of the school or to cooperate with their children's teacher. Parents of many immigrant children coming from countries with rigid and conventional school systems are very different from the culturally deprived socially rejected or feckless parents of children under social handicap; in fact, they are much more akin to the extreme status-dissenters among English parents, for the problem can often be that the parents' expectations of school are far more severe than the school's own views. Clearly, it is advisable for a school not only to seek to make itself understood in individual families but to seek out the leaders of the different ethnic groups and invite their cooperation as intermediaries. This is usually much more easily done for groups, other than West Indians, which are well organized and have their own cultural leaders. Part of the difficulty of West Indian groups is their loss of the established social control by the extended family—granny is often left behind and the young mother does not have her support or that of other relations. Here more direct advice is likely to be needed.

I have chosen questions that are examples only of the many which need to be answered and which present constantly changing difficulties to schools. But I hope that they are sufficient to make the point that the difficulties are different in degree rather than in kind from those of English subcultures that are alien to the expectations of a meritocratic ethic. The problems of immigrant children are not easy, but they are anything but uniform. In fact, each immigrant subculture has greater similarity to some English counterpart than it has to many other groups of immigrants. Experienced and sympathetic teachers are well aware that the problems of cooperating with immigrant families are as diverse as are those of cooperating with native English ones.

Chapter 8

Evaluation, Appraisal, and Counselling

A SCHOOL HAS two independent tasks in the field of evaluation and appraisal which are all too often confused: evaluating its curriculum and appraising its students.

1. EVALUATION OF CURRICULUM

At present a school's results in public examinations are often looked to as a way of evaluating its curriculum. Indeed examinations are the nation's traditional method of quality control. To rely on them for this purpose is damaging not only because of the known inadequacy of our examination techniques but also because of the way they distort the work of any school which bases its self-concept on this kind of achievement. So long as the nation uses public examinations as its means of certification at 16 and 18, it is an essential part of the school's care for its students to prepare them well. But good schools are well aware that to use these examinations to evaluate the school's curriculum is to denigrate or ignore important aspects of its work, as for instance the studies of pupils not entering examinations and the unexamined work, such as minority work in sixth forms, of those who are preparing for public certification.

At present the only valid means that a school has for evaluating its curriculum in comparison with that of other schools are the standardized attainment tests. So long as teachers do not suppose that these tests have anything to say about individuals except when used diagnostically, standardized tests undertaken by a year-group can be a useful occasional guide to those who want a rough estimate of how their pupils' average attainment compares with the sample used in standardizing these national tests. Of course the school's cohort is bound to be skewed by external factors, but cautiously interpreted these tests can be useful to a group of teachers working with a year-group.

Unfortunately, the standardized tests available at the moment are limited in what they test as attainment. Undoubtedly one of the tasks facing those engaged in a new and more open kind of schooling will be to engage with test and measurement experts to devise new kinds of attainment tests. Before this can be done, they will need to formulate with precision the kinds of behaviours that they wish to evaluate. This will require in turn two prior stages, a first during which they work reflectively, keeping careful records of the kinds of requirements that they find emerging in process, and a second which sets up close collaboration in research projects among a number of schools with psychometrists, through which they formulate their criteria with refinement and coherence.

It is regrettable that development of new curricula has lagged behind the psychometrists' development of highly sophisticated techniques for evaluation. Nevertheless, it does not follow that those who are engaged in this developmental work should feel hampered, even guilty, because they are not yet ready to say which aspects of a highly diversified curriculum should have priority in a new scheme of evaluation.

For the time being, teachers working in new curricula have to trust their subjective impression (which they undoubtedly have) that the model which they are developing is satisfactory. They will do well also to invite observers less committed than they to report impartially and informally on classroom work in progress and on contact they have with pupils, and either among themselves or with such observers to devise simple internal tests as a feedback to guide them in their explorations of curriculum.

2. APPRAISAL AND COUNSELLING OF STUDENTS

Far more fundamental to the well-being of the pupil in the school is that teachers should evolve good techniques for the appraisal of the individual. A group of experienced teachers reports: "The charge most memorably and bitterly made against their schools by the young workers we interviewed was that 'our teachers didn't know us'—or worse—'our teachers didn't *want* to know us' ... If the young themselves can so directly put the finger on the central weak spot in their schooling, we can at least be guided by them."[1] If one does not have good tools one is not likely to enjoy a task or to be deeply involved in it, and it is arguable that it is the inadequacy of our arrangements for appraisal as much as any harshness or indifference which leads to the failures in contact of which these young people complained.

Any consideration of appraisal in the collaborative school must be based on a firm foundation of personal concern with the growth of persons. In this chapter the values expressed earlier in the book are taken for granted. It is not enough to be well-intentioned; we need also to be skilful. The whole scene of collaborative learning is one intended to help teachers to perceive their students more clearly through a more intimate and friendly complex of relationships with them than anything the traditional schooling makes possible. But this will still be at the level of personal "hunch," and perhaps in some cases meagre and uncomprehending, unless the school sets about also to create effective records and closer networks of communication *about* its students than those we have today. They are in an advantageous position, for whereas the old-fashioned curriculum required the individual teacher to focus on large groups of students, the modern curriculum enables groups of teachers to collaborate in observing individual characteristics and progress.[2] In this situation the subjectivity of diverse individual teachers has positive value.

[1] K. Rudge in Fourth Report
[2] For the work of the focus-group of teachers see pp. 235ff.

A. THE PRESENT SITUATION—*another caricature?*

The proposals that follow are not such as to add to the work of the teacher in an English school, with his very heavy teaching schedule, but should permit him to deploy his energies more fruitfully. The present state of affairs is not satisfactory.

(i) *Day-to-day appraisal*

The present ethos and practice of the school demands that teachers spend a great deal of time "marking" work. Much of this marking would be better done by the pupil himself. Much would be better not done at all, for a reason of principle: since it is based on quantification of diverse individuals' attainments at identical pieces of work it draws the student's and teacher's attention away from diagnosing strengths and weaknesses to placing against imaginary standards. Much of it would better not be done at all because it is badly done: English teachers are appallingly ignorant of the requirements of properly objective teacher-made tests. They happily impute values to the questions composing a test, although this can be done properly only by comparison with a large and carefully selected sample of students' work. They also attribute marks to answers given in tests, essays, and so on on the basis of the subjective impressions of the individual teacher. It is quite arguable that a group of teachers (perhaps with the advice of the students themselves) giving their impressions of work provide as good a guess as any as to the promise of development and the continuing needs indicated by students' essay-type answers; but this is not what happens. In practice in the daily life of the school, the pupil is at the mercy of the subjective impressions of one individual working in isolation, who may be quite out of sympathy with his cognitive style, the values he expresses, and his personality.

(ii) *School examinations*

As if the falsity engendered by these ineffectual markings of classroom tests and homework were not enough, at the end of each term, or twice a year, "internal examinations" are held, which ritualize our daily errors. The marking of these examinations is quantified, in order that the marks can be added up, in order that a rank order of pupils throughout the spectrum of school lessons can be obtained (although there are anomalies here: music included but not art, or vice versa, and so on). The whole cavort might be thought to be haphazard and disingenuous. It is, however, haphazard and ingenuous, and this is professionally more heinous, for students really believe these values that we place upon them, because we have faith in them ourselves. It is here that the self-fulfilling prophecy operates, in the heart of the school's cataloguing system. (A colleague of mine having made, late at night, a mistake in his sums made an elaborate chart in which one pupil was placed near the top of his class's rank order when he should have been in the middle: next term that pupil was near the top, in all subjects.)

The internal examination is one of the ways in which we encourage conformity and damage potential. The whole occasion has a solemnity, a ritual of observance, which must suggest to the child that the results have meaning, that, even if he is not being "known" as our school leavers asked to be known (see page 214), he is at least being assessed by people who know what they are doing. Again, we celebrate the presence of an emperor who isn't there.

(iii) *School reports*

Finally, the system of reports for parents requires teachers termly or annually to add to these lists of marks some well-considered comments on the pupil's progress. Either they know a great deal more than can be whittled down to a phrase or two, or (and this applies especially to those who see an individual child only once a week) they have far too superficial an acquaintance to justify arbitrary statements. But we perform the ritual. The form teacher, who in fact may see very little of the child if he teaches him only occasionally or not at all, comments yet again. A tutor who knows a little of his work may add a comment of some value. The head's signature shows that he accepts responsibility for this strange *ragout*. The document is sent to the parents—and no-one, not child, not parent, not teacher, is very much the wiser.

B. AN INTERIM PROPOSAL

It is beyond my competence to forecast the new developments of appraisal which could emerge from a close partnership in research projects of experienced teachers with psychologists specializing in the study of personality and with experts in tests and measurement. At present, all we can look for, and it will be a vast improvement on what we have had until now, is a simple appraisal system which makes use of teachers' perceptions of students and students' self-perceptions, while openly admitting their subjectivity. What we need are records which help us to look at the child in the round on a spot-check basis and also to recognize changes in his behaviour.

A fourfold model

In all future plans, we can expect a fourfold system to be valuable, which will have a place for four elements of appraisal. These are:

1. Observing the child here and now:
   (*a*) his performance on tasks (both self-imposed and required); and
   (*b*) the kinds of cognitive, affective, and psychomotor behaviours that he evinces; and their inter-relationships, which are our guide to who he is.

2. Mapping his development:
   (a) the changes in his performances at tasks; and
   (b) the changes in the kinds of behaviours that he evinces; and their changing inter-relationships, which are our guide to who he is becoming.

In all these cells, there is a place for the student's self-appraisal.

A note on self-appraisal

In learning to understand a little better what he *is*, and why he does what he does, and who he might become, we shall be denying ourselves the perceptions of a good pair of eyes (potentially the best if he has retained or learned a sustaining confidence in himself and his own judgment) if we ignore the student's own appraisal of himself. Self-appraisal is helpful not only in itself but in the cognitive dissonance set up for teachers and pupil between the pupil's own assessment of himself and his teachers', which should create an important stimulus to his self-understanding and growth as well as to their understanding of him. Similarly it is in the diagnostic discussion of students' work with them, in which we can invite them to appraise their own performance and their development over a period of time, that students increasingly become close partners in programming their own education. This tutorial relationship is, of course, familiar to all good teachers. My point is that the conditions of collaborative learning make it easier to apply it widely than when the teacher works through class teaching methods, and that this advantage will not be fully exploited unless the child's own viewpoint on himself and his work is seen as a necessary component of the school's appraisal records. In the long run of his life, after all, and at every instant, it is what he knows, feels and believes about himself that is important for him, and it is our task through our faith in him to help him to secure his faith in himself in the process of his self-enquiry.

In the fourfold model each cell is important. If we emphasize the dynamic cells, 2(a) and (b), at the expense of observing the child as he is here and now, we shall find ourselves over-emphasizing our predictions of the future. It is unlikely with our present traditions that we shall emphasize what the child brings to a learning situation, 1(b), and his general personality development, 2(b), at the expense of noting his performance, 1(a) and 2(a), but to do so would be to evade our prime responsibility for children's learning; and indeed there is some precedent for this in the attitude of some schools to their so-called "Newsom children," pupils whom they may agree to some extent to like, but have decided to be pretty well ineducable.

The dynamic cells of the model, 2(a) and (b), build into the appraisal system two processes of great value, the concept of *trend-watching* and that of the student's *development through relative strengths*. The first process is essential if we are to have a generous enough time-scale for observing development and the second is essential for supporting and facilitating individual achievement.[1]

Finally, cells 1(b) and 2(b) should make the school's appraisal system into a flag of freedom for the individual, ensuring constantly that he is being allowed to emerge in his unique combination of traits, is being accepted as a personality and not seen simply as the sum of his performances. It is when these two cells are not sufficiently prominent in teachers' minds that the whole processing into conformity represented by ideas of "objectives for a unit of work" of which I have complained becomes possible (see pp. 87-8).

Cells 1(a) and (b)—The child here-and-now

Clearly the quality of our whole appraisal system cannot be better than the quality of our observation of the child here and now. Cell 1(a), our observation of task-performance, will have to be a good deal more sophisticated than it has been in the

---

[1] L. A. Smith describes these concepts, which he had used in appraisal for many years in Second Report, pp. 46-55

past. Standardized attainment tests have their place in this cell, but only if they are used diagnostically. To use them as evidence of anything more than what the child's strengths and weaknesses were at the particular moment of the test is to misuse them as we once misused the I.Q. test, when we supposed it to reveal to us the secret of a child's potential. Used diagnostically, to note for instance whether he succeeds in items drawing on higher mental processes or relies mainly on memory-recall, or in combination with an I.Q. test as a cross-check of attainment which might have been expected at the time against that observed in specific tests of reading and so on, they have value. On the other hand, these tests are not so important that taking them should be ritualized into public occasions. They are better related to a phased observation of individual students than executed *en masse*.

Attainment on standardized publicly available tests can safely be quantified, so long as the quantification is subsidiary to a diagnostic purpose. All appraisal other than this will have to be verbally formulated, and this is helpful because it ensures that the teacher's subjectivity is acknowledged. In these other kinds of appraisal we can be far more imaginative than is usual in schools today, looking to guided discussion and to role-playing for instance, if retrospective examinations are required for any reason.

In a very free situation such as IDE/M demands, which is the desideratum of the whole Fourfold Curriculum, appraisal of students' performance will largely be in terms of their performance at tasks they have chosen themselves. This obviates the whole notion of identical testing of different individuals. Hence teachers find themselves free to attend, much more than they have been able to in the past, to the way in which in their daily work pupils set about choosing tasks, identifying problems, planning their work, communicating their findings through various media, and seeing how one piece of work leads on to others or relates to the proceedings of other clusters of children. It is in this process of observation, incidentally, far more than through retrospective analysis, that they are able to note the individual contributions of pupils to common enterprises. Once the work is complete, if group process has been satisfactory, it should not be either easy or important to undertake that kind of analysis.

I realize of course that apart from performance at standardized attainment tests, the distinction between cells 1(*a*) and 1(*b*) should not be overdrawn. It is impossible to say of any one child in any series of situations whether, for instance, he has come up with a great many ideas because the subject matter has interested him, because he believed he was being successful, because he had done a great deal of work, or because he is a person gifted with "ideational fluency." For this reason a school's appraisal sheets cannot be divided into two halves, one indicating behaviour in school processes and the other suggesting characteristics which it seems that the child brings to any situation he enters. I believe, however, that if we do not make determined efforts to look for these characteristics we may miss them, and hence the child, altogether.

Cell 1(*b*) is the one for which we have least precedent, and which creates the most difficult problem. My suggestions can only be quite tentative. In part the problems are similar to those of Cell 1(*a*), namely to choose, from a wide selection of possibilities, which traits should be noticed and recorded. The difference is that when we look at the aspects of behaviour which together suggest personality traits (which we certainly need to recognize and respect and which would help us to understand a pupil's performance at school tasks) there is an additional difficulty of choosing models to generate the questions we should ask. A use of a Bloom model, for instance, would be very fruitful, but it would give us a very different outcome from a model, such as that of Guilford, which emphasizes different cognitive styles.

To take one or two concepts out of context from several psychologists' theoretical models would be to remove them from the theory that makes them meaningful, and which they summarize. This would be quite improper. Yet to use more than one model in its entirety at a time would require an appraisal sheet so elaborate that it would not be used. My feeling at present is, therefore, that teachers should agree a series of lenses to be used over a period of a year or so. At times they may use a home grown scheme which might be based, for instance, on ranges of observed behaviours arising from the ideas of *enquiry*, *making*, and *dialogue*, or it might consist of the traits they find through diaries and anecdotal records that they do in fact observe (supplemented and modified according to conscience). At times they can use more formal three-dimensional models or taxonomies, such as those of Guilford and of Bloom, (but not limited to these of course).

One aspect of each student which should recur through the years is a note of the kinds of work situation in which he seems to prosper. This would include observation of whether he works best at times in isolation or prefers continuing collaboration, of what part he plays most readily in collaborative work, whether he is most at ease "inventing," "designing," or "maintaining," and in what circumstances he seems to dry up and prefer to "do" what others have planned—(see page 106). It would also include notes of what material appears to "fascinate" him for "the suggestion emerges that human talent . . . can be comprehended in terms of categories of fascination."[1] Over the years of a student's life this kind of observation need not be arduous, and would ensure that aspects of him once noted could be kept at the forefront of teachers' minds in the future.

The problem remains of the format of the appraisal sheet. A suggestion made by Edwin Mason and myself has been used by some schools to their satisfaction.[2] This was a grid similar to those used for assessing attainment in terms of objectives, with a note across the top of behaviours (which would, as I have now suggested, vary from time to time), and the children's names listed down the left-hand side.

---

[1] This important suggestion of Franklin J. Shaw is developed in Sidney M. Jourard and Dan C. Overlade, edd., *Reconciliation: A Theory of Man Transcending* (D. van Nostrand, 1966), Ch. 6, pp. 63-76
[2] Second Report, pp. 48-9

One feature of this sheet seemed to us important: we suggested that only positively desirable behaviours (including cognitive, affective, and psychomotor) should be noted. The teacher would put in ticks or letters as these behaviours were noted. Our belief was that if teachers are to work through relative strengths it is not desirable to complicate this sheet with failures or deviance, which can be amply described in anecdotal records.

If each teacher has a copy of the same sheet, with the behaviours that are being looked for agreed beforehand by a focus-group of teachers (although the individual teacher has space to add others with which he is specially preoccupied) profiles begin to emerge that are a great deal more revealing than anything we have had in the past. When they are compared, or transferred to cumulative sheets, several things happen. Some children's behaviours have barely been noticed, and it then becomes a task for the group to see whether this was because all the tasks given have been beyond them or because of their being rather unnoticeable children, of the kind whose reports in the traditional system would have been largely fictitious because no teacher could admit to knowing so little about them. About other children there is a strong divergence of opinion, and it then becomes part of the group-process of the focus-group to question whether this is due to the child having certain rather specific talents noted by specialists in their own field, or to problems of compatibility between teacher and student which may lead to a halo effect, positive or negative. In either case, the sheets act as a guide to future action of the group.

These sheets are valuable aide-memoires for teachers who are involved in a continuing process of collaborative appraisal. It may be best quite rapidly to transfer them into brief summaries of children looked at in turn on a rota system.

Cells 2(a) and (b)—Trend-watching

The appraisal system includes not only the elements used but the context of their use. For the mass ritual of seasonal examinations, with the appalling pressure they involve for teachers, we should substitute a regular system of *case conferences*, in which the profiles of children selected in turn are examined in detail so that characteristics here and now and also progress and development are regularly noted. This is a year-round process. Probably two conferences a year is ample for most children, although there will be those who present special problems. For such a pupil the case conference may well be a relatively formal affair, involving the presence of social workers from outside the school interested in him or his family circumstances. As I have already suggested, the child's appraisal of himself, as well as the things noticed about him by the school and other welfare agencies is part of the evidence for a case conference. It goes without saying that his parents can be consulted, not merely informed.

The success which teachers from day to day, and also at the case conference, make of their essential task of *trend-watching* depends on the qualities of the evidence they use for their appraisal, but also on the skill and self-discipline with which they interpret the changes they notice from one case conference to another, for it is the case conference that are engaged with cells 2(a) and (b) noting the child's progress and development through time. Two temptations sit there for the purpose of being avoided: one is to suppose that comparisons of an individual's marks in successive objective attainment tests give accurate evidence of improvement or decline. They cannot be used for this purpose. The second is to suppose that it is proper to extrapolate from his past progress to the expectations we can have of him later. In watching trends we recognize that very often children traverse plateaus of learning. But they may also experience periods of actual regression. The skill and sympathy of teachers is required to estimate whether this is a valuable regression, such as may come if an adolescent has not fully lived through earlier more childish stages. (A girl I knew was rebellious only on her very last day at school on the grounds "I never have been naughty, and it's my last chance ever.") On the other hand, other cases of regression in social and in cognitive behaviours may be symptomatic of anxieties that should not go unnoticed. Finally, we have to get rid of any ideas of fixed ages for passing fixed points, for this is to neglect the need to structure learning according to the needs of the learner.

C. COUNSELLING

The primary purpose of appraisal is to make a good basis for counselling, and a secondary purpose is to make possible an effective partnership with parents on behalf of the child. The position of counsellor is little known in England. I believe we have to attribute this fact to our education having been subject-centred and vocationally biased. For the pupil has been assessed on his separate performance at different subjects, and the advice given to him as an individual has largely been in the hands of a Careers Teacher and Youth Employment Officer. In some large schools the house staff have taken over some pastoral duties, but this is very different from setting up a formal counselling system, since no special training is provided for house staff such as is given to counsellors in, say, the U.S.A. or Sweden. Since 1965 a small number of counsellors is being trained at Universities, but valuable as are the insights they should bring to the few schools they work in, this cannot be said to be a scale of undertaking which can mean that official counsellors are going to be part of the expected school staff. The same is true of teacher social-workers, although since they are normally thought to be required mainly in schools in deprived areas it is more realistic to speak of them as a practical possibility for a proportion of schools.

It cannot be any part of this book to examine in detail the very difficult question of inter-professional services in the school, but it is reasonable to look at the requirements of ordinary teachers if they are to fulfil (at any rate in some respects) the role filled in other parts of the world by welfare specialists.

If teachers have evolved an effective appraisal system they will have much of the evidence they need for counselling the individual. But they also need access to expert consultants who recognize teachers' expertise and close acquaintance with the individual child but can help them to interpret evidence in cases they find difficult to understand or to handle. Our psychological services are meagre but almost more serious is the failure of communication that schools often complain of, and it is alarming to learn that from the side of some School Psychological Services and School Welfare Departments this exclusion is deliberate.[1]

Professor John Pierce-Jones's study in the United States[2] indicated the value to teachers of having trained consultants available with whom they could discuss difficulties, rather than having the counsellor within the school meeting the children himself. Probably this for the English scene is the way through. Certainly a much closer partnership is required with all expert services than the schools have hitherto enjoyed. The problem then of cooperation with psychological and social services is two-fold: we should have teachers (or part-time workers) with sufficient specialized in-service (or possibly pre-service) training to make them competent in referral, so that students whose problems are of a kind or intensity which teachers cannot deal with or which arise from family situations can be referred. This is an important service that the school can give not only to the students themselves but to their families as well, since poor behaviour at school can be the first sign of serious disturbance in the home which social workers could alleviate. Secondly, we need to have much more support from other agencies, including psychiatric services, about

[1] cf. Margery G. Cooper, *School Refusal: An Inquiry into the part played by School and Home* (Educational Research, 1966), pp. 223 ff. "In many cases, knowledge of diagnosis and treatment was withheld from school personnel."
[2] John Pierce-Jones, *Texas Research in Child Behaviour Consultation: Conceptual Model, Experimental Strategies and Preliminary Results,* University of Texas (Mimeograph)

behaviour problems which do not require referral but which may, if badly handled, become serious.

Counselling consists mainly of the pastoral care, more fully understood now, of all the young people in the school. Although the techniques should be client-centred in the sense that students arrive at their own interpretation of their problems and their own decisions for action, it can be seen as advisory, not solely consultative; that is to say, in the day-to-day collaborative working, teachers can take the initiative when they see difficulties arising. On the other hand in a truly open situation, when teachers go around the school looking *available* to those who wish to consult them, students will tend, as in any good cafeteria system, to seek out the teacher who they feel can at that moment best help them. This is another reason that it is important to have good records easily available, since the teacher of their choice may not be well acquainted with his self-chosen clients.

In the day-to-day in-play of collaborative learning one of the new skills that teachers have to develop is to watch trends. The main use of this skill is to enable them to see how far it is possible to go in allowing students to programme their own learning, and when guidance is necessary. They should think in terms of diversified routes, for the student needs a satisfactory feedback to his efforts in learning if he is to progress through identifying his *relative strengths*. These are more important aids to progress than the attempt to plot his passing fancies: "In a child of moderate ability, his interests may be detected as those aspects of his behaviour which appear within his profile as 'relative strengths': it being assumed that interest is usually nurtured by attainment."[1]

Relative strengths are very clearly indicated by the clusters of ticks that appear on his appraisal sheet, by the diary of the work he has done, and in some cases by his use of the Special-interests cell of the curriculum. Perhaps the most important task of a focus-group is to consider how flexible they can afford

L. A. Smith, in Second Report. p. 54

to be in allowing students to programme their own work. A child may well prosper, for instance, in the literary aspects of IDE/M but continue to flinch at using mathematical language. A focus-group in its early days is likely to hustle the child into approved routes too quickly, until it has allowed itself the experience of seeing how satisfactorily students in fact come to fill gaps in their programme, once they have experienced the success they need. A more confident focus-group is able to agree more readily to leave the student on his chosen tack and then find ways of phasing in mathematics through the Remedial Section, having shown him that it is useful to him; or they may decide to leave this particular child for a long time to follow his own route, because temperamentally it is important for him, or because there are such difficulties in his life at the moment that it would be very wrong to add to its harshness challenges that he has shown us he does not feel up to meeting. One of the functions, after all, of the Remedial Section is to allow children quickly to work through programmes they need, either in small groups or independently, as the need becomes plain to them through the process of their work or because of some new ambition they develop for the future.

In counselling, parents are to be welcomed as partners. In many cases they need to be educated to act in partnership with the school. Most school reports as at present sent out to parents do not give the evidence that they need if they are to act as fellow-counsellors to their children. I have already suggested that groups of teachers should have a regular routine of case conferences on a few children rather than an occasional burst of, almost inevitably, ill-directed judgments and should hope to draw on parents' views. One of the outcomes of the case conference is the subsequent report to parents, which now does not come at any fixed moment of the school year. A short essay-type report, based on the case conference summary is what the parent needs to have after the child's case has been fully discussed. For this I can do no better than commend the format used by L. A. Smith at his school. This contained five elements:

1. Identification of relative strengths of the student: a general statement of encouragement.
2. The school's proposals (arrived at through discussions between teachers and the student) as to the programme for the next period of work, which it has devised to help the pupil to develop through his relative strengths.
3. Suggestions as to the ways parents might help in the educational processes, with special reference to 2.
4. A general statement appraising the student's performance relative to others of his age.
5. A positive statement giving a description of the student's participation as a member of the school community.

The design of this report is a precise practical expression of the values implicit in the appraisal and counselling of a collaborative school.[1]

---

[1] An interesting improvement on the usual report was described by F. Lorenz, a head teacher, on BBC TV ("School and Home," 1st June 1968) after this had been written. He has two-way reports, in which parents report also. Add self-reporting, and a comprehensive document would emerge.

Chapter 9

Changing Roles in a Changing Situation

1. CHANGING ROLES FOR TEACHERS

The older school was an organization for imparting information and values accepted by the adult world. The new school I propose is an organism involved in living: its members explore new possibilities of moral order, new developments in knowledge, new kinds of internal social relationships and new relationships with the larger community. Increasingly, teachers themselves become involved in creative work, and those concerned with the creative arts and crafts increasingly are at the centre of the teachers' groups. Finally pupils and teachers value observation of what actually is, and of persons as they actually are, that is to say they are engaged in dialogue. All this is very different from the enclosed and dogmatic education that was appropriate when the culture to be transmitted was relatively static.

It follows that the kind of society that a school is is greatly changing, and this means that the relationships and self-concepts of teachers as well as taught need to be looked at.

It is not possible in a general survey of this kind to undertake a detailed discussion of the role of the head teacher and of his colleagues, who are known today significantly as "assistant teachers" led by "heads of department"; but it is worth at least referring to this question, partly because it suggests that some of the criteria selection committees have had for their choice of head teachers are now inappropriate and may well delay needful change, partly in the hope that

THE HEAD TEACHER

No full-scale study has been made in England of the role-expectations of a head teacher in relation to pupils, to colleagues within the school, and to the Local Education Authority, but in practice we recognize the kinds of presuppositions that belong to a closed society. The head's task is to ensure that through a well-organized chain of command through his heads of department a fixed foreknown task is effectively carried out. William Taylor has recently suggested that three traditions have combined to create the role-model of the head:

> The differing traditions of instructor/proprietor, the post-Arnoldian gentleman scholar, and the elementary school "master" with his monitors and assistants, have each made their contribution to this conception. In certain respects their influence has been in the same direction, encouraging a substantial measure of localized charisma, a somewhat authoritarian attitude to staff as well as pupils, and a protective role with respect to the influences of parents and the community on the work of the school.[1]

These three very different traditions all belong to a static social system and also to a very different national situation from that of the United States, for instance, where for decades schools have been required by the community to play their part in establishing a common national culture.

Basil Bernstein has recently described the underlying concepts of purity—and one might add parsimony—underlying our traditional educational system:

> The concept of knowledge was one that partook of the "sacred": its organization and dissemination was intimately related to the principles of social control. Knowledge (on this view) is dangerous,

---

[1] W. Taylor, "Should Headmasters Also be Trained?," (review of W. G. Walker, *The Principal at Work*, University of Queensland Press, 1965), *Forum*, VIII, No. 2 (Spring, 1966), pp. 67f.

it cannot be exchanged like money, it must be confined to special well-chosen persons and even divorced from practical concerns. The forms of knowledge must always be bounded and well insulated from each other . . . Specialization makes knowledge safe and protects the vital principles of social order. . . .

Education in breadth, with its implications of mixture of categories, arouses in educational guardians an abhorrence and disgust like the sentiments aroused by incest. This is understandable because education in breadth arouses fears of the dissolution of the principles of social order.[1]

As pillars of the established social order, head teachers have expected and received a large measure of autonomy, so that they are free not only from parental "interference" but also from control of the curriculum by officers or elected members of the Local Education Authority. The result has been that schools are very much the expression of the head's personality and any experienced visitor going into a school yard and watching the way pupils move about and behave to each other can very quickly make a good guess as to the personality of the head teacher whom he will shortly meet.

I shall touch later on the problem of going out to meet the community—not only parents, but the other social agencies and the people of the neighbourhood served by the school. For the moment there is the simpler problem of the internal relationships of the school. For here the "collective ferment" of small groups, and the greater individuation of teachers that occurs in a situation where the creative contribution of each is valued, assist the head teacher who is anxious to develop a closer partnership with the staff.

I have sometimes shocked teachers by suggesting that whereas in the past we have had a hierarchical image of the power structure in a school as a triangle with the head at the top, a better model today would be the relationship in which a social worker described in his own unit, as an inverted triangle, with the leader at the base, supporting the senior experienced staff who in their turn support the more junior, allowing the more difficult problems to filter down to him. The notion

[1] Basil Bernstein, "Open Schools, Open Society?" *New Society* (14th Sept., 1967)

of *supportive leadership* is an important one for schools. But it is not dynamic enough to indicate the creative function of the modern head, who must encourage a sense of purpose without recourse to domination, acting as a consultant, recognizing and nursing growth points, sponsoring research, and ensuring communication, and thereby ensuring that all have an overview of the life and development of the school. The analogy with the catalyst is sometimes used, but does not deserve to be pressed, for the essence of a catalyst is that its presence speeds up change but that it is itself unchanged. To call him or her a catalyst is to see the head teacher as still outside the system, whereas in a society that is moving towards "organic solidarity" from "mechanical solidarity"[1] all its members can be engaged in dialogue, can be open to change, in fact can grow.

In this context, a head teacher can be seen as an expressive rather than an instrumental leader if this is temperamentally appropriate for him, and others can then take on some of the instrumental tasks which have usually been his. We can look therefore to persons who elicit rather than impose or even "inspire," and the selection committee can freely select as head teachers people much more in line with the new kind of teacher whose work and attitudes I have discussed in this book. It follows that good qualifications in an academic subject and the experience of running a large subject department—may not be of such importance as they have been in the past (although of course not to be despised). We can hope to see also as heads and deputy heads more teachers from the studios and workshops. Many of them are at least as generally well read as colleagues in academic departments and have an equal ability to come to terms with new developments in other disciplines, have a close knowledge of young people based on years of personal contact with them in creative work or physical education, and have into the bargain the character-

---

[1] Basil Bernstein, ibid. Dr. Bernstein's article consists mainly of an analysis of the new trends in secondary schools which are the theme of this book, in terms of Durkheim's distinction between "organic" and "mechanical" solidarity.

istic of "dominance" which enables them to assure to others the freedom they themselves need and value.

Again, as Parsons and Bales have shown in their study of the family, expressive leadership is a role to which women in our culture are well accustomed,[1] so that once the new role of the head teacher comes to be better understood there should be less fear of appointing women to the headships of co-educational schools, a fear which is leading to a loss of scope for women teachers and a wastage of their talent.

Once we move away from the concept of the head teacher as a high priest, handing on a tradition, or a "personality" of an imposing kind, we shall begin to recognize the great need for preparation for his or her role. It is one of the great lacunae in our system of in-service courses for experienced teachers that this is so much the exception. We shall see also that courses for present or future heads must include very considerable elements of group process, since this so signally enables people, through experiencing (and surviving) honesty in human relationships, to develop trust in self and others.

TEACHERS WITH TEACHERS

In an organically realized society persons have far greater significance than in one that relies on mechanical solidarity, for " . . . organic solidarity presupposes a society whose social integration arises out of *differences* between individuals . . . (which) . . . become crystallized into *achieved* roles."[2]

Something of this process has been outlined in my description of Model C (pages 69ff.), the classroom situation in which students and teachers transact with one another in a fully personal way. This model is appropriate also when we come to look at the collaborative learning process of teachers relating to one another. The nucleus of energy for teachers is the *focus-group*.

---

[1] Talcott Parsons and Robert F. Bales, *Family, Socialization and Interaction Process* (Free Press of Glencoe, 1955)
[2] Basil Bernstein, op. cit.

It is interdisciplinary focus-groups that are the most novel aspect of the collaborative school, but where these are well-established there emerges a tendency for other groups of teachers, concerned with autonomous or 'orbital' studies to cluster together in the same kind of way.

The first step of all the heads and senior teachers who have moved towards the reforms I have described is to invite teachers willing to experiment to form an interdisciplinary focus-group. They nearly always work in the first instance with first year students, a decision that recognizes the needs of young pupils coming from the stability of the junior school day and also defers to the initial fears of specialist teachers that to experiment later in the pupil's school life might upset his chances in external examinations. In each school it has been possible to find ready volunteers for this first experimental year, and a year later to add a second group, and again a third. And so the process should continue, for the satisfaction of the teachers in their new creative group work as well as the improved learning of the youngsters continues to convert teachers who were cautious or even antagonistic at the beginning.

The interdisciplinary focus-group, concerned with a division or year-group of some 150 children for perhaps 50 per cent. of their time-table has four main functions, each of which requires them to play a variety of roles:

    A. Planning phases of work.
    B. Observation and support during phases of work.
    C. Recording and appraising a phase of work.
    D. Appraising the progress of individual students.

A. Planning Work

During the process of *making ready*[1] for any phase of IDE/M there are some roles common to all members of a focus-group, while others become differentiated. In considering the kinds of questions which might arise during the coming phase of

---

[1] L. A. Smith, "Starting IDE," *IDEAS*, No. 1

work, every member of the group puts forward in a non-judgmental "brainstorming" session any notions that occur to him, drawing on his non-professional interests as well as the specialism that he represents; only in this way can the group have confidence that they can prepare the necessary resources. But each member will also have special skills.

* First and foremost, each represents one or more subject disciplines and can assess what contribution these can make to the work in hand and also what previous work children have done in them which will be relevant, and what special skills or concepts of the disciplines are likely to be embraced by different children with different kinds of attainment in the division or year-group.
* Beyond that, each is likely to have some personal competence for the many tasks of the group outside his official qualifications. Most teachers have interests and skills which engage them out of school but have had little place in their teaching hitherto.
* I have already suggested that a teacher with experience of dealing with children who have special learning difficulties has much to give, and will be especially concerned with preparing assignments for them to enable them to play their full part in the common ploy.
* It is essential to each focus-group to have at least one representative of one of the arts among its number; in fact, at least one head wisely made up her first focus-group from teachers most of whom had a known interest in some form of art.
* Each teacher, as representative of his discipline, calls on the advice of other members of that subject department for specialist resources, but there is need, too, for one person to specialize in audio-visual aids and to be charged with ensuring that films and so on are known and ordered.
* A new function, which should be represented in the school's staffing (though not of course in each focus-group) is the specialist in graphic design who can see to it that the school's own resources are presented as professionally as what it

draws on from outside; communication with this specialist is another task.

* The focus-group does not work on its own in IDE/M. Other teachers form a peripheral group, who are sometimes timetabled in to work in IDE/M when members of the focus-group are drawn away for other aspects of the Fourfold Curriculum, and someone has the task of communicating with these, warning them of the kinds of questions on which children will be consulting them.

B. *Observation and support during phases of work*

The value of IDE/M to students depends very largely on the quality of the teacher's observation, his diagnosis of their needs, and the advice he gives them. He is an adviser and he is a consultant helping them with difficulties of which they are aware. But in addition to this relationship with individuals and "clusters" teachers require an over-all view as grouping specialists,[1] so as to ensure that students collaborate in the clusters most rewarding for their developing work. Teachers working as focus-groups in fact report that they spend most of their weekly planning period discussing the progress of students. For this purpose one of the best traditions of the good primary school is important: the regular noting of actual work undertaken by each student in IDE/M.[2] Only in this way can the focus group be sure that all students' work is observed, and the process is important also for the purposes of trend-watching and development through relative strengths.

C. *Recording and appraising a phase of work*

A great deal of creative effort goes into the planning of a phase of work, and it would be regrettable if there were no

---

[1] L. A. Smith, "Starting IDE," *IDEAS*, No. 1
[2] Anthony Smith (Pilot Course No. 8) reports a very simple basis for this: his pupils plan their work in advance in written form and then briefly discuss with him how far they have completed their plans.

feedback to suggest for future reference what questions in fact proved important to the young and fruitful in the learning to which they led, what kinds of resources were required, available and actually used, and so on. The production of a regular diary of this kind has been proposed by the Curriculum Laboratory to schools working with it on special projects. It is an important first stage out of which hypotheses should emerge which will make possible more formal researches, and we should hope in due course to create a model with which the work could be recorded in an orderly way to make some comparisons possible. This is a first essential step towards an appraisal of the new curriculum as an environment for learning.

D. *Appraising the progress of individual students*

This vital part of the school's work falls largely on the focus-group, at any rate during the early years of secondary schooling. The members of the focus-group see the students more frequently than others can, and do so in a situation which demands and enables freedom of choices. This freedom to choose can reveal the student's aptitudes, personal characteristics, and compatibilities or difficulties in relationships with others and can do so on a larger canvas and in greater detail than can any other cell of the curriculum.

It is of course a tradition of great importance in English schools that for each pupil there is one named teacher who has a special responsibility for him, whether the basis of organization is forms, "houses" or an amalgam of the two. It may be that forms (or "Division Groups") will become outmoded as new buildings become available which do not set students apart in small boxes, and the concept of houses is frequently under fire. However this may be, the individual tutor is an essential feature of the school's counselling and appraisal system, and it is desirable that for the early years of schooling the teacher mainly charged with an individual child's welfare should be a member of the focus-group working with him. If this is quite impossible each child should still have a focus-group tutor who will keep in close touch with his main tutor. (Later on a tutor may well be concerned with the pupil in his special interest work.)

It is manifest that the contribution of the focus-group to the appraisal and counselling systems of the school is a very important aspect of its work (see pp. 214ff.).

The roles of the teachers in a focus-group, in their dealings with one another and with sources of help in school and out of school, are so various that they do not allow of any concept of hierarchy. A focus-group *may* perhaps have a chairman of committee, but it will not have a boss. In fact, the main reason why I propose a maximum of 180 pupils working together in IDE/M is that a focus-group of more than six would be likely to become hierarchical and to subdivide into conflicting sub-groups. If it did, it would be depriving its members of the profit and even therapy that arise from mutual trust in collaborative learning. Heads of departments have their functions, and so do resources experts and teachers charged specially with questions of referral to other agencies and so on. But within the focus-group they do not claim *ascribed* status of that kind, but achieve the status that the quality of their collaboration justifies. A young teacher, coming into his first job, will need as he has always done the support of experienced professional colleagues—and one of the advantages of focus-grouping is that he can seek advice and help quite naturally from people working so closely with him—but the focus-group is based on the assumption of his equality with them.

One feature of the present hierarchy of schools which should not be allowed to hamper progress towards a more open schooling is the narrow basis on which special increases to salary are made. At present nearly all major increments go to Heads of Subject Departments. We should anticipate the development of a much wider variety of positions carrying special responsibility. These will surely include recognition of such tasks as curriculum planning; obtaining and making new resources for learning; scanning research relevant to secondary schooling, such as problems of the gifted or socially handicapped and new insights on grouping, curriculum and appraisal; general oversight of the welfare services of the school and of referral to other agencies; supervision of students on pre-service teaching practice or visits of observation; liaison with industry, further education, and other agencies concerned with the young; facilitation of the progress of older students into adult life and continuing contact with 16-year-old leavers who do not wish to break their ties with the school (often the task of the Youth Tutor). I do not even want this list to be exhaustive. My point simply is that when we acknowledge in the reward structure of the school the great variety of services the school offers to the young we shall free all teachers from the effects of a subject-based hierarchy narrowly conceived. Excellence in a subject discipline and an over-riding concern for the quality of learning in it throughout a school have, of course, a continuing claim to recognition, but so have other qualifications and tasks.

2. *PROFESSIONAL COLLABORATION: Schools, L.E.As, Universities, and Colleges.*

A group of teachers reported not long ago a feeling

> that they are at the bottom rung of a great hierarchy of officials, whose attitude they expect to be critical and restrictive. The salary scale of the profession, with its sharp division between head teachers and others, and between officials and teachers, reflects a sense of values very different from that obtaining in many other countries. Old attitudes are revealed even in our nomenclature which speaks of Authorities and Inspectors, rather than of specialists, consultants or partners.[1]

Let us contrast their feelings about their position (which the emphasis in the salary scale on executive powers seems, as they suggest, to confirm) with Dr. Alice Miel's comment of the requirements of a professional person:

---

[1] First Report, p. 17

Only the person who has an opportunity to use considerable judgment of his own in how he carries out his responsibilities and judgment as to the ways he will use time, energy and resources, can operate as the kind of professional person we need in the schools. Only such a person can, in turn, deal with each student as an individual whose dignity is to be maintained and advanced.[1]

A comparison with the medical or legal profession may add another dimension to our understanding of the educational hierarchy. The great specialist physician or surgeon, we may imagine, and the great counsel or international lawyer, recognize a professional equality or at least fraternity with the everyday G.P. or the small lawyer that we do not expect the Vice-Chancellor of a University or a Regius Professor to feel for the infant teacher. The teacher is conscious of having very little professional status vis-à-vis either the educational administrator or the established teacher in Higher Education. Even within schools, there is a hierarchy that sharply discriminates between heads, heads of departments and the ordinary assistant teacher (and incidentally that often posits a difference of status between heads of academic and other departments). This is a situation typical of the organization that relies on "mechanical solidarity,"[1] which of its nature emphasizes ascribed status.

Yet there is an anomaly. There are persons superior even to the professional hierarchs, to whom the Government of the day looks for advice on policy-making. Even the "educational guardians"[2] need guarding, it seems, for the tradition of the large-scale Government Reports on education remains, by which the Secretary of State seeking for recommendations on policy appoints a Committee to report to him within terms of reference of his selection; these Committees are usually chaired by, and consist in good proportion of, people not presently connected with education, even though the Committee's area of investigation may often not be such as

---

[1] A. Miel, "Innovation and People," *Educational Leadership*, XXII, 589 (May, 1965)
[2] Basil Bernstein, "Open Schools, Open Society?" *New Society* (14 Sept. 1967)

to lead to large-scale administrative decisions, but would seem to demand an intimate understanding of day-to-day educational problems. I mean no ill-will to chairmen and members of these committees (usually ad hoc appointments to the Central Advisory Council for Education) when I say that the most valuable parts of their reports are the research that they are able to finance.

These occasional large-scale Reports are bound to be marmoreal in character, monuments at best to the best thinking of a while ago. This encourages retrospective thinking. We judge our progress by how far we have implemented a Report which was written perhaps a decade before; in fact, people still enquire whether the Hadow proposals made in 1926, for abolishing all-age schools, are yet implemented, although for some time now a number of teachers have been looking enviously at the ten-year schools in other countries. The damage done can be extremely serious when, as with the Newsom Report, the terms of reference are inept; for the Committee was invited to consider the education of young people of average and below average ability, as if that phrase still had meaning and as if the education of all children in the secondary school did not require urgent attention.

But even if the series of Reports had been well planned by successive Ministers and even if the Newsom Committee had escaped this net and had produced a richly well-informed Report, one of a quality comparable to the more recent Plowden Report, this is not the flexible dynamic system for policy-making that we need in a rapidly evolving situation. For that we must look to new kinds of partnerships. The Schools Council should have an important role especially if, when it completes its present commitment to a rather random sponsoring of large-scale projects, some leading to providing resources that are bound to be rapidly obsolescent, it moves on to create a more flexible programme, providing more serious research on the one hand and on the other a stream of information about developments at home and abroad, set in the context of well-analysed theoretical discussion, and supported by good information-retrieval systems which would enable schools to obtaih and correlate resources effectively.

But ultimately the schools will come most readily to good decisions and become more truly congruent in their culture if new occasions and modes of collaboration can be evolved of teachers in different schools, of teachers with representatives of L.E.A.s, and of both with H.M.I.s, and also of teachers in schools with their fellow teachers in Universities and Colleges of Education who are concerned with schooling. "The teacher . . . needs . . . the kind of democratic supportive leadership that we enjoin him to give to children."[1]

Increasingly, it seems, L.E.A.s are appointing officers who see themselves not as inspectors but as advisers. There is good evidence of what a supportive L.E.A. can achieve, for anyone concerned with English education could name certain outstanding L.E.A.s where the average teacher is far above the national average in competence, and the best teach superbly. This happens when an L.E.A. sets out to support teachers, helping them with resources, providing good in-service courses, being open to consultation and personal contact with individuals, consulting them about buildings and in general creating a solidarity of an organic kind. But the teachers who made the melancholy comment I have referred to (on p. 240) came from many different L.E.A.s and were agreed that as a rule neither heads nor individual teachers were invited into such a partnership. Today, L.E.A.s which now want to encourage change meet sometimes with surly responses from teachers who are suspicious of such overtures because there has been a history of misunderstanding between two levels of a bureaucratic machine. There are similar traditions of mistrust between teachers in schools and those in "Higher Education," mistrust of a kind very damaging to progress since it perpetuates a dangerous distinction between theory and practice.

If we think of the nature of creative behaviour in any medium it becomes clear that new kinds of collaboration are

[1] First Report, p. 18

required right across the teaching profession to enable it to meet new situations aptly and with imagination. Any creative act has its own rhythm: it demands an intense awareness and preoccupation with the material, followed by a period when the mind is switched off or allowed to play. Out of this can spring invention, often experienced as a quite unexpected imaginative leap. There follows a stage of vigorous and purposeful convergence in design.[1] The evidence on which educational decisions must be based is so wide-ranging that no one person can experience both the intense direct preoccupation with individual children, who change under our eyes as new experiences are offered to them, and an intense preoccupation with the knowledge about children and adults that is becoming available through the human sciences. Add to this the need to be preoccupied with the ever-changing environment and our new ways of understanding and controlling it, with the variety of cultural and sub-cultural trends in our society and with the range of possible human behaviours which our developing knowledge of other societies provides, and it becomes totally inept for those who are primarily educational theorists and those who are primarily practical teachers in schools to work in isolation from each other.

One of the ways in which collaboration can be achieved (despite administrative difficulties about differing rates and terms of payment) is the development of far more exchanges between teachers in schools, those in Further Education (who have much experience of value to schools) and others in Universities and Colleges. Far more mixed appointments are needed: a person who is half school-teacher and half University-teacher should not be almost as mythical as a centaur.

A further way is through a change of heart (or perhaps one should say the use of the "method of intelligence")[2] by many of the Universities and Colleges which organize in-service courses. Even today courses take place in Universities where teachers' main contact with University staff is to sit in rows and

[1] cf. for a summary, H. Rugg, *Imagination* (Harper and Row, 1963), Chs 1 and 2
[2] See pages 93f., above

listen to them at lectures, where they produce essays on questions not of their own choosing, and where at the end they are required to submit to tests and examinations as unsound in design as any they have set their pupils. It is an impertinence to suppose that experienced teachers should come to Colleges and Universities for instruction of a didactic kind. Such assumptions of superiority ensure that many theorists in Higher Education will not profit from their contact with their colleagues in schools.

This book is largely the outcome of nearly three years of a very different kind of course, in which College staff and school staffs have joined in collaborative study of problems in secondary schooling that have led to policy decisions. A far more important outcome of this collaboration has been the radical reform of schools which these teachers are now creating, each after his own style, but in line with the general policies to which we have all become committed.

As tutors, the staff of the Curriculum Laboratory have always been clear that our first responsibility was to look to the well-being of members of the courses, supporting them in so far as we could through a difficult process of reappraisal of values they have lived with for years. But we have always recognized a complete mutuality between tutors and course-members. It happened that we were tutors, but equally well it might have been they (and may on another occasion be so), and often we have looked to them for help and advice. In this collaboration we have not been catalysts; far from it. Each of us knows himself deeply indebted to members of these courses for increased emotional, social, and intellectual well-being. It is the confidence that comes of this relationship which reinforces our optimism about what young people could become if this mutuality (adjusted, of course, to developmental differences, but fundamentally identical) could be achieved in schools.

This kind of collaboration need not be confined to in-service courses. If L.E.A.s can move from inspection towards advice and support, Universities and Colleges can move from instruction towards a consultative role, offering a service of special expertise, say, in techniques for effective flexible grouping, in audio-visual aids, in programming, or in new developments in subject and interdisciplinary teaching. The new work of teachers in focus-groups, the more heuristic methods in autonomous studies, the programming required for effective "remedial" services, and the more diverse work of students involved in "orbital work" will all mean that teachers will be looking for new resources and new kinds of support.

We come inevitably to the problem of where the responsibility for curriculum change must rest. In traditional theory it rests with the teacher; but, although some teachers have used their freedom, curriculum change has partly gone by default, has partly been gleaned from syllabuses for external examinations, has partly come from the pioneer work of subject specialist associations and from the endeavours of H.M.I.s and L.E.A. Inspectors.

The only justification that teachers have for claiming initiative in curriculum change is that they know their students. This is an irrefutable argument, providing that they do come to know them, better than they have in the past. The pattern that emerges as the best for curriculum reform in England is that teachers working closely with students in school plan their curriculum flexibly according to those students' diverse needs and preoccupations. But to do so they will draw on the help of other teachers through private communication networks and through Teachers' Centres; and they will draw also on the help of L.E.A.s and of teachers in Further and Higher Education in a much closer and freer collaboration than they have known. This is the division of labour appropriate to their work, which will enable them to create what A. K. Rice has called a "congruent culture":

> The culture, together with the structure, forms the texture of an institution, gives it its "life" within which individuals can exist and know something about where they are, can move and know something about whence they come and where they go. The culture ... covers a wide range of behaviour—methods of work, skills and know-

ledge, attitudes towards authority and discipline, and the less conscious conventions and taboos. In any institution "cultural congruence," the extent to which the culture "fits" the task of the institutions, is as important for effective task performance as structural fit.[1]

3. SCHOOL AND COMMUNITY

A "POROUS" SCHOOL

I have deliberately concentrated attention in this book on the internal relationships of the school, believing that authentic change within the school will of its own dynamism create new relationships with parents and with the community at large. Many barriers to communication dissolve when people enjoying the full support of collaborative group work find the world less threatening and understand more fully the defences they have put up against it. Increasingly, too, the speed of change and our growing understanding of the complexity of human development make it clear that education is too big a task for any one group of people to take for its own: we need all the help the community can give to the school.

Again, when a school cares for its students as persons, it becomes aware—as so many teachers have over the years—of the lacunae in the social scene where community should be. One of the most urgent tasks of the coming years is for all of us to find ways of advancing community, in concept and in actuality, in Britain: we can no longer make do with nostalgia for the rural and urban villages of the past.

Finally, it is part of the mood of the period in which we live to recognize that children are not chattels. No-one possesses them, save themselves. The school increasingly sees itself as an enabling institution, helping children to explore themselves as they are and might be, and as facilitating during their school-time and at the end of it a smooth passage to other sources of work and leisure.

[1] A. K. Rice, *Learning for Leadership* (Tavistock Publications, 1965), p. 43

All in all, as the privacy of knowledge[1] fades, the school increasingly becomes a porous community. The extent to which this may happen is uncertain. It may be that the era of the existence of schools as places to go to every day is coming to an end. But if they are going to fade away, as some predict, they will leave damage behind them unless in the coming decade (and starting immediately) we all collaborate to make them good places for the young to live in.

The precise means whereby schools can achieve a richer complex of collaboration with the community are a matter for delicate analysis—of home-school relationships, for instance, of inter-professional services, and of more sensitive cooperation between school and employers. Perfunctory treatment of the subject would be worse than to acknowledge the area of investigation but leave it to one side, as I am doing. I would like only to suggest certain general comments, which follow from some of the general concepts about relationships that I have proposed.

If we apply the concept of a focus unit working with peripheral support, the school's assessment of its place in the community should be based on a recognition of what is its unique function, the task which would not be accomplished if the school did not exist, and what functions it shares with other agencies. The school's unique function is its care for the cognitive growth of the young. It is through the educational system that the nation focuses its attention on this aspect of its members' lives. It is true that we have now come to understand more fully than half a century ago the close relationship of attitudes to cognitive growth, and the fact that exploratory and creative thinking reflect personality as well as intellect. It follows that schooling must be living, as I have suggested; not only the privacy but the primacy of knowledge is fading. But we should not conclude from this that the school should make a take-over bid for all aspects of the child's development just because these affect his cognitive growth: that would be to revert to the ways of the ambitious

[1] See pages 231-2

grammar school which deliberately aimed to cut the child off from his roots in family and neighbourhood unless they matched its culture.[1] A better conclusion is to recognize that others are equally concerned in his social and emotional development, indeed it is the parents' prime parental task to focus on this. Here the school's offering is peripheral, and close collaboration on behalf of the child is necessary between all the socializing institutions (home, neighbourhood, school) concerned with him.

In inviting the more intimate cooperation of parents in their pupils' education, the school may well meet a good deal of resistance to change in education. Parents as a rule opt for the status quo: thus selective schools have their adherents even among parents whose children did not "pass the 11 plus;" coeducational schools are often not welcomed by parents who are used to separate schooling, and vice versa. A generation of parents who have been accustomed to think of examination results as the sole or main criterion for judging a school can be suspicious of teachers' attempts to reduce the area of influence of the examination system. There is always too the tendency to think, when new developments are proposed to ameliorate the condition of the young, Well, I went through it and it did me no harm. But despite these difficulties, parents must be drawn in to support the child in all the key decisions he is helped to make about his education, and teachers need to recognize behind the anxiety of some parents and the passivity or resentment of others a parent's plain concern for the individual child. In some cases they find they need to educate parents in the skill of loving their own children. Sometimes this seems impossible where a family has completely broken down, but even then the school acts on behalf of parents, not as a rival.

It also follows, in my view, that take-over bids which see the school as the centre of the community need to be watched with care. The school uses, on behalf of the community,

[1] cf. B. Jackson and F. Marsden, *Education and the Working Class* (Routledge and Kegan Paul, 1962).

valuable sites and equipment, and one of the ways in which it can contribute to life around it is to make these available, to offer places where adults can come to learn or just to get on with their useful chores. But in doing this its role is to offer facilities—for parents to work alongside their children for instance, and for mid-adolescents to continue to keep in touch with the environment which they left abruptly at 15 or 16—and to offer friendships. In this collaboration again the school is an equal partner but no more.

It is admirable to see schools which are not possessive, where during the school day mothers come in with younger children to the clinic, or to classes. This is in line with the humanising developments which begin to break down the isolation of secondary school students by inviting them to help to provide additional resources for learning for those younger children whom we too rigidly separate from them in infant and junior schools.[1] We should welcome any communal developments of this kind which heal the arbitrary gashes inflicted by administrative procedure on what should be an unhampered period of growing up, growing older—and growing old.

In this context, it is not the professional task of teachers to take on the teaching of the community at large. If they choose to do so, they should be rewarded for it, but on the whole they are likely to be better engaged studying, even teaching, elsewhere, enjoying the occupations that they enjoy and growing in the society of adults rather than spending their evenings in school, Of course, they may want to do that and then it would be impertinent to prevent them; but one of the things a head teacher needs to help his staff to guard against is a tendency to allow themselves to be too exclusively engrossed in school—and the reason often given, that this is an opportunity to get to know their pupils, is no longer relevant, since in collaborative learning they will be getting to know them in the course of every day.

[1] See also, C. M. James, "Childhood Towards Adolescence: the Forgotten Years," *IDEAS*, No. 5, 1968

CHANGING ROLES IN A CHANGING SITUATION

A more useful occupation for some teachers at least, as they become increasingly experienced in human relationships through the climate of their daily work, may be to help to create new kinds of neighbouring, of quite informal kinds, in which people can become better able to communicate with each other and so develop the kind of "collective ferment" which alone will generate and regenerate community life.

TOWARDS COLLABORATION

Parents and teachers need each other. They may not like each other—and there is a long history of mistrust especially where there are class differences—but on behalf of the children they must learn to collaborate.

Teachers and industrialists and other employers need each other. They may not like each other, and in fact often have very unpleasing stereotypes of the "typical school" or the "typical employer." But on behalf of the smooth transition from school and the hope of young people of finding appropriate employment in which their growth can continue, they must learn to collaborate.

Teachers and social workers, youth leaders, psychologists, and others concerned with youth, need each other. They may not like each other, and in fact there is a long history of mutual disregard. But if young people are to have the support they need in order to cope with the sickness of the society we have created (the sickness in themselves, in us and in our institutions) they must learn to collaborate.

The people who first see the need to collaborate are the people who must set up the process of collaboration. In many cases traditional jealousies and misconceptions make the first steps embarrassing, if not painful, but if the teachers of a collaborative school recognize the need they will have acquired also the skills and attitudes demanded.

For the process of neighbouring is the process of collaborative learning, no more and no less.

Glossary of English Educational Terms

Department of Education and Science. The educational office of the central government.

Eleven-plus. A test at the end of primary schooling to decide whether a student should go to a selective or non-selective school. At one time an extremely critical moment in the lives of all children in the maintained (equals U.S. public) school system in England and Wales. Less widespread now with powerful move towards comprehensive secondary schools, and now based, where it continues, solely or mainly, on teachers' recommendations.

Examinations. There are three public examinations for school students, two usually taken at 16, one at 18, although passes can be picked up in various subjects at any age. They are G.C.E. 'O' level and 'A' level (General Certificate of Education and Ordinary and Advanced Level), and C.S.E. (Certificate of Secondary Education). All are single-subject, not group exams with grades given on each subject. Wide choice of subjects.
1. G.C.E. 'O' level. Taken usually at 16. Target population about the 'top' 20%. Students take anything from one to ten or even more subjects, seven being usual for college-bound and similar students.
2. G.C.E. 'A' level. Taken usually at 18. Students take one to three or four subjects, usually interrelated owing to the specialized nature of English university education. Five 'O's and two or three 'A's at good grades are standard qualifications of university candidates.
3. C.S.E. Started in 1960's to provide certification at 16 at rather lower level than 'O' level, say next 20%, grade 1 C.S.E. being taken as equivalent to 'O'. Important distinction is that C.S.E. is teacher-controlled on regional basis, also that under Mode 3, one of three available 'modes' of examining, a school proposes its own syllabus and method of examining, the work being moderated by other teachers; work over two years may be presented. The least disruptive form of examining for innovative schools.

GLOSSARY

Inspectors. Two kinds. H.M.I.'s (*Her Majesty's Inspectors*), on the staff of Department of Education and Science, and L.E.A. Inspectors, on the staff of Local Education Authorities, the latter often now called consultants or advisers.

Local Education Authorities (L.E.As). School districts. With less than 200 for all England and Wales, they are much larger than most American school systems, and this makes many differences in the relationship to the immediate community.

Nuffield Projects. The Nuffield Foundation is a private foundation which led the way in funding curriculum studies in the 1960's before the setting up of the Schools Council.

Prefects. Senior pupils traditionally charged with custodial duties under the guidance of teachers.

Raising of the School Leaving Age (RSLA). Compulsory education at present runs from 5 to 15. Minimum leaving age to be raised to 16 in 1972/3. Originally planned for 1970, RSLA has been a source of a good deal of re-thinking of the curriculum. Worth noting that with 'O' level and C.S.E. at 16, students leaving school at 16 are not usually thought of as "dropouts" in England as they are in the States.

Reports. The Department of Education and Science periodically sets up ad hoc committees of generally interested persons, including some professional teachers and educators, to report on educational matters. The three of most concern to this book are the Crowther Report (1959) concerning ages 15-18, the Newsom Report (1964) concerning ages 13-16 "of average and less than average ability," and the Plowden Report (1966) on primary schooling. Usually known by names of chairmen.

Schools. Types of schools by age. Two main plans in current use are:
1. Infant School, 5-7 } Primary school
   Junior School, 7-11 }
   Secondary School, 11-18
2. First School, 5-9
   Middle School, 9-13
   Secondary School, 13-18

This book was written about Plan 1, the standard plan in most L.E.A.s until quite recently. Middle schools are now becoming more common, sometimes on educational grounds, frequently because with the move to comprehensive schools Plan 2 is more economical in buildings.

N.B.: In England, "going to school" is used only to refer to education under 18, the colloquial use of it for college or university being unknown, although some parts of universities are known officially as Schools.

Types of Secondary School.
  1. Grammar schools. Selective secondary schools. Grammar school population varies according to L.E.A. policy from some 15% to an occasional 60%, about 22% being usual.
  2. Secondary Modern Schools. Non-selective, i.e. select-minus schools. Accepting full normal range other than those selected for grammar school. Taken together, grammar schools and secondary modern schools are described as the bipartite system, originally proposed as a tripartite system to include technical schools.

Comprehensive Schools. Schools accepting the full normal range. Some so-called comprehensive schools are not fully so since a reduced number of grammar schools are retained alongside them.

Forms in Schools. In English schools children are grouped by age, traditionally in one-year chronological age groups, increasingly at younger ages in mixed ages, but still by age, not by grade. This book is about secondary schools (11-18), so the forms referred to run as follows: 1st = 11/12, 2nd = 12/13, 3rd = 13/14, 4th = 14/15 (last year of compulsory schooling until 1972/3), 5th = 15/16 (usual year for 'O' level and C.S.E.; will be last year of compulsory schooling). Sixth form covers the last two years of schooling (equals high school juniors and seniors in the United States), i.e. 16/17 and 17/18, usually called Lower and Upper Sixth respectively.

N.B.: It is correct to speak of English practice, or practice in England and Wales, rather than British practice, because the educational traditions and planning of Scotland are different in many respects. There is a separate Scottish Education Office, not subject to the Department of Education and Science in Whitehall.

Streaming and Setting. Streaming is (attempted) homogeneous grouping within an age-group according to performance in all subjects lumped together, or sometimes in Maths and English together. Setting is homogeneous grouping according to performance in individual subjects. For other kinds of grouping see pp. 175ff.

Head Teachers in Schools. School Principals.

Index

GENERAL INDEX

Italic numerals indicate main references

Adolescence, 7, 14f, 38f, 90, 102, 113, 119, 130; needs, 18, 33, 122, 200; frustration, 15-16, 108-9; life-tasks, 24, 122; mid-, 18, 34, 48, 127, 153, 156, 158, *159*, 164, 177
Age, chronological, 165, 176, 185f, 191; developmental, 176, 179f, 186
Aggression, 71, 110, 150
Anxiety, 75, 116, 167, 180, 225, 249
Appraisal, 17, 72, *212*,ff 217, 222, 226, 227, 238f; case-conferences, 207, 224, 228; diagnosis, 60, 87, 127, 200, 213, 218, 220, 237; reports, 216f, 228, 229; trend-watching, 93f, 94, 97, 219, 224f, 227, 237; self-, 157, 217ff
Areas of Investigation, 66, 68, 103, 127, 146, 153, 154, 156, 165
Assignments, 60, 81, 189, 236
Attainment, 25, 165, *198*, 212, 213, 220, 221, 222, 224, 227, 236; grouping by, 176, 181, 182, 183, 184, 193
Autonomous Studies, 61, *128-30*, 142-3, 150, 165, 178, 185, 189-90, 197, 209, 235

Boys, 110, 155, 161, 186
Buildings, 187, 188, 189, 194, 238, 243

Change, social and cultural, 13, 21, 29, 33, 35, 102-3
Child-centred education, 13-14, 42, 65
Children, exceptional, *195*f; gifted, 126, 194, 195, *196*ff, 240
Class lessons, 31, *53-7*, 58, 60, 61, 129, 138, 186-8, 196; -room organizing, 52, 62-3
Clusters, 43, 57, 61, 63, 66, 68, 77, 129, 154, 186-8, 190, *191*ff, 193f, 237
Cognitive styles, 37, 61, 172, 196, 221
Collaboration, 62, 107; collaborative learning, 13, 44, *52-77*, 97, 149, 166, 198, 214, 218, 234, 239, 245, 251
"Collective ferment," 51, 191, 232, 251
Communication, 13, 35, 60, *111*, 129, 146-7, 202, 233
Community, 20, 39, 41, 60, 162, *247-51*
Competition, 15, 24, 74, 48, 63, 198
Comprehensive schools, 37, 47, 182, 183, 187, 204, 220

Concepts, 36, 38, 63, 68, 81, 103, 126, 128, 136, 142-3, 146, 150, 154, 168, 169, 193
Concerns, 24, 51, 54, 56, 76, 81, 122, 123, 126, 145, 146, 206
Consultants, 50, 52, 57, 61, 65, 189, 226, 233, 237, 240, 243, 246
Counselling, 66, 75, 212, *225*ff
Courses, In-service, 244-5; Pilot, 7, 26, 38, 44, 45, 116, 135, 160, 205, 207, 253
Culture, 27, 35, 40, 41, 48, 53, 94, 164, 184, 210, 246, 249; inclusive, 35, 37, 40, 48
Curriculum, content of, 26, 50, 51, *78*ff, *88*ff, 97, 102, 112, 119, 122, 140f, *148*ff, 209, 214, 232, 240, 246; evaluation of, *212*ff; planning, 46, 82, 239, 246; rationale of, *78*ff, 123; Fourfold, 50, 61, 81, 103, *125*ff, 126, 132, 149, 176, 188, 198, 220, 237

Decision-making, 62, 64, *65*ff, 66, 67, 73, 97, 117, 168, 199, 227, 248
Deprivation, 7, 32, 57, 80, *204*ff, 208
Development, social, 35, 46; personal, 61, 118, 122, 158, 172; sexual, 54, 110, 159
Dialogue, 11, 26, 68, 76, 95, *112-21*, 127, 149, 150, 153, 222; /oblivion, 95-6, 123
Discovery, 17, 64, 112, 137
Diversity, personal, 13, 16, 39, 43, 53, 60, 75, 124, 132, Ch. 7, 175, 234; in curriculum, 29, 52, 53, 88, 165, 246; in environment, 29, 53, 125, 155, 166
Divisiveness, in adult life, 34, 135, 185; in school, 132, Ch. 7, 175
Dominance, 30-1, 54, 196, 234

Education, Colleges of, 51, 58, 90, 164, *240*ff, 243, 244, 245, 246; Further, 164, 244; see also Secondary; Universities
Education, economic function, 27f, 112, 173; ends and means, 27, 86, 122; as selective agency, 27, 46
Educ. Development Center, 166, 168
Elites, 33, 35, 39, 48, 50, 163
Elementary School Teaching Project, 206
Enquiry, 64, 68, 76, 95, *98*ff, 127, 128, 162, 165, 170, 191, 192, 1.93, 222; as experi-

ment, explanation and exploration, 100-2, 142, 166-7; /apathy, 95, 101, 123; see also Interdisciplinary
Environment, 94-6, 109, 122, 154-5, 164, 203-4
Evaluation, 86, *212*ff
Examinations, 17, 24, 31, 50, 78, 86, 133-5, 160, 162, 190, 209, 212, 216, 220, 235, 249
Experience, 13, 21, 38, 68, 76, 115, 118, 121, 124, 142, 146, 177; having *an*, 121, 136

Family, extended, 19; nuclear, 19, 23, 75, 177; see also Home
Fear, 20, 21-2, 70-2, 155
Focus-groups of teachers, 11, 52, 68, 69, 90, 128, 129, 151, 170, 187, 189, 205, 223, 227, 228, 234, *235*, 246, 248; and peripheral groups, 237, 248, 249

Games, 118, 168
Girls, 31, 110, 153, 158, 161, 186, 200
Goldsmiths' College Curriculum Laboratory, 7, 9, 63, 98, 116, 134, 245, 253
Grouping, 60, 159, *175*ff, 187, 193, 198-9, 202, 240; family-, 176f; flexible, 57, *60*ff; friendship-, 179, 191, 193; by grading, 59, 181; see also Clusters; Tasks
Groups, 17, 62, 67, 69, 76, 119, 131, 228; Division, 189, 191, 193, 238; Main, 60, 66, 187, 188, 189, 191, 193, 194
Growth, 41, 56, 172, 185, 201; cognitive, 117, 142, 144, 248

Head teachers, 45, *231*ff, 240, 243, 250
Home, 15, 18-19, 20, 22, 23, 30, 70, 76, 80, 173, 205, 210-11, 224, 225, 228, 232, 248-9
"Humanities," 34, 39, 132, 133, 139, 149

Identity, 62, 67, 109, 118, 153, 156, 172
Immigrants, 173, 195, *208*ff
Individualized studies, *59*ff, 61, 62, 189, 190, 74-5, 129, 190-1; see also Diversity
Industry, 17, 20, 24, 35, 39, 161, 240, 248, 251; Indus. Training Boards, 28, 160-1
Integrated studies, 38, 126, 128, 132, 133, 138, 142
I.Q., 29, 71, 105, 181, 183, 199, 220
Interdisciplinary studies, 24, 36, 37, 49, 61, 82, 90, 120, 126, *127*f, *132*ff, 136, *144*ff, 159, 188, 197, 235; /intra-disciplinary, 61, 82, 126, 127; Enquiry (IDE) and Making (IDM), 49, 50, 66, 98, 99, 126-8, *132*ff, 141ff, 148, 151, 152, 156, 163-4, *165*ff, 168, 169, 185, 188, 189, 190, 194,
197, 203, 209, 220, 228, 237, 239
Interests, 55, 67, 89, 155, 159, 164, 176, 177
International Evaluation of Achievement, 51, 182
Interprofessional services, 225, 248
Involvement, 12, 25, 43, 104, 116, 160

Knowledge, 44, 109, 128, 144, 147, 164, 231, 248; see also Obsolescence

Leadership, 40, 135, 198; expressive, 233, 234; supportive, 233, 243, 246, 249
Learners, roles of, Ch. 2; retarded, 200f
Living, 12, 41, *94*ff, 96, 113, 122, 124, 148
Local Education Authorities, 51, 231, 232, *240*ff, 243, 245, 246

Making, 76, 95, 99, 102, *105*ff, 112, 115, 127, 149, 162, 167, 170, 195, 222; design, 95, 106, 198, 222; doing, 106, 107, 108, 115, 222; hypotheses, 34, 66, 101, 109, 137, 142, 152, 160, 195; invention, 34, 41, 54, 95, 106, 193, 194, 222; maintenance, 106, 198, 222; /passivity, 95, 123
Mental processes, higher, 147, 220
Minorities, *195*ff
Models, 152, 222, 225
Motivation, 12, 27, 53, 55, 66, 72, 79, 118, *126*, 174, 195, 205

Needs, 24, 40f, 64, 125, 127, 176, 180, 191; expressive, 18, 72
Neighbourhood, 80, 176, 179, 204, 232, 249
Nuffield Foundation, 33, 136, 148

Objectives, in curriculum planning, 66, *81*ff, 82, 84, 85, 91, 97, 122, 219, 222
Observation, 15, 117, 118, 124, 148, 152, 214, 220, *235*, 237
Obsolescence, 21, 44, 57, 88-9, 147
Organic solidarity, 51, 234, 238, 241, 243

Participation, 39, 43, 64, 67, 115, 192
Persistence, 16, 105, 155, 173
Personality traits, 31, 55, 143, 169, 183, 217, 219, 221, 24
Person-centred schooling, 42, 40, 160
Personal relationships, 7, 40, 54, 81
Persons, *69*ff; perception of, 14, 18, 45, 55, 60, 62, 69, 97, 148, 214, 217
Phantasy, 18, 109, 113, 118, 155
Phases of work, 59, 68, 91, 136, 154; planning, 136, 154, *165*ff, 220, *235*, 237f
Play, 41, 52, 116, 120-1

INDEX

Poetry, 105, 186, 193
Political socialization, 39-40, 149, 162
Power, 20, 39-40, 54, 56, 74, 158, 232
Practical studies/theoretical, 109; practical-theoretical, 41, 110-11
Pre-vocational studies, 66, 160, 225
Primary school, 7, 12, 13, 14, 18, 52, 63, 70, 115, 117, 149, 151, 152, 153, 154, 166, 177, 179, 203, 204, 235, 237, 250
Problems, identifying and solving, 18, 28-9, 34, 38, 44, 66-8, 103, 140, 169, 220
Programmed learning, 60, 81, 126, 129, 131, 180, 183, 198, 199, 218, 228, 246; National Centre for, 183
Proprium, 15, 54, 85, 105

Race, 73, 209
Realism, 16, 108f, 109, 113, 120
Regression, 206, 224, 225
Relative strengths, 13, 33, 45f, 56, 60, 90, 124, 196, 209, 219, 227, 229, 237
Remedial education, 15, 151, 156, 201, 202, 246; in the Fourfold Curriculum, 61, 126, 127, *129f*, 158, 180, 185, 189, 197, 202, 228; and examinations, 162, 170
Reports, Government, 241; Crowther, 28, 96, 134, 161; Hadow (1926), 14; Newsom, 39, 108, 134, 200, 204, 242; Norwood, 134; Plowden, 149, 242; *Early Leaving*, 179
Research, 20, 46, 148, 188, 217, 233, 239
Resources, 9, 51, 68, 112, 187, 236, 239, 243

Schools Council, 242; publications, 37, 39, 64, 86, 108, 133, 139, 148; and examinations, 86, 148, 242
Secondary education, 7, 18, 22, 23; and change, 7-8, 19, 20, 25, 41, 67, 76, 112, 174, 249; new model of, 20, 26, 40; as selective agency, 27; values, 77
Secondary school, 19, 44, 47, 91, 102, 183, 240ff, 249; school day, *15*ff, 38, 51, 54, 56, 77, 129, 131, 138, 151, *188*ff, 197; "porous," 119, 247; social climate, 40, 45, 58, 62, 65, 67, 70, 77, 104, 112, 139, 170, 231; social life, 56, 158, stages, 151-8; welfare services, 179, 205, 226, 240
Security, 18, 45, 69, 72, 151, 189
Self-concepts, 22, 25, 56, 65, 72, 110, 118, 119, 120, 124, 157; -discovery, 9, 17, 55-6, 119, 150, 203, 218
Setting, 176, 182, 185
Sixth form, 34, 145, 157, 163f, 212
Skills, 17, 44, 63, 66, 72, 126, 130, 164, 166, 167, 171, 190, 191, 236; enquiry, *103-4*, 124, 136; literacy, 103, 203
Social class, 20, 25, 195, 204-5, 211, 251; and dominance, 196, 234; language, 172, 173, 206, 209; middle class values, 47, 48, 73, 173, 174; of the school, 173, 208; working class, 7, 31, 47, 48, 67, 73, 173, 174, 208, 249; and success, 138
Social services, 205, 207, 224-6, 232, 251
Social studies, 133-5, 140, 162, 169, 244
Special Interests ("Orbital" work), 61, 127, *131*f, 151, 156, 158, 160, 164, 185, 191, 197, 203, 209, 227, 232, 235, 239, 246
Status, 23, 32, 33, 47, 72, 160
Streaming, 29, 30, 38, 39, 175, 176, *181-5*, 198, 199, 204; see also Grouping
Subject-disciplines, 68, 103, 126, 128-9, 138-46, 167, 187, 197, 236; and enquiry, 38, 89, 145, 146, 149; new, 147; structure of, 128, 141-4; arts, 38, 77, 99, 108f, 119-21, 129, 189, 193, 216, 236; drama, 52, 120, 121, 153, 169, 189, 193, 195; sciences, behavioural and social, 18, 34, 38, 39, 139, 149, 150, 244; natural, 33, 34, 38, 99, 100, 105, 146, 149, 185, 189; movement, 112, 120, 169, 189, 193; technical, 33-4, 109-10, 134, 188, 198; mathematics, 40, 71, 77, 108, 182, 185, 197; various, 38-40, 52, 77, 133, 146, 148, 153, 154, 169, 186, 189, 197, 216, 233; see also Autonomous Studies; Humanities; Social Studies
Success, 30, 63, 72, 90, 109, 172
Sweden, 29, 33, 51, 183, 225

Talent, 25, 28-30, 39, 51, 88; creative, 23, 25, 30-3, 112, 203; destroying, 171ff
Tasks, 15, 54, 69, 109, 183, 191, 194, 220
Teachers, 7, 8, 16, 18, 20, 25, 43f, 49, 74, 137, 173, 234ff, 243, 251; collaboration of, 57; -compatibility, 176, 178, 223; and curriculum planning, 127; pastoral role, *46*ff, 56, 74, 225, 227; professionals, 20, 127, 148, 240; roles, changing, *Chs. 2 and 9*, 62ff, 123-4; as specialists, 44, 46, *49*f, 61, 68, 131, 223, 235; status, achieved/ascribed, 32, 47, 234, 239, 241; student-, 46, 56, 58, 226, 234; women, 234; Teachers Centres, 51, 246
Team-teaching, 44, 53, *57*ff, 61, 69, 139
Technological aids, 8, 57, 60, 131, 180, 189, 236, 246; society, 18, 27, 28, 40, 66
Thinking, convergent/divergent, 25, 52; 107, 195; creative, 16, 25, 32, 105, 248,

critical, 31, 90, 107, 166; grammar of 92, 150; productive, 107, 141, 142, 166, 167; systemic, 147, 154, 197
Thirteen-year-olds, 34, 130, 155-7
Truth, 65, 74, 76, 142, 234

Unauthenticity, 45, 55, 75-6, 120
UNESCO, 81, 87
United States, 39, 60, 70, 85, 114, 132, 140f, 165, 201, 225, 226, 231
Universities, 25, 30, 90, 163, 240-7, 241, 243, 244, 245
Use, 69, 114, 115, 117; and values, 112

Values, 48, 49, 76, 84, 113, 124, 161, 167, 201; in curriculum, 81

Waste, 28, 29
Wonder, 112, 113, 114, 119
Work, 121, 161; and leisure, 157, 174, 247; and love, 69, 70, 122; and play, 52; rhythms of, 112, 167; world of, 103

Youth services, 225; tutors, 240
Youth, 110, 133, 144, 251; well-spent, 42, 113, 115, 122f

AUTHOR INDEX

Abel-Smith, B., 204
Allport, G. W., 15, 54, 159
Amaria, R., 183, 199, 203
Bales, R. F., 234
Banks, O., 22
Berelson, B., 192
Berne, E., 118
Bernstein, B., 173, 232-4
Bettelheim, B., 70
Biran, L. A., 183, 199, 203
Bloom, B. S., 84, 221f
Brameld, T., 40, 77
Brembeck, C. S., 24
Bruner, J. S., 44, 111, 117, 144
Buber, M., 117
Burstall, C., 172
Burt, Sir Cyril, 134
Cattell, R. B., 30f
Cooley, W. W., 100
Cooper, M. G., 226
Daniels, J. C., 185
Davis, D. R., 200
Dewey, J., 136f
Dickinson, E., 33
Dickson, G. E., 46
Dienes, Z. P., 147
Douglas, J. W. B., 173, 174, 182, 185
Erikson, E. H., 69, 110
Floud, J. E., 174
Freud, S., 21, 69, 153, 160
Guilford, J. P., 198, 221f
Halsey, A. H., 174
Hanson, J. W., 24
Hargreaves, D. H., 173
Hodgson, A., 166
Holt, J., 70ff

Hudson, L., 34, 50
Husén, T., 51
Jackson, B., 23, 249
Jackson, Lord, 36
James, C. M., 7, 49, 130, 159, 250
James, J., 151
Jones, J., 151, 168
Klein, J., 73
Kogan, N., 31, 155, 196, 200
Krathwohl, D. R., 84
Lawton, D., 133
Leith, G. O. M., 183, 199, 203
Lewis, J., 157
Lippitt, R., 68
Maccoby, M., 114
Macdonald, J. B., 99, 138
McGregor, O. R., 167
Marcouse, R., 116
Marsden F., 23, 249
Mason, A. E., 43, 59, 128, 130, 155, 222
Mauger, S., 99
Miel, A., 140f, 241
Miller, R. I., 93
Modiano, N., 114
Mogford, B., 100
Morris, J. M., 171
Moustakas, C. E., 119
Musgrove, F. W., 18f, 22
Padgett, T., 169
Parsons, T., 234
Patterson, F., 168
Phillips, G. D., 111
Piaget, J., 113, 153, 160
Pidgeon, D. A., 59, 182
Pierce-Jones, J., 226

Read, Sir Herbert, 175
Reed, M. B., Jr., 100
Reuchlin, M., 35
Rice, A. K., 246f
Riesman, D., 70
Riessman, F., 201
Roane, F., 72
Robertson, S. M., 70, 99, 144
Rogers, C. R., 67
Rugg, H., 244
Russell Davis, D., 200
Sands, O., 80
Sewell, E., 104
Smith, L. A., 24, 63, 131f, 179, 191, 219, 227, 229, 235, 237
Steiner, G. A., 192
Svensson, N. E., 183-4
Swift, D. F., 23
Tanner, J. M., 179
Taylor, W., 231
Tawney, R. H., 48
Townsend, P., 204
Van Thil, W., 93
Wallach, A., 31, 155, 196, 200
Wastnedge, E. R., 65
Way, B., 99, 120
Weinstein, G., 123, 206
White, R. K., 68, 136
Whitehead, A. N., 83, 137, 143
Whitely, W. M., 185
Wiersma, W., 46
Wolf, R. M., 205f
Zarat, E., 138
Zweig, F., 23